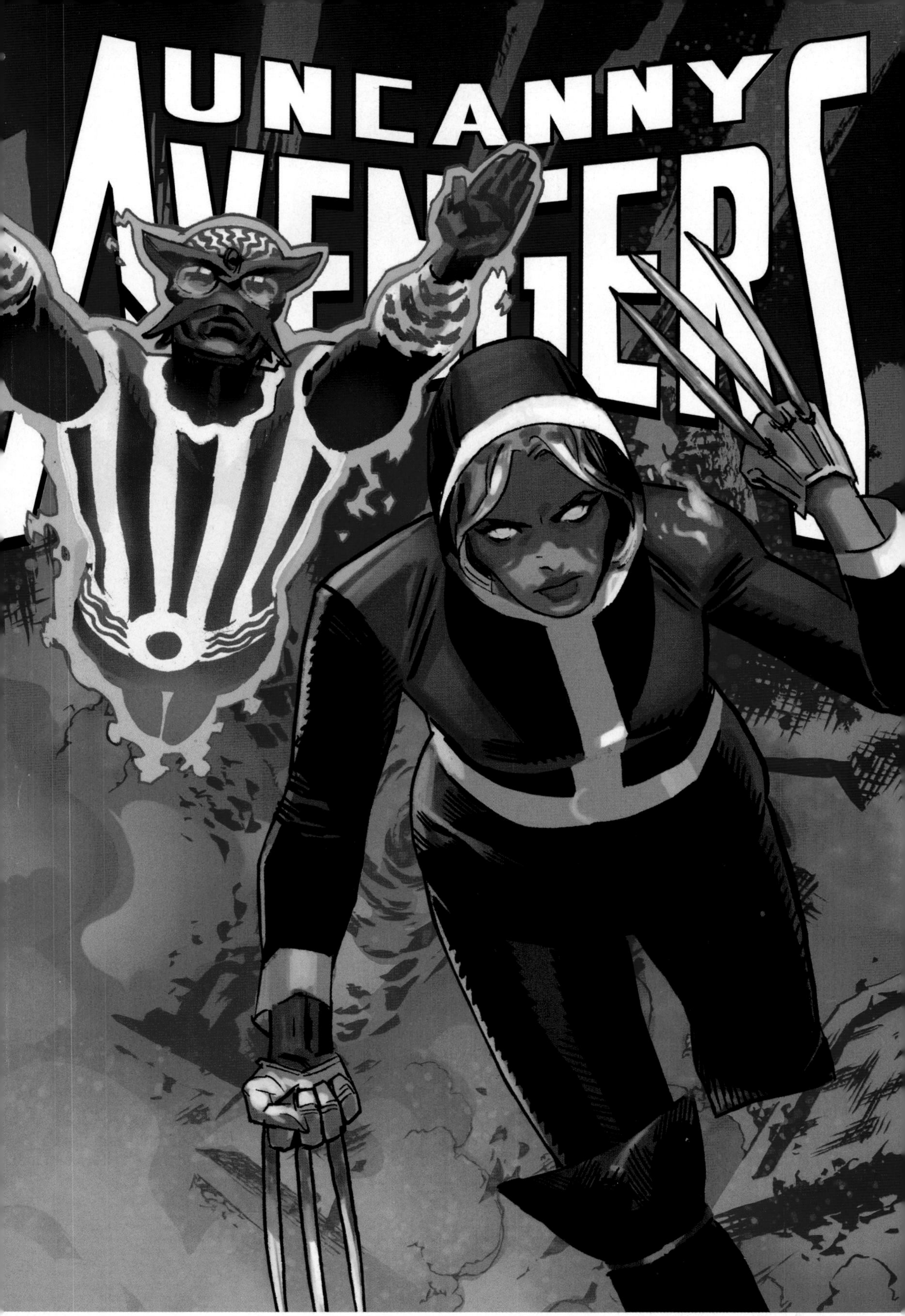
UNCANNY
AVENGERS

RAGNAROK NOW

PREVIOUSLY

Uriel and Eimin, the twin heirs to the throne of Apocalypse and protégés of the time-traveling mastermind Kang, h
arrived on present day Earth, leaving a trail of destruction in their wake: They have felled a Celestial, obliterated
Peak space station and fractured the Avengers Unity Squad.

As the divided Avengers scatter across the globe in search of the Apocalypse Twins, they are assaulted by the F
Horsemen of Death — reanimated avatars of the Avengers' fallen teammates and family members. While Won
Man is ambushed by his brother, the Grim Reaper, Thor is attacked by the Sentry, a former teammate he slaye
battle. Wolverine is confronted by his son, Daken, whom he drowned, and the Scarlet Witch is abducted by d
X-Man Banshee.

As Havok, Captain America and Wasp infiltrate the twins' base in the hopes of breaking their hold over the Earth, U
and Eimin make a daunting offer to the Scarlet Witch: to be the savior of mutantkind, to end the war between man
mutant by using her powers to rapture the entire mutant race to a new homeworld.

UNCANNY AVENGERS VOL. 3: RAGNAROK NOW. Contains material originally published in magazine form as UNCANNY AVENGERS #12-17. First printing 2014. ISBN# 978-0-7851-8483-6. Published by M
WORLDWIDE, INC., a subsidiary of MARVEL ENTERTAINMENT, LLC. OFFICE OF PUBLICATION: 135 West 50th Street, New York, NY 10020. Copyright © 2014 Marvel Characters, Inc. All rights reserved. All cha
featured in this issue and the distinctive names and likenesses thereof, and all related indicia are trademarks of Marvel Characters, Inc. No similarity between any of the names, characters, persons, and/or insti
in this magazine with those of any living or dead person or institution is intended, and any such similarity which may exist is purely coincidental. Printed in the U.S.A. ALAN FINE, EVP - Office of the President,
Worldwide, Inc. and EVP & CMO Marvel Characters B.V.; DAN BUCKLEY, Publisher & President - Print, Animation & Digital Divisions; JOE QUESADA, Chief Creative Officer; TOM BREVOORT, SVP of Publishing; DAVID BC
SVP of Operations & Procurement, Publishing; C.B. CEBULSKI, SVP of Creator & Content Development; DAVID GABRIEL, SVP Print, Sales & Marketing; JIM O'KEEFE, VP of Operations & Logistics; DAN CARR, Exe
Director of Publishing Technology; SUSAN CRESPI, Editorial Operations Manager; ALEX MORALES, Publishing Operations Manager; STAN LEE, Chairman Emeritus. For information regarding advertising in Marvel C
or on Marvel.com, please contact Niza Disla, Director of Marvel Partnerships, at ndisla@marvel.com. For Marvel subscription inquiries, please call 800-217-9158. Manufactured between 1/24/2014 and 3/1(
by R.R. DONNELLEY, INC., SALEM, VA, USA.

10 9 8 7 6 5 4 3 2 1

LEGO and the Minifigure figurine are trademarks or copyrights of the LEGO Group of Companies. ©2013 The LEGO Group. Characters featured in particular decorations are not commercial products and might
available for purchase.

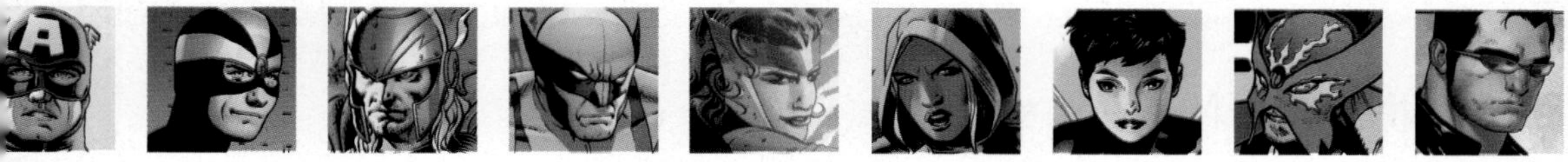

APTAIN MERICA | HAVOK | THOR | WOLVERINE | SCARLET WITCH | ROGUE | WASP | SUNFIRE | WONDER MAN

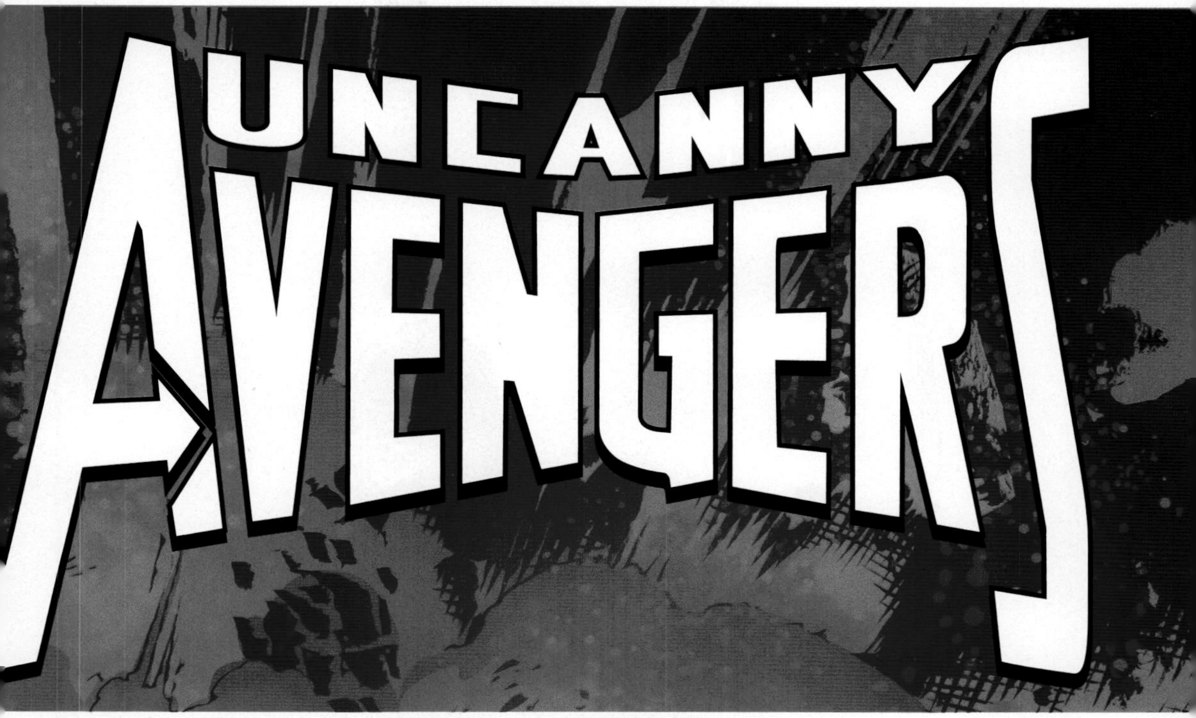
UNCANNY
AVENGERS

RAGNAROK NOW

WRITER: **RICK REMENDER**

#12
ARTIST
SALVADOR LARROCA
COLOR ARTIST
FRANK MARTIN
COVER ART
JOHN CASSADAY & LAURA MARTIN

#13
ARTIST
DANIEL ACUÑA
COVER ART
JOHN CASSADAY & LAURA MARTIN

#14-17
PENCILER: **STEVE McNIVEN**
INKERS: **JOHN DELL** (#14-16) & **JAY LEISTEN** (#15-17)
WITH **DEXTER VINES** (#15)
COLOR ARTIST: **LAURA MARTIN**
COVER ART: **STEVE McNIVEN**
WITH **JUSTIN PONSOR** (#14-16) & **DAVE McCAIG** (#17)

LETTERER: **VC'S CLAYTON COWLES**
EDITORS: **TOM BREVOORT** WITH **DANIEL KETCHUM**

COLLECTION EDITOR: JENNIFER GRÜNWALD
ASSOCIATE MANAGING EDITOR: ALEX STARBUCK
EDITOR, SPECIAL PROJECTS: MARK D. BEAZLEY
SENIOR EDITOR, SPECIAL PROJECTS: JEFF YOUNGQUIST
SVP PRINT, SALES & MARKETING: DAVID GABRIEL
BOOK DESIGN: JEFF POWELL AND RODOLFO MURAGUCHI

EDITOR IN CHIEF: AXEL ALONSO
CHIEF CREATIVE OFFICER: JOE QUESADA
PUBLISHER: DAN BUCKLEY
EXECUTIVE PRODUCER: ALAN FINE

UNCANNY AVENGERS #12

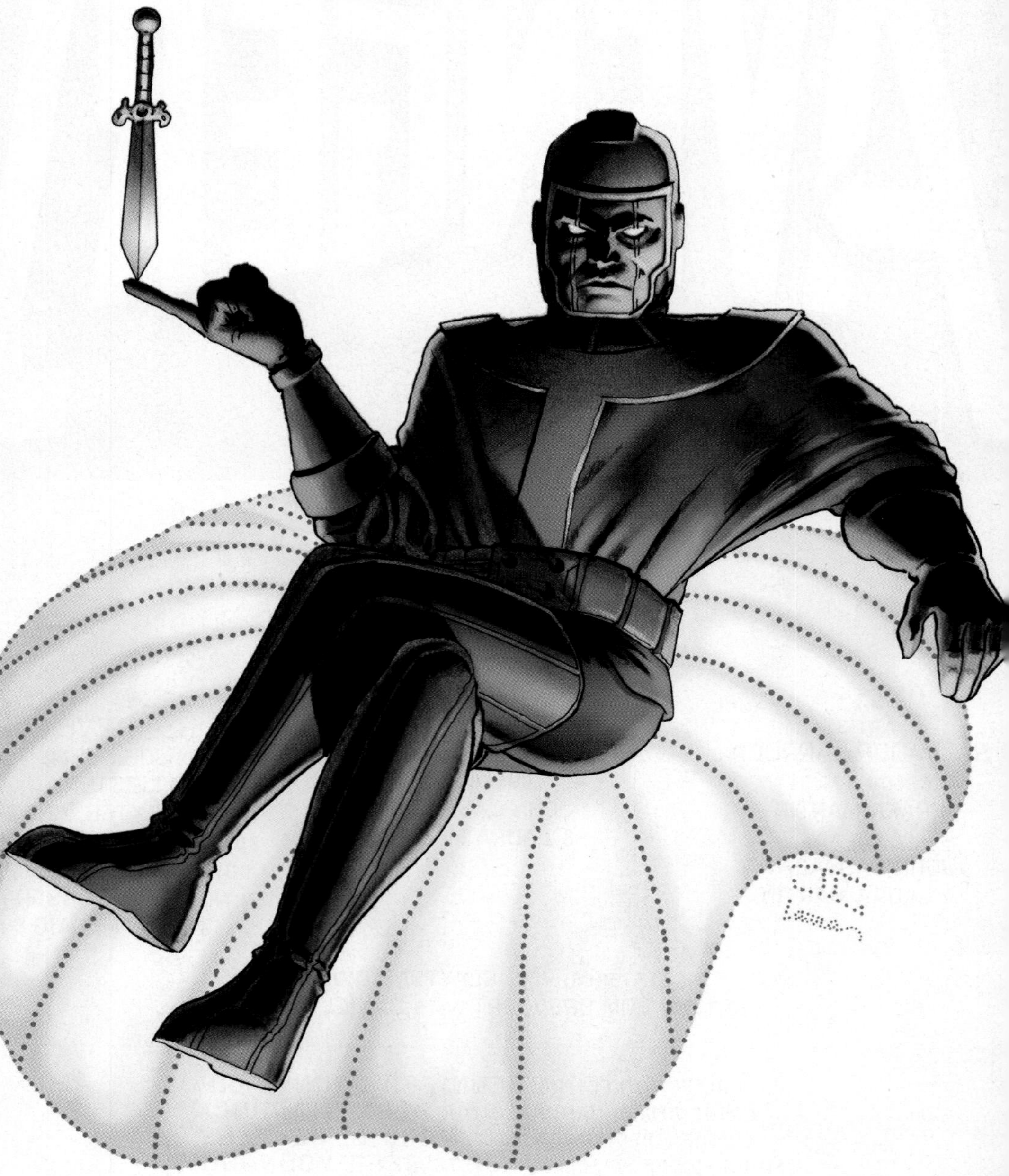

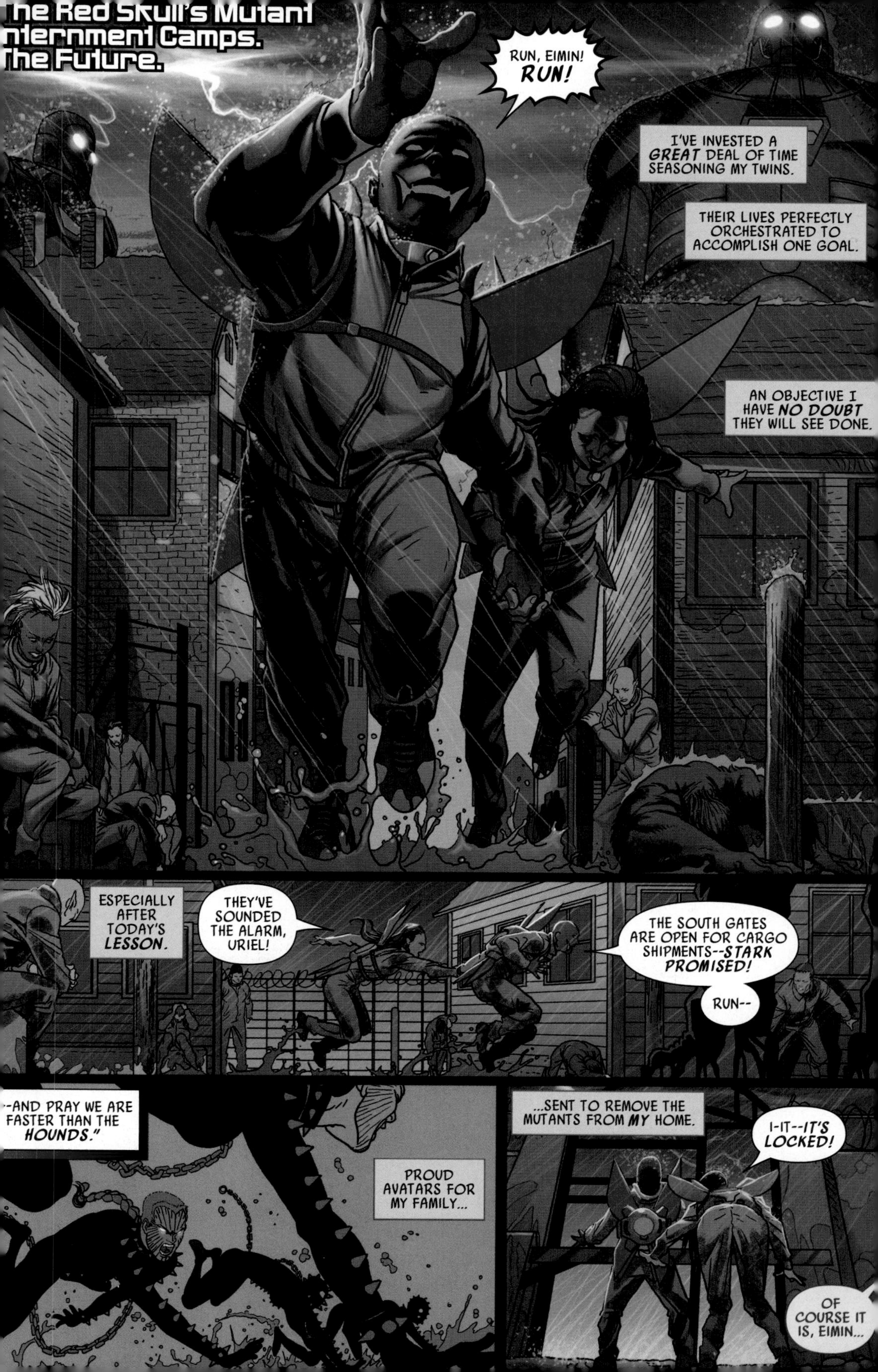
The Red Skull's Mutant
Internment Camps.
The Future.
RUN, EIMIN! RUN!
I'VE INVESTED A GREAT DEAL OF TIME SEASONING MY TWINS.
THEIR LIVES PERFECTLY ORCHESTRATED TO ACCOMPLISH ONE GOAL.
AN OBJECTIVE I HAVE NO DOUBT THEY WILL SEE DONE.
ESPECIALLY AFTER TODAY'S LESSON.
THEY'VE SOUNDED THE ALARM, URIEL!
THE SOUTH GATES ARE OPEN FOR CARGO SHIPMENTS--STARK PROMISED!
RUN--
--AND PRAY WE ARE FASTER THAN THE HOUNDS."
PROUD AVATARS FOR MY FAMILY...
...SENT TO REMOVE THE MUTANTS FROM MY HOME.
I-IT--IT'S LOCKED!
OF COURSE IT IS, EIMIN...

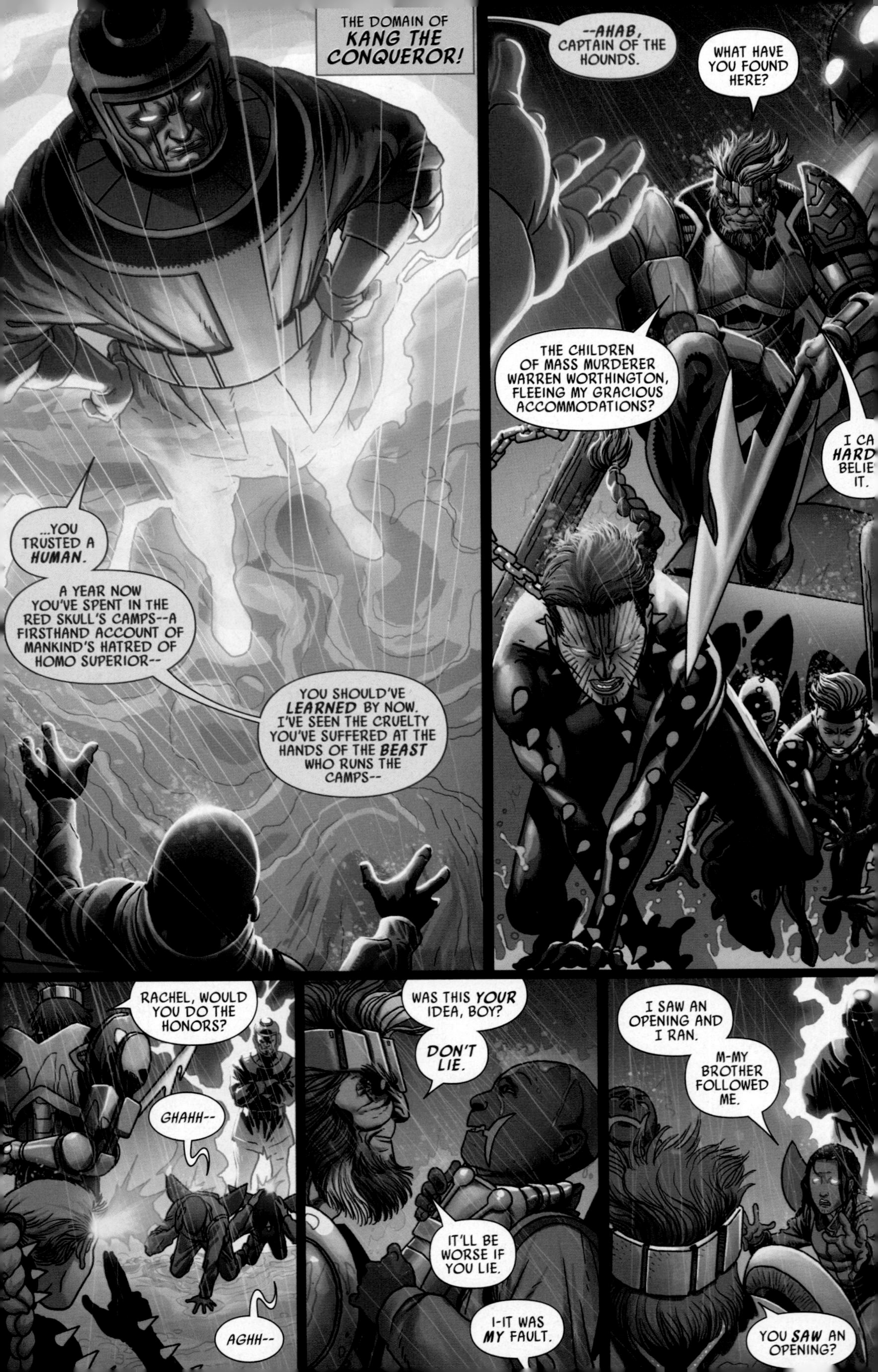
THE DOMAIN OF KANG THE CONQUEROR!
...YOU TRUSTED A HUMAN.
A YEAR NOW YOU'VE SPENT IN THE RED SKULL'S CAMPS--A FIRSTHAND ACCOUNT OF MANKIND'S HATRED OF HOMO SUPERIOR--
YOU SHOULD'VE LEARNED BY NOW. I'VE SEEN THE CRUELTY YOU'VE SUFFERED AT THE HANDS OF THE BEAST WHO RUNS THE CAMPS--
--AHAB, CAPTAIN OF THE HOUNDS.
WHAT HAVE YOU FOUND HERE?
THE CHILDREN OF MASS MURDERER WARREN WORTHINGTON, FLEEING MY GRACIOUS ACCOMMODATIONS?
RACHEL, WOULD YOU DO THE HONORS?
GHAHH--
AGHH--
WAS THIS YOUR IDEA, BOY?
DON'T LIE.
IT'LL BE WORSE IF YOU LIE.
I-IT WAS MY FAULT.
I SAW AN OPENING AND I RAN.
M-MY BROTHER FOLLOWED ME.
YOU SAW AN OPENING?

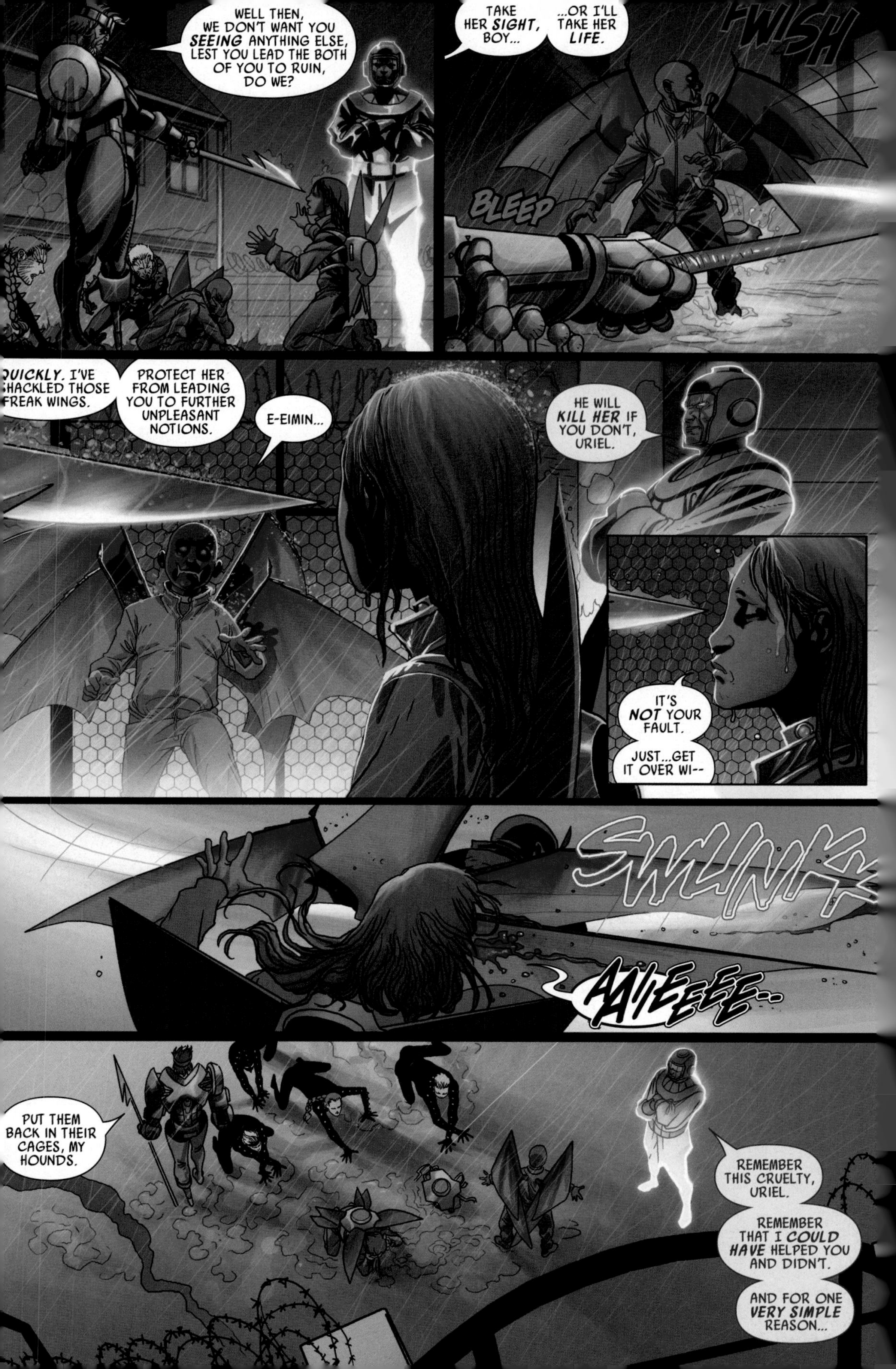

WELL THEN, WE DON'T WANT YOU SEEING ANYTHING ELSE, LEST YOU LEAD THE BOTH OF YOU TO RUIN, DO WE?
TAKE HER SIGHT, BOY...
...OR I'LL TAKE HER LIFE.
FWISH
BLEEP
QUICKLY. I'VE SHACKLED THOSE FREAK WINGS.
PROTECT HER FROM LEADING YOU TO FURTHER UNPLEASANT NOTIONS.
E-EIMIN...
HE WILL KILL HER IF YOU DON'T, URIEL.
IT'S NOT YOUR FAULT.
JUST...GET IT OVER WI--
SWUNK
AAIEEEE..
PUT THEM BACK IN THEIR CAGES, MY HOUNDS.
REMEMBER THIS CRUELTY, URIEL.
REMEMBER THAT I COULD HAVE HELPED YOU AND DIDN'T.
AND FOR ONE VERY SIMPLE REASON...

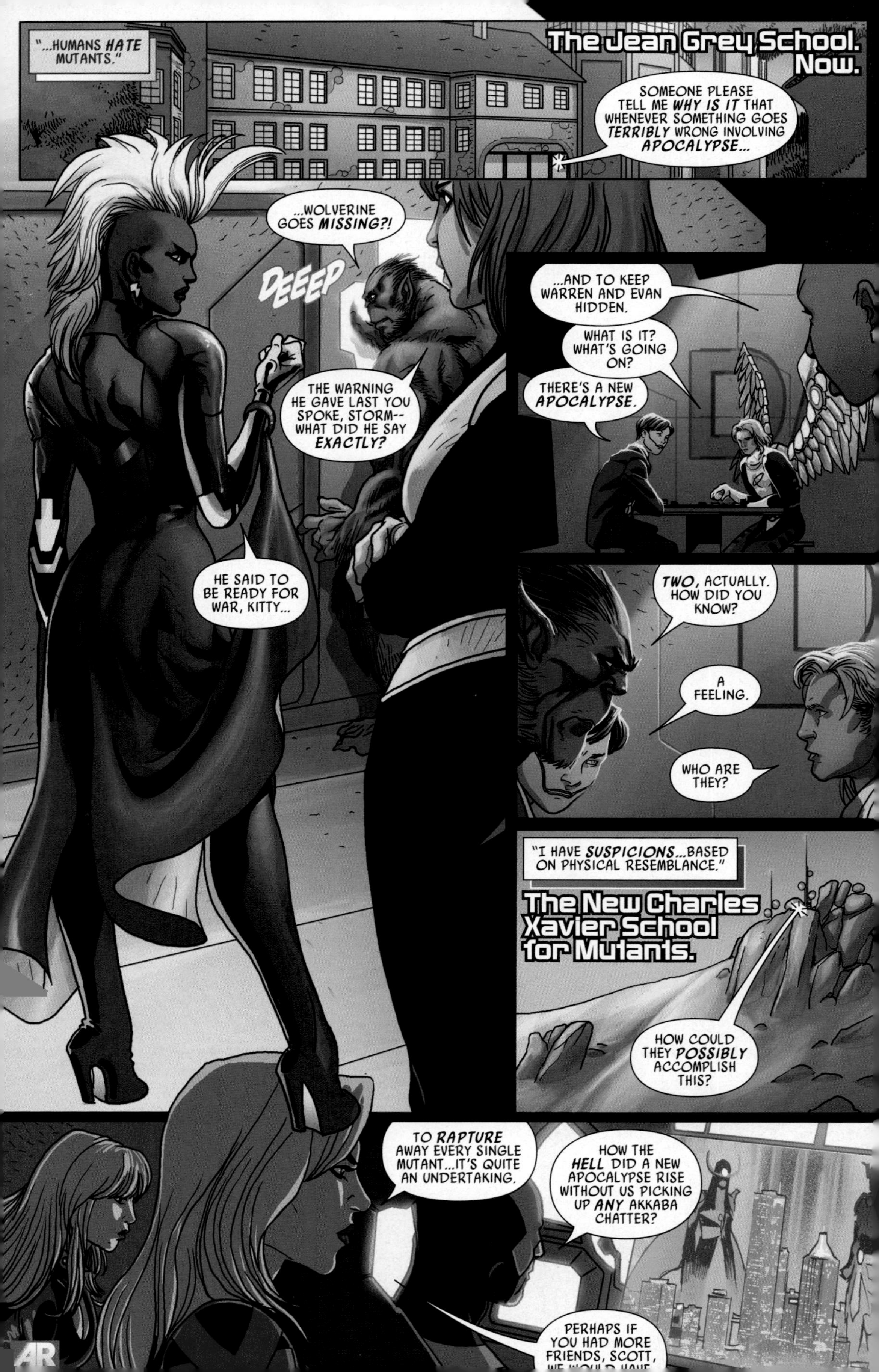
"...HUMANS HATE MUTANTS."
The Jean Grey School. Now.
SOMEONE PLEASE TELL ME WHY IS IT THAT WHENEVER SOMETHING GOES TERRIBLY WRONG INVOLVING APOCALYPSE...
...WOLVERINE GOES MISSING?!
DEEEP
THE WARNING HE GAVE LAST YOU SPOKE, STORM-- WHAT DID HE SAY EXACTLY?
HE SAID TO BE READY FOR WAR, KITTY...
...AND TO KEEP WARREN AND EVAN HIDDEN.
WHAT IS IT? WHAT'S GOING ON?
THERE'S A NEW APOCALYPSE.
TWO, ACTUALLY. HOW DID YOU KNOW?
A FEELING.
WHO ARE THEY?
"I HAVE SUSPICIONS...BASED ON PHYSICAL RESEMBLANCE."
The New Charles Xavier School for Mutants.
HOW COULD THEY POSSIBLY ACCOMPLISH THIS?
TO RAPTURE AWAY EVERY SINGLE MUTANT...IT'S QUITE AN UNDERTAKING.
HOW THE HELL DID A NEW APOCALYPSE RISE WITHOUT US PICKING UP ANY AKKABA CHATTER?
PERHAPS IF YOU HAD MORE FRIENDS, SCOTT,

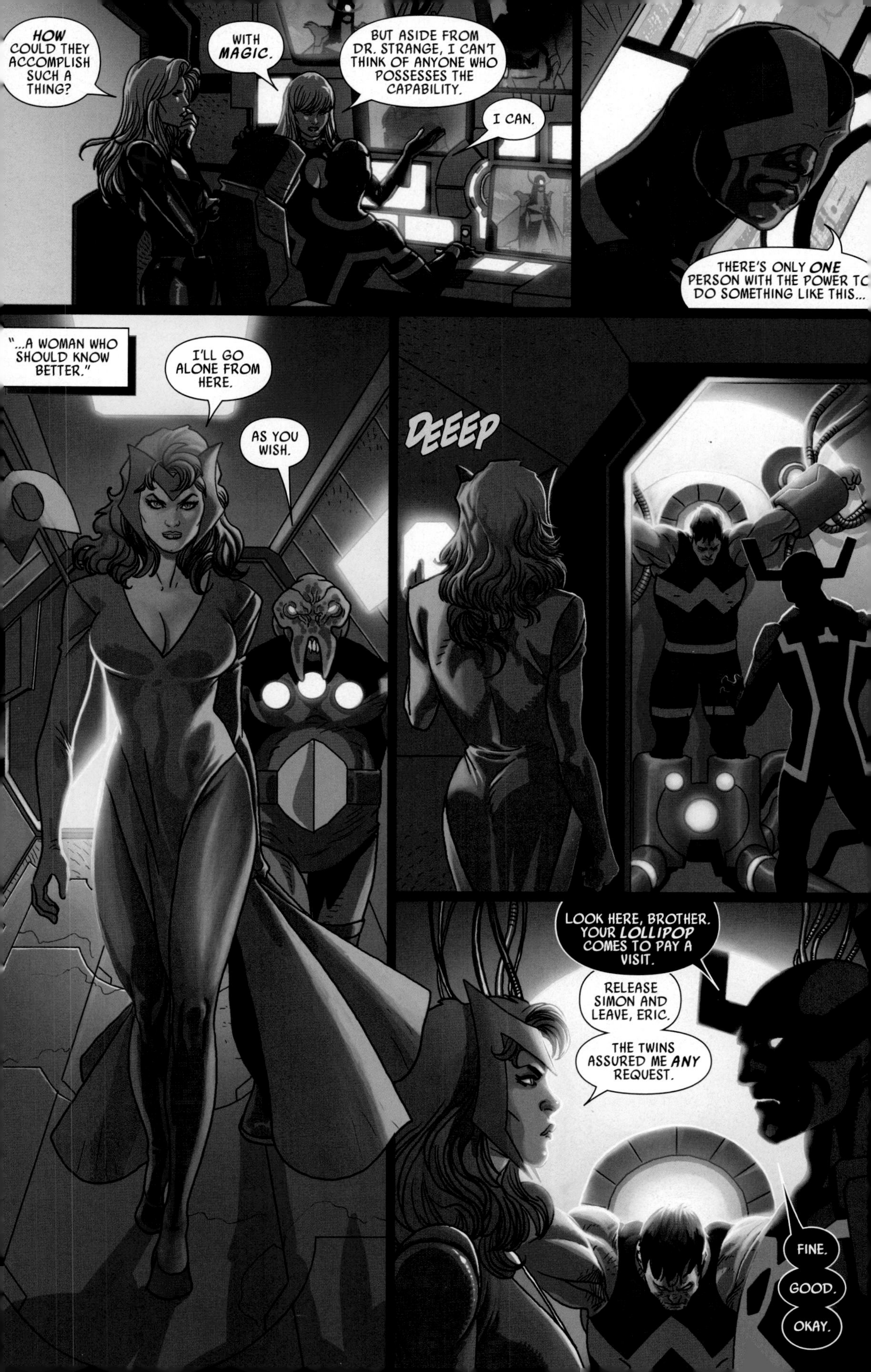
HOW COULD THEY ACCOMPLISH SUCH A THING?
WITH MAGIC.
BUT ASIDE FROM DR. STRANGE, I CAN'T THINK OF ANYONE WHO POSSESSES THE CAPABILITY.
I CAN.
THERE'S ONLY ONE PERSON WITH THE POWER TO DO SOMETHING LIKE THIS...
"...A WOMAN WHO SHOULD KNOW BETTER."
I'LL GO ALONE FROM HERE.
AS YOU WISH.
DEEEP
LOOK HERE, BROTHER. YOUR LOLLIPOP COMES TO PAY A VISIT.
RELEASE SIMON AND LEAVE, ERIC.
THE TWINS ASSURED ME ANY REQUEST.
FINE.
GOOD.
OKAY.

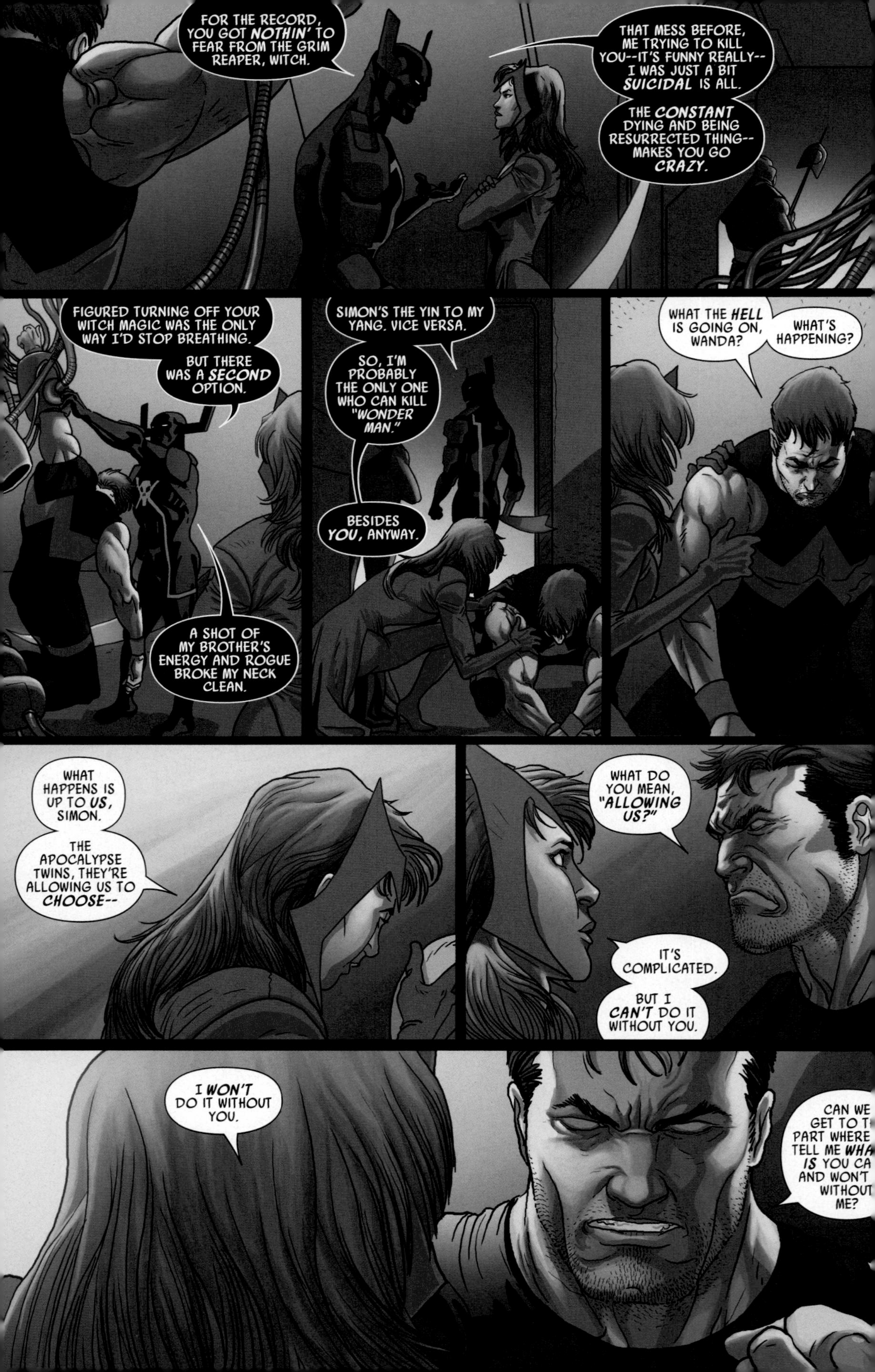
FOR THE RECORD, YOU GOT NOTHIN' TO FEAR FROM THE GRIM REAPER, WITCH.
THAT MESS BEFORE, ME TRYING TO KILL YOU--IT'S FUNNY REALLY--I WAS JUST A BIT SUICIDAL IS ALL.
THE CONSTANT DYING AND BEING RESURRECTED THING--MAKES YOU GO CRAZY.
FIGURED TURNING OFF YOUR WITCH MAGIC WAS THE ONLY WAY I'D STOP BREATHING.
BUT THERE WAS A SECOND OPTION.
A SHOT OF MY BROTHER'S ENERGY AND ROGUE BROKE MY NECK CLEAN.
SIMON'S THE YIN TO MY YANG. VICE VERSA.
SO, I'M PROBABLY THE ONLY ONE WHO CAN KILL "WONDER MAN."
BESIDES YOU, ANYWAY.
WHAT THE HELL IS GOING ON, WANDA?
WHAT'S HAPPENING?
WHAT HAPPENS IS UP TO US, SIMON.
THE APOCALYPSE TWINS, THEY'RE ALLOWING US TO CHOOSE--
WHAT DO YOU MEAN, "ALLOWING US?"
IT'S COMPLICATED.
BUT I CAN'T DO IT WITHOUT YOU.
I WON'T DO IT WITHOUT YOU.

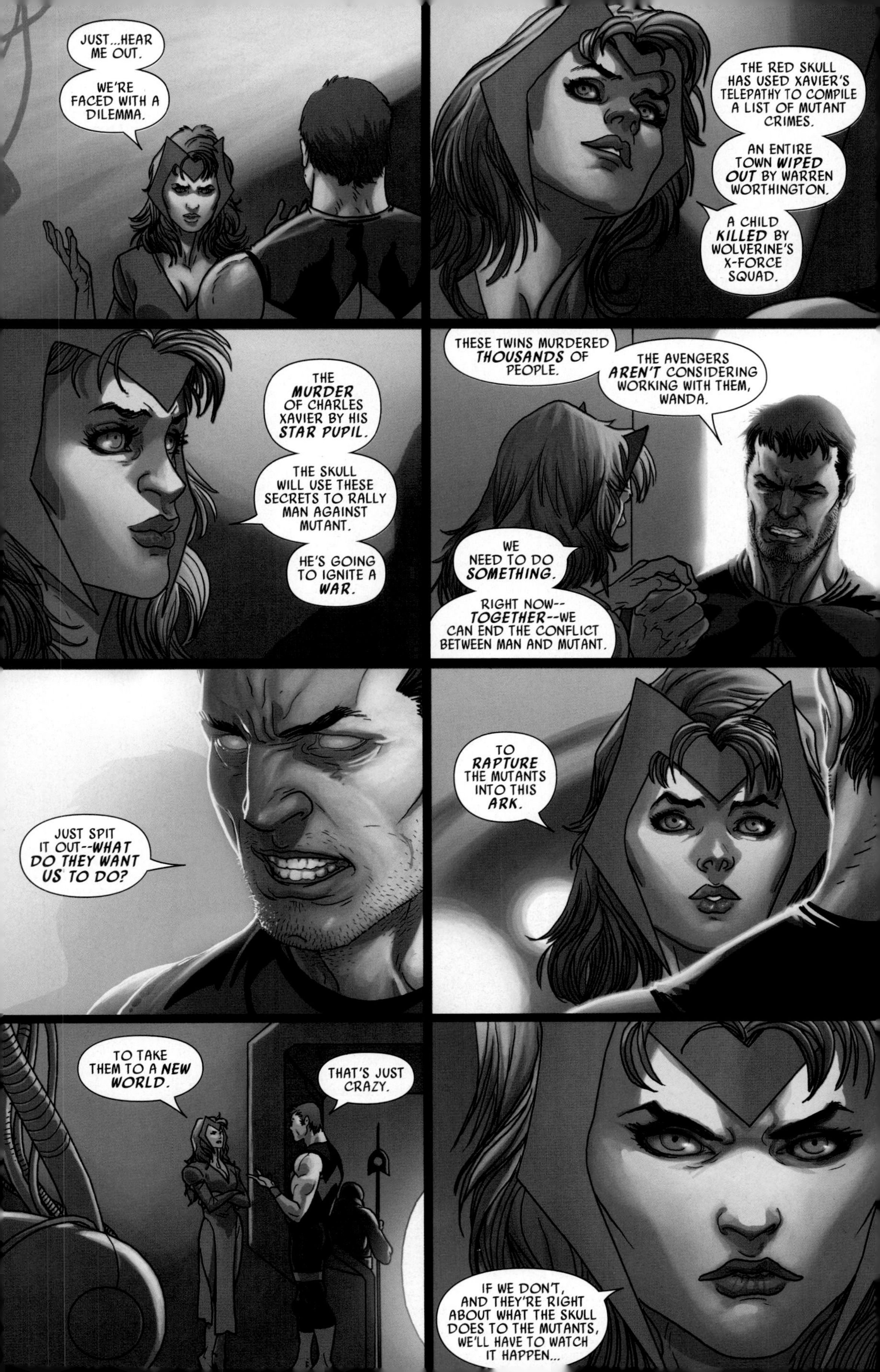
JUST...HEAR ME OUT.
WE'RE FACED WITH A DILEMMA.
THE RED SKULL HAS USED XAVIER'S TELEPATHY TO COMPILE A LIST OF MUTANT CRIMES.
AN ENTIRE TOWN WIPED OUT BY WARREN WORTHINGTON.
A CHILD KILLED BY WOLVERINE'S X-FORCE SQUAD.
THE MURDER OF CHARLES XAVIER BY HIS STAR PUPIL.
THE SKULL WILL USE THESE SECRETS TO RALLY MAN AGAINST MUTANT.
HE'S GOING TO IGNITE A WAR.
THESE TWINS MURDERED THOUSANDS OF PEOPLE.
THE AVENGERS AREN'T CONSIDERING WORKING WITH THEM, WANDA.
WE NEED TO DO SOMETHING.
RIGHT NOW--TOGETHER--WE CAN END THE CONFLICT BETWEEN MAN AND MUTANT.
JUST SPIT IT OUT--WHAT DO THEY WANT US TO DO?
TO RAPTURE THE MUTANTS INTO THIS ARK.
TO TAKE THEM TO A NEW WORLD.
THAT'S JUST CRAZY.
IF WE DON'T, AND THEY'RE RIGHT ABOUT WHAT THE SKULL DOES TO THE MUTANTS, WE'LL HAVE TO WATCH IT HAPPEN...

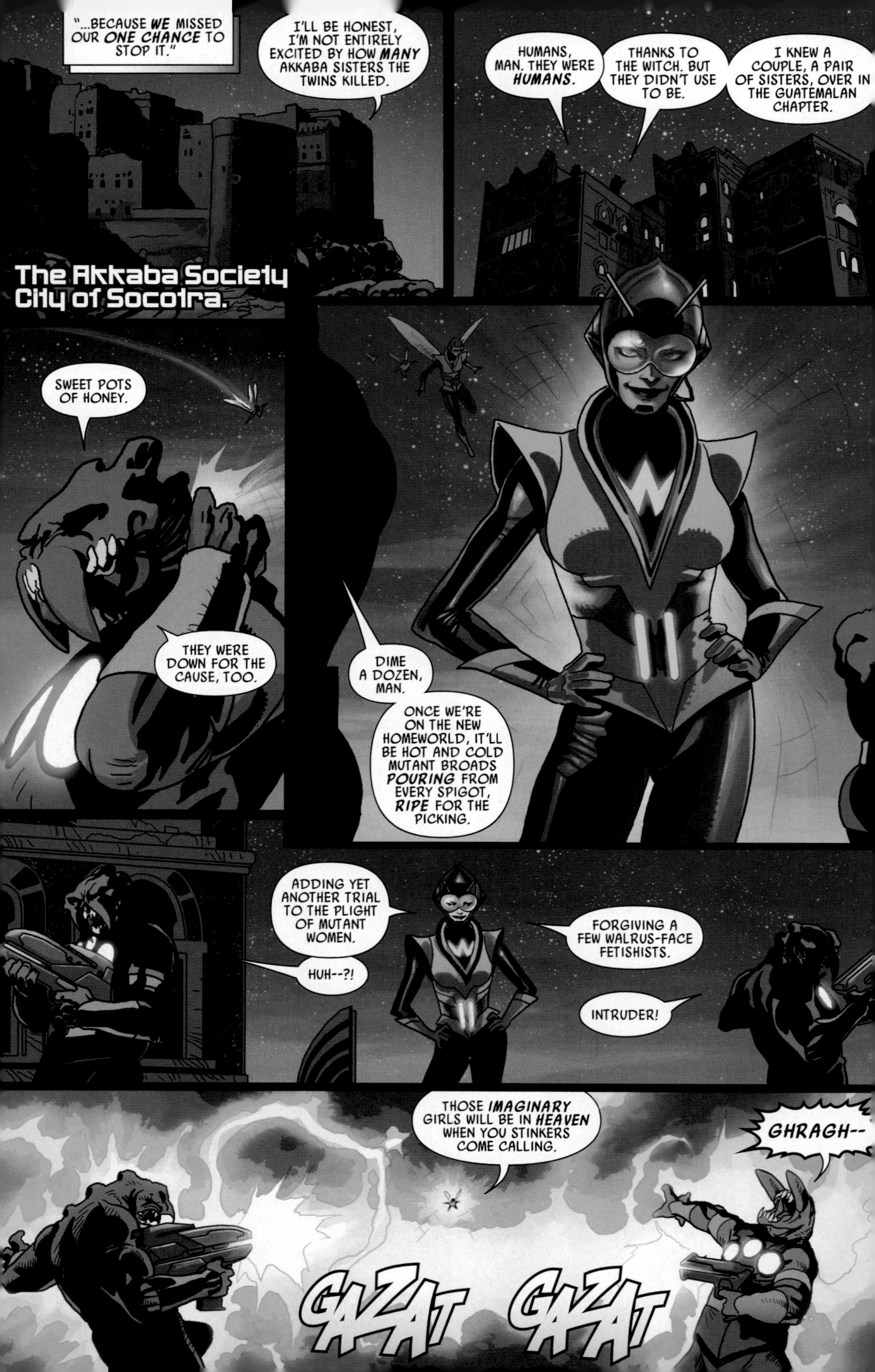
"...BECAUSE WE MISSED OUR ONE CHANCE TO STOP IT."
I'LL BE HONEST, I'M NOT ENTIRELY EXCITED BY HOW MANY AKKABA SISTERS THE TWINS KILLED.
The Akkaba Society
City of Socotra.
HUMANS, MAN. THEY WERE HUMANS.
THANKS TO THE WITCH. BUT THEY DIDN'T USE TO BE.
I KNEW A COUPLE, A PAIR OF SISTERS, OVER IN THE GUATEMALAN CHAPTER.
SWEET POTS OF HONEY.
THEY WERE DOWN FOR THE CAUSE, TOO.
DIME A DOZEN, MAN.
ONCE WE'RE ON THE NEW HOMEWORLD, IT'LL BE HOT AND COLD MUTANT BROADS POURING FROM EVERY SPIGOT, RIPE FOR THE PICKING.
ADDING YET ANOTHER TRIAL TO THE PLIGHT OF MUTANT WOMEN.
HUH--?!
FORGIVING A FEW WALRUS-FACE FETISHISTS.
INTRUDER!
THOSE IMAGINARY GIRLS WILL BE IN HEAVEN WHEN YOU STINKERS COME CALLING.
GHRAGH--
GAZAT
GAZAT

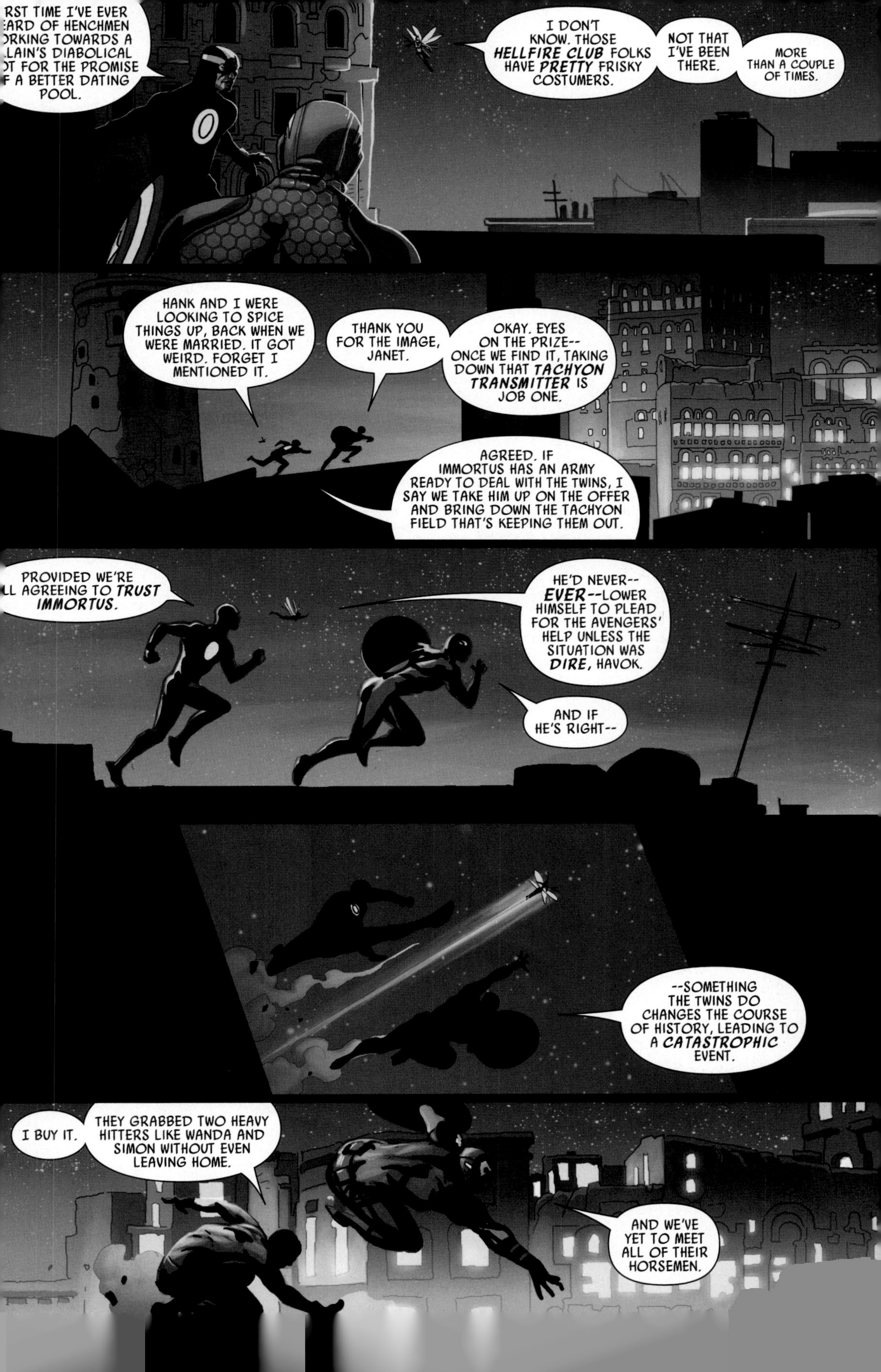
RST TIME I'VE EVER EARD OF HENCHMEN ORKING TOWARDS A LAIN'S DIABOLICAL OT FOR THE PROMISE F A BETTER DATING POOL.
I DON'T KNOW. THOSE HELLFIRE CLUB FOLKS HAVE PRETTY FRISKY COSTUMERS.
NOT THAT I'VE BEEN THERE.
MORE THAN A COUPLE OF TIMES.
HANK AND I WERE LOOKING TO SPICE THINGS UP, BACK WHEN WE WERE MARRIED. IT GOT WEIRD. FORGET I MENTIONED IT.
THANK YOU FOR THE IMAGE, JANET.
OKAY. EYES ON THE PRIZE-- ONCE WE FIND IT, TAKING DOWN THAT TACHYON TRANSMITTER IS JOB ONE.
AGREED. IF IMMORTUS HAS AN ARMY READY TO DEAL WITH THE TWINS, I SAY WE TAKE HIM UP ON THE OFFER AND BRING DOWN THE TACHYON FIELD THAT'S KEEPING THEM OUT.
PROVIDED WE'RE LL AGREEING TO TRUST IMMORTUS.
HE'D NEVER-- EVER--LOWER HIMSELF TO PLEAD FOR THE AVENGERS' HELP UNLESS THE SITUATION WAS DIRE, HAVOK.
AND IF HE'S RIGHT--
--SOMETHING THE TWINS DO CHANGES THE COURSE OF HISTORY, LEADING TO A CATASTROPHIC EVENT.
I BUY IT.
THEY GRABBED TWO HEAVY HITTERS LIKE WANDA AND SIMON WITHOUT EVEN LEAVING HOME.
AND WE'VE YET TO MEET ALL OF THEIR HORSEMEN.

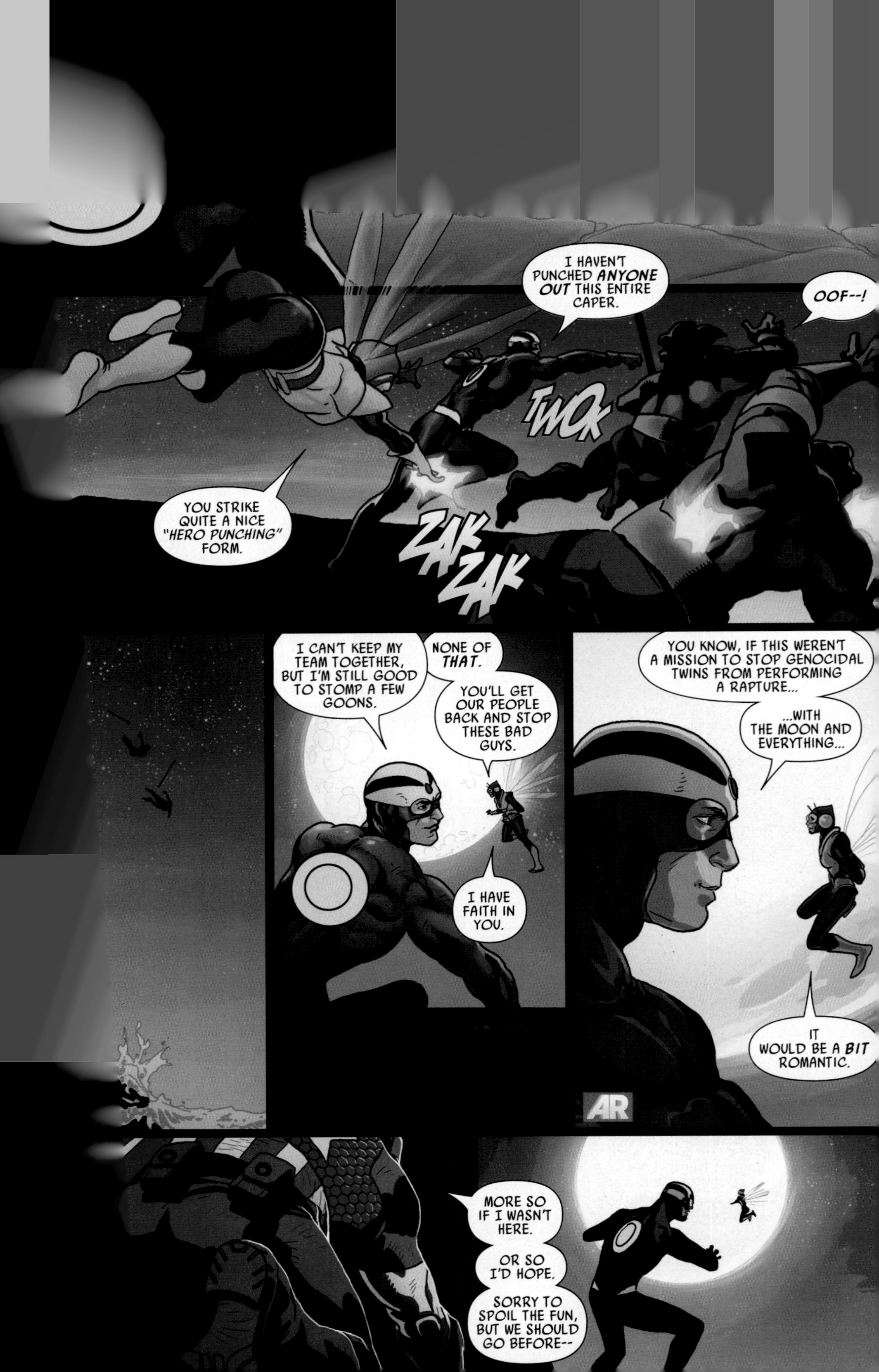
I HAVEN'T PUNCHED ANYONE OUT THIS ENTIRE CAPER.
OOF--!
TWOK
YOU STRIKE QUITE A NICE "HERO PUNCHING" FORM.
ZAK ZAK
I CAN'T KEEP MY TEAM TOGETHER, BUT I'M STILL GOOD TO STOMP A FEW GOONS.
NONE OF THAT.
YOU'LL GET OUR PEOPLE BACK AND STOP THESE BAD GUYS.
I HAVE FAITH IN YOU.
YOU KNOW, IF THIS WEREN'T A MISSION TO STOP GENOCIDAL TWINS FROM PERFORMING A RAPTURE...
...WITH THE MOON AND EVERYTHING...
IT WOULD BE A BIT ROMANTIC.
MORE SO IF I WASN'T HERE.
OR SO I'D HOPE.
SORRY TO SPOIL THE FUN, BUT WE SHOULD GO BEFORE--

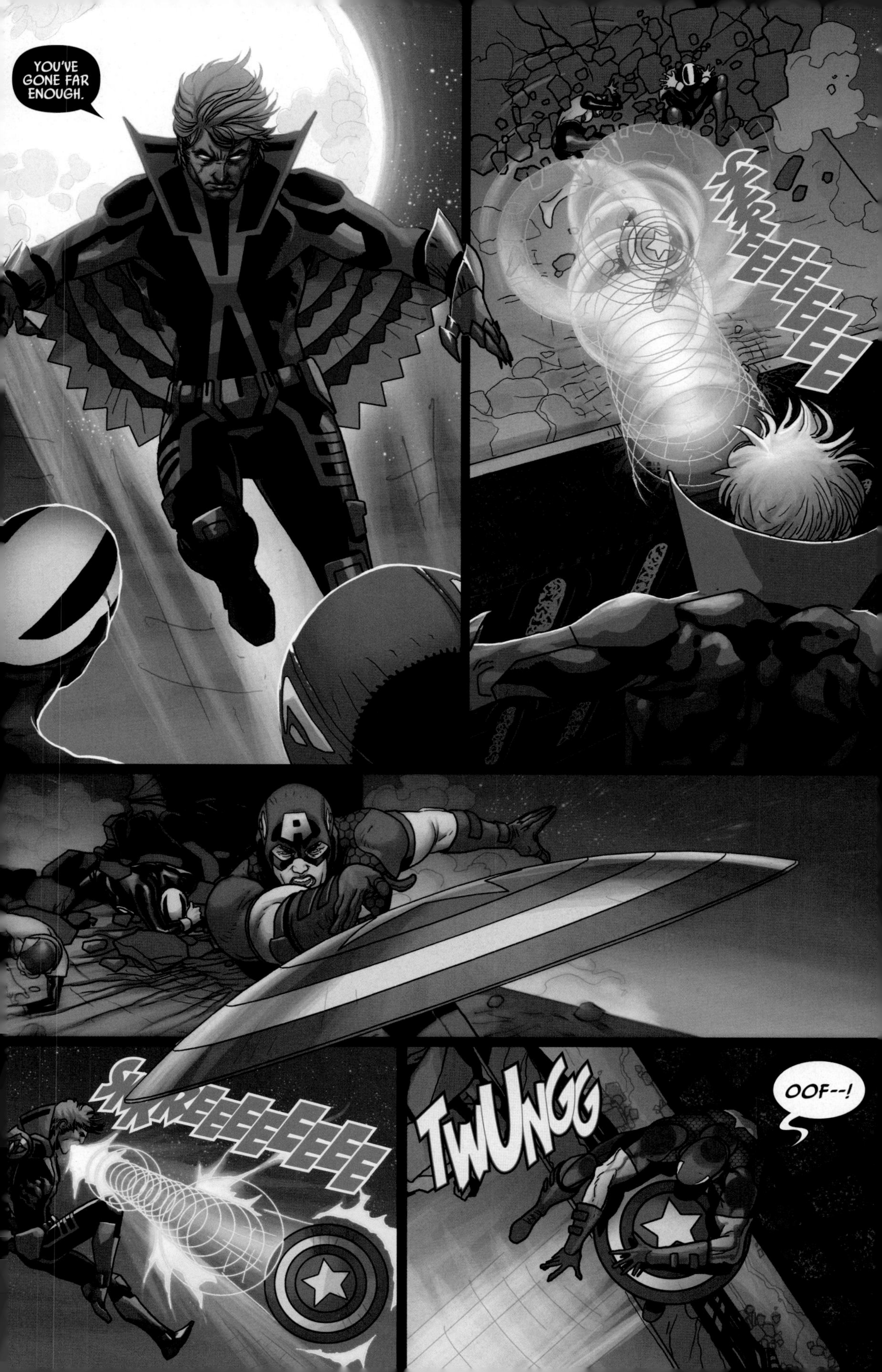

YOU'VE GONE FAR ENOUGH.
SKREEEEEEEE
SKREEEEEEEEEEE
TWUNGG
OOF--!

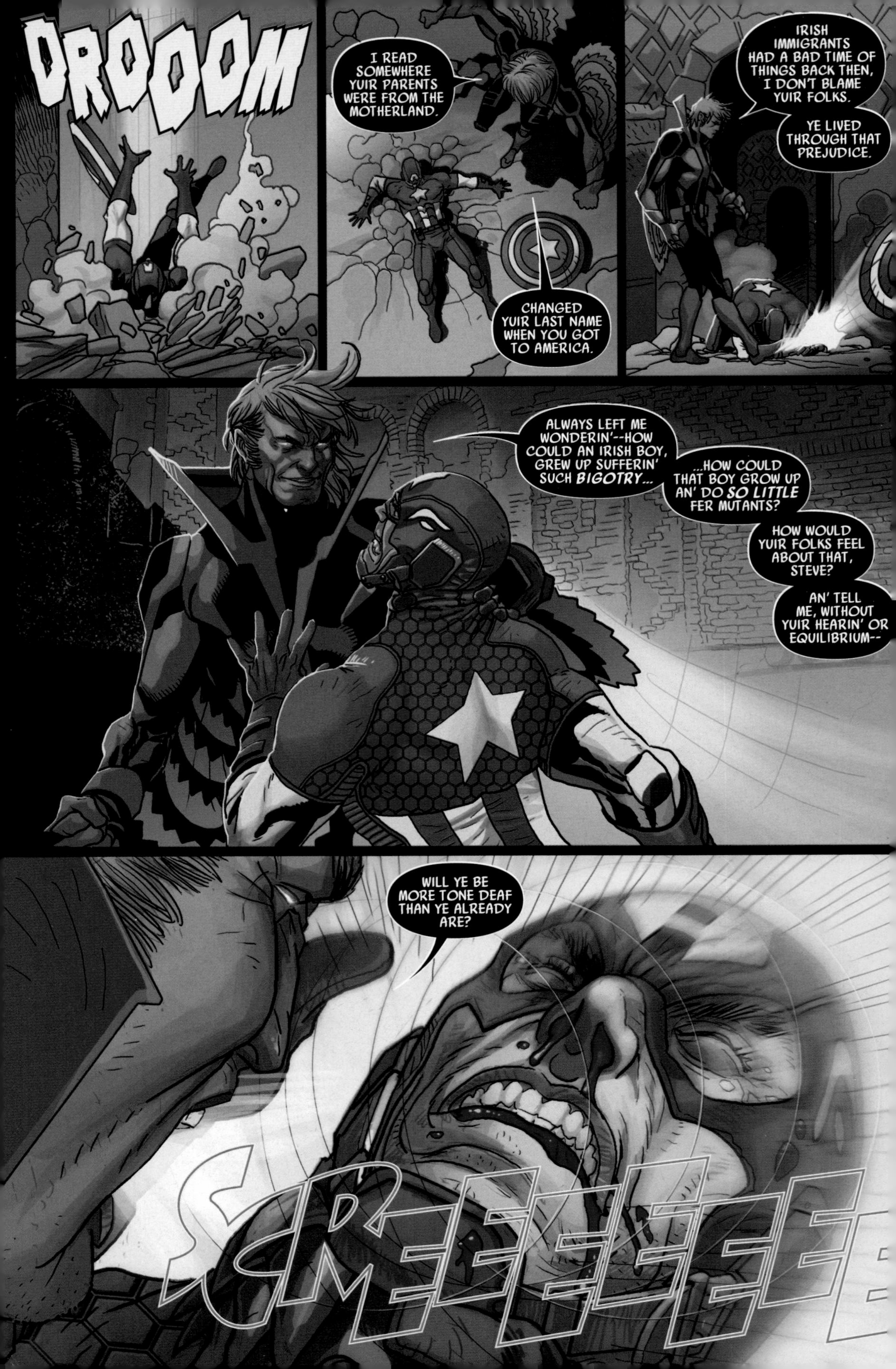
DROOOM
I READ SOMEWHERE YUIR PARENTS WERE FROM THE MOTHERLAND.
CHANGED YUIR LAST NAME WHEN YOU GOT TO AMERICA.
IRISH IMMIGRANTS HAD A BAD TIME OF THINGS BACK THEN, I DON'T BLAME YUIR FOLKS.
YE LIVED THROUGH THAT PREJUDICE.
ALWAYS LEFT ME WONDERIN'--HOW COULD AN IRISH BOY, GREW UP SUFFERIN' SUCH BIGOTRY...
...HOW COULD THAT BOY GROW UP AN' DO SO LITTLE FER MUTANTS?
HOW WOULD YUIR FOLKS FEEL ABOUT THAT, STEVE?
AN' TELL ME, WITHOUT YUIR HEARIN' OR EQUILIBRIUM--
WILL YE BE MORE TONE DEAF THAN YE ALREADY ARE?
SCREEEEEEE

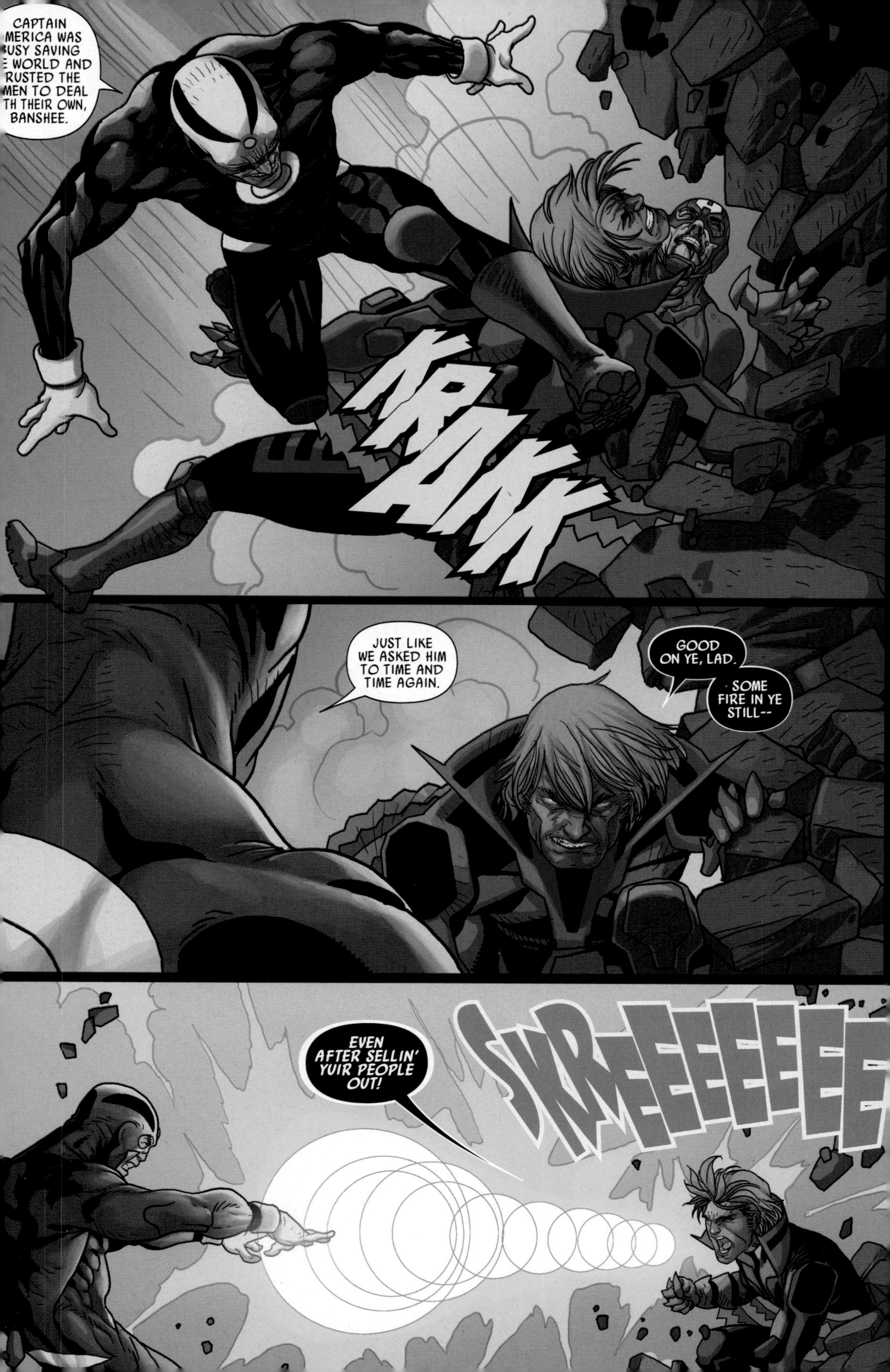
CAPTAIN
MERICA WAS
BUSY SAVING
E WORLD AND
RUSTED THE
MEN TO DEAL
TH THEIR OWN,
BANSHEE.
KRAKK
JUST LIKE WE ASKED HIM TO TIME AND TIME AGAIN.
GOOD ON YE, LAD.
SOME FIRE IN YE STILL--
EVEN AFTER SELLIN' YUIR PEOPLE OUT!
SKREEEEEEEEE

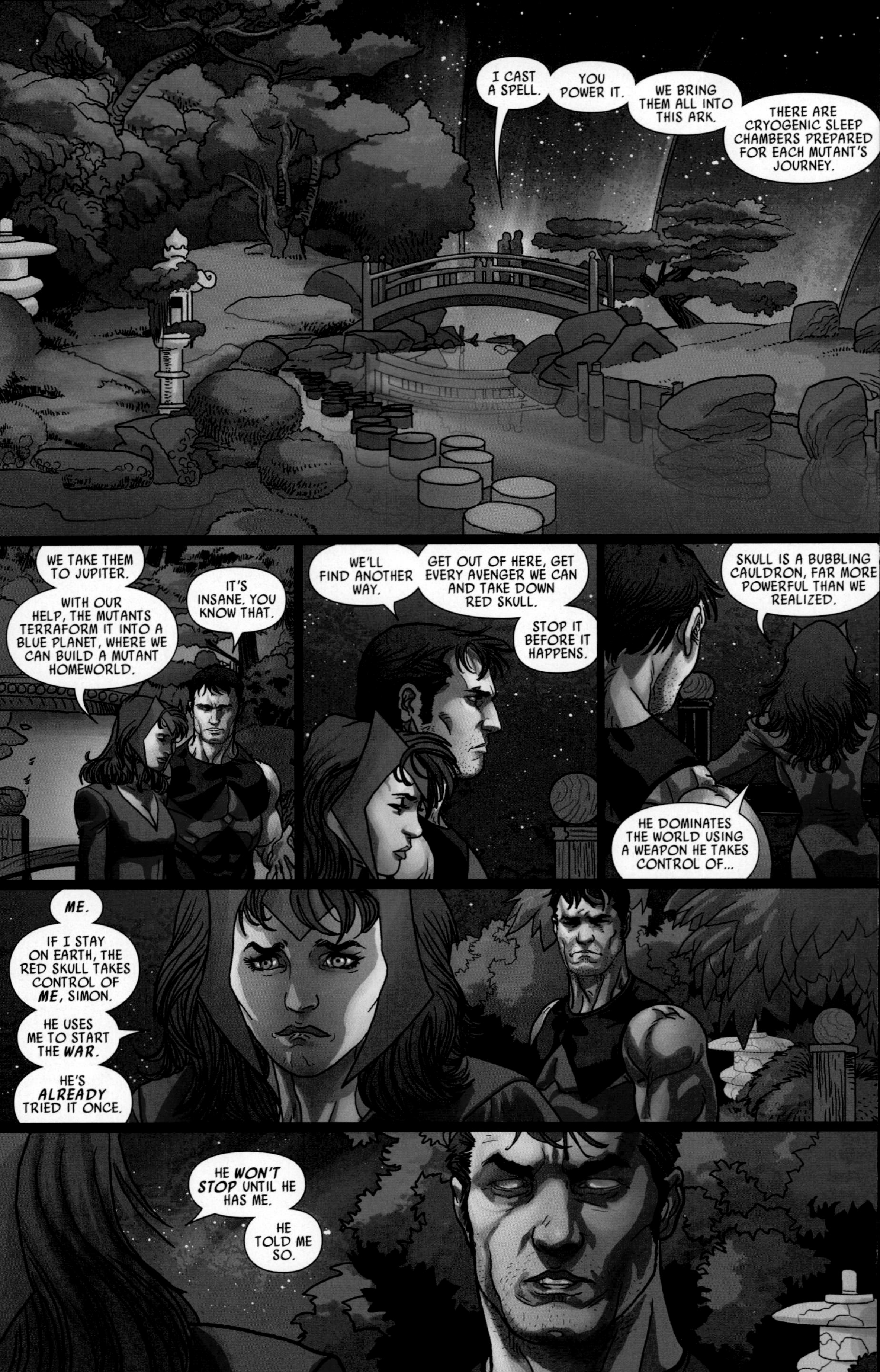
I CAST A SPELL.
YOU POWER IT.
WE BRING THEM ALL INTO THIS ARK.
THERE ARE CRYOGENIC SLEEP CHAMBERS PREPARED FOR EACH MUTANT'S JOURNEY.
WE TAKE THEM TO JUPITER.
WITH OUR HELP, THE MUTANTS TERRAFORM IT INTO A BLUE PLANET, WHERE WE CAN BUILD A MUTANT HOMEWORLD.
IT'S INSANE. YOU KNOW THAT.
WE'LL FIND ANOTHER WAY.
GET OUT OF HERE, GET EVERY AVENGER WE CAN AND TAKE DOWN RED SKULL.
STOP IT BEFORE IT HAPPENS.
SKULL IS A BUBBLING CAULDRON, FAR MORE POWERFUL THAN WE REALIZED.
HE DOMINATES THE WORLD USING A WEAPON HE TAKES CONTROL OF...
ME.
IF I STAY ON EARTH, THE RED SKULL TAKES CONTROL OF ME, SIMON.
HE USES ME TO START THE WAR.
HE'S ALREADY TRIED IT ONCE.
HE WON'T STOP UNTIL HE HAS ME.
HE TOLD ME SO.

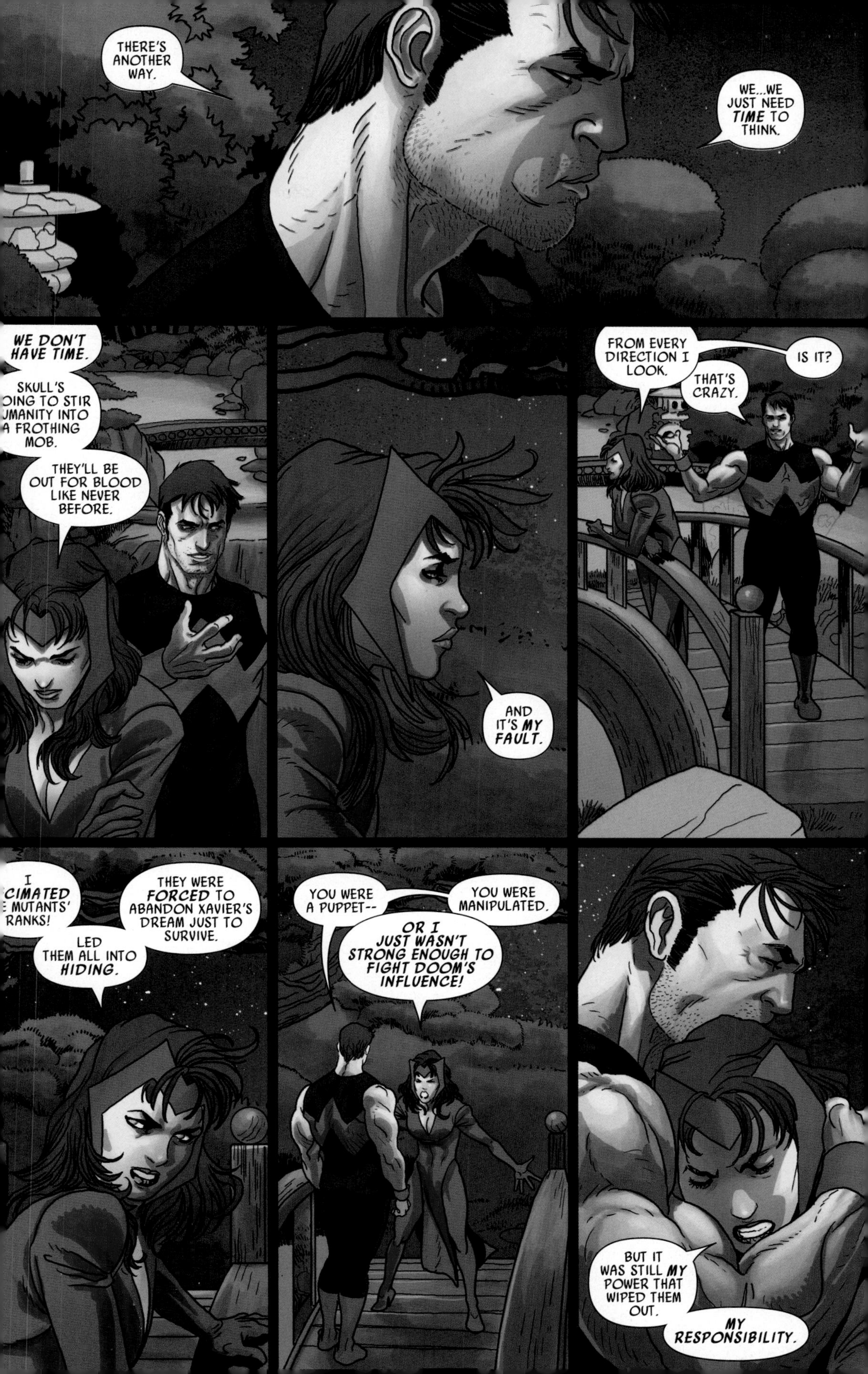
THERE'S ANOTHER WAY.
WE...WE JUST NEED *TIME* TO THINK.
WE DON'T HAVE TIME.
SKULL'S OING TO STIR UMANITY INTO A FROTHING MOB.
THEY'LL BE OUT FOR BLOOD LIKE NEVER BEFORE.
AND IT'S ***MY FAULT.***
FROM EVERY DIRECTION I LOOK.
THAT'S CRAZY.
IS IT?
I ***CIMATED*** E MUTANTS' RANKS!
LED THEM ALL INTO ***HIDING.***
THEY WERE ***FORCED*** TO ABANDON XAVIER'S DREAM JUST TO SURVIVE.
YOU WERE A PUPPET--
YOU WERE MANIPULATED.
OR I JUST WASN'T STRONG ENOUGH TO FIGHT DOOM'S INFLUENCE!
BUT IT WAS STILL ***MY*** POWER THAT WIPED THEM OUT.
MY RESPONSIBILITY.

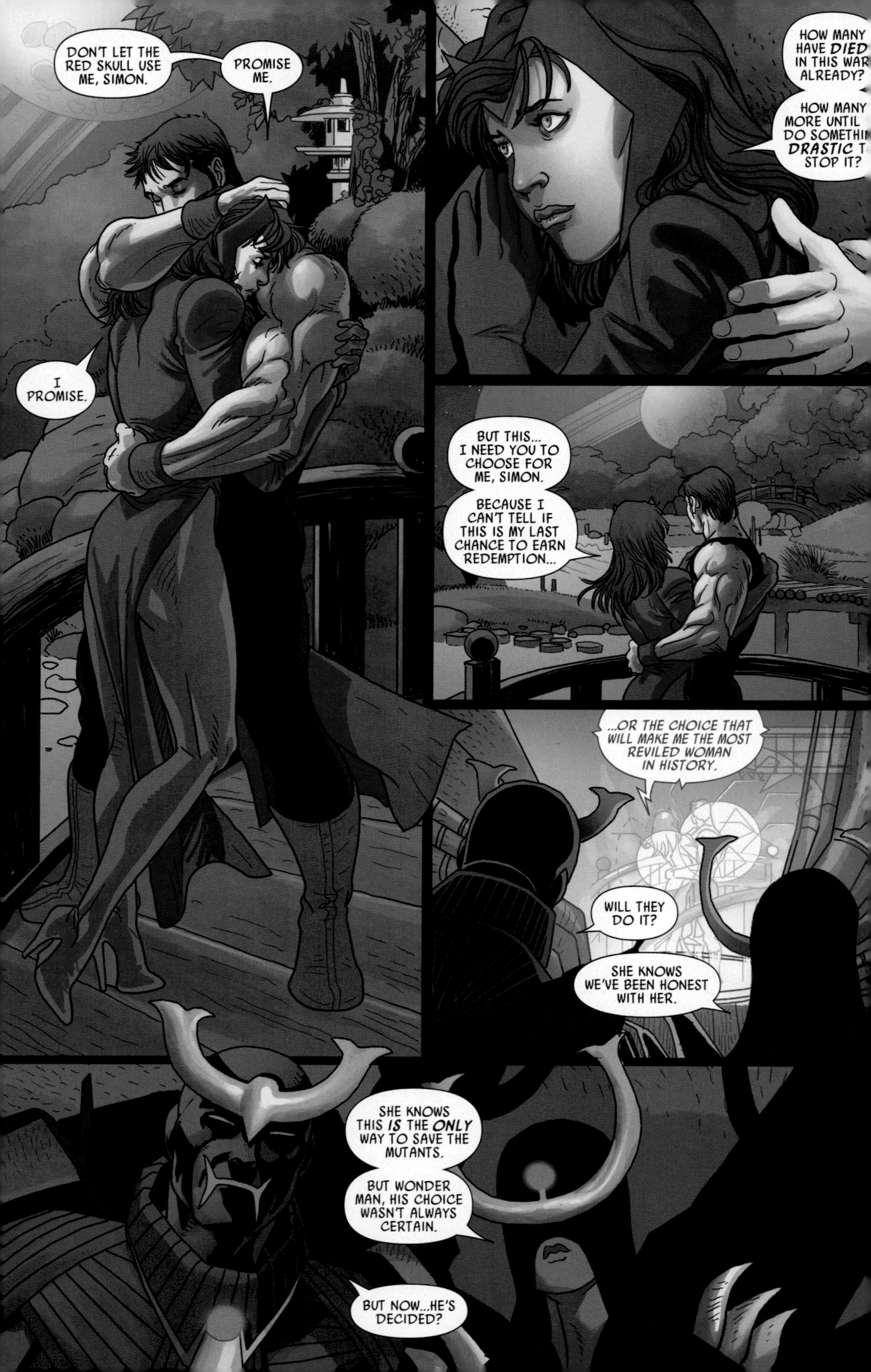
DON'T LET THE RED SKULL USE ME, SIMON.
PROMISE ME.
I PROMISE.
HOW MANY HAVE DIED IN THIS WAR ALREADY?
HOW MANY MORE UNTIL DO SOMETHI DRASTIC T STOP IT?
BUT THIS... I NEED YOU TO CHOOSE FOR ME, SIMON.
BECAUSE I CAN'T TELL IF THIS IS MY LAST CHANCE TO EARN REDEMPTION...
...OR THE CHOICE THAT WILL MAKE ME THE MOST REVILED WOMAN IN HISTORY.
WILL THEY DO IT?
SHE KNOWS WE'VE BEEN HONEST WITH HER.
SHE KNOWS THIS IS THE ONLY WAY TO SAVE THE MUTANTS.
BUT WONDER MAN, HIS CHOICE WASN'T ALWAYS CERTAIN.
BUT NOW...HE'S DECIDED?

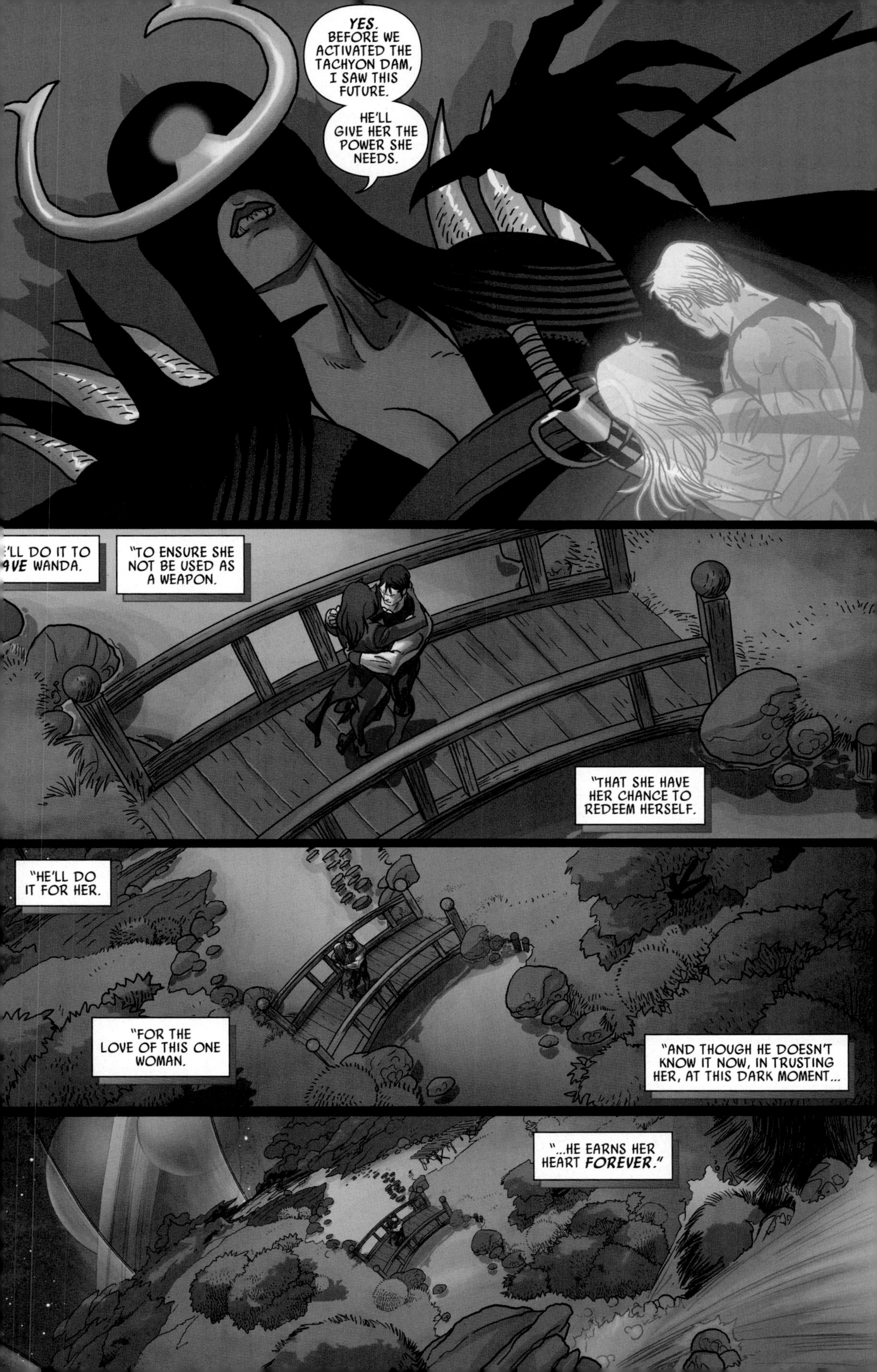
YES. BEFORE WE ACTIVATED THE TACHYON DAM, I SAW THIS FUTURE.
HE'LL GIVE HER THE POWER SHE NEEDS.
'LL DO IT TO AVE WANDA.
"TO ENSURE SHE NOT BE USED AS A WEAPON.
"THAT SHE HAVE HER CHANCE TO REDEEM HERSELF.
"HE'LL DO IT FOR HER.
"FOR THE LOVE OF THIS ONE WOMAN.
"AND THOUGH HE DOESN'T KNOW IT NOW, IN TRUSTING HER, AT THIS DARK MOMENT...
"...HE EARNS HER HEART FOREVER."

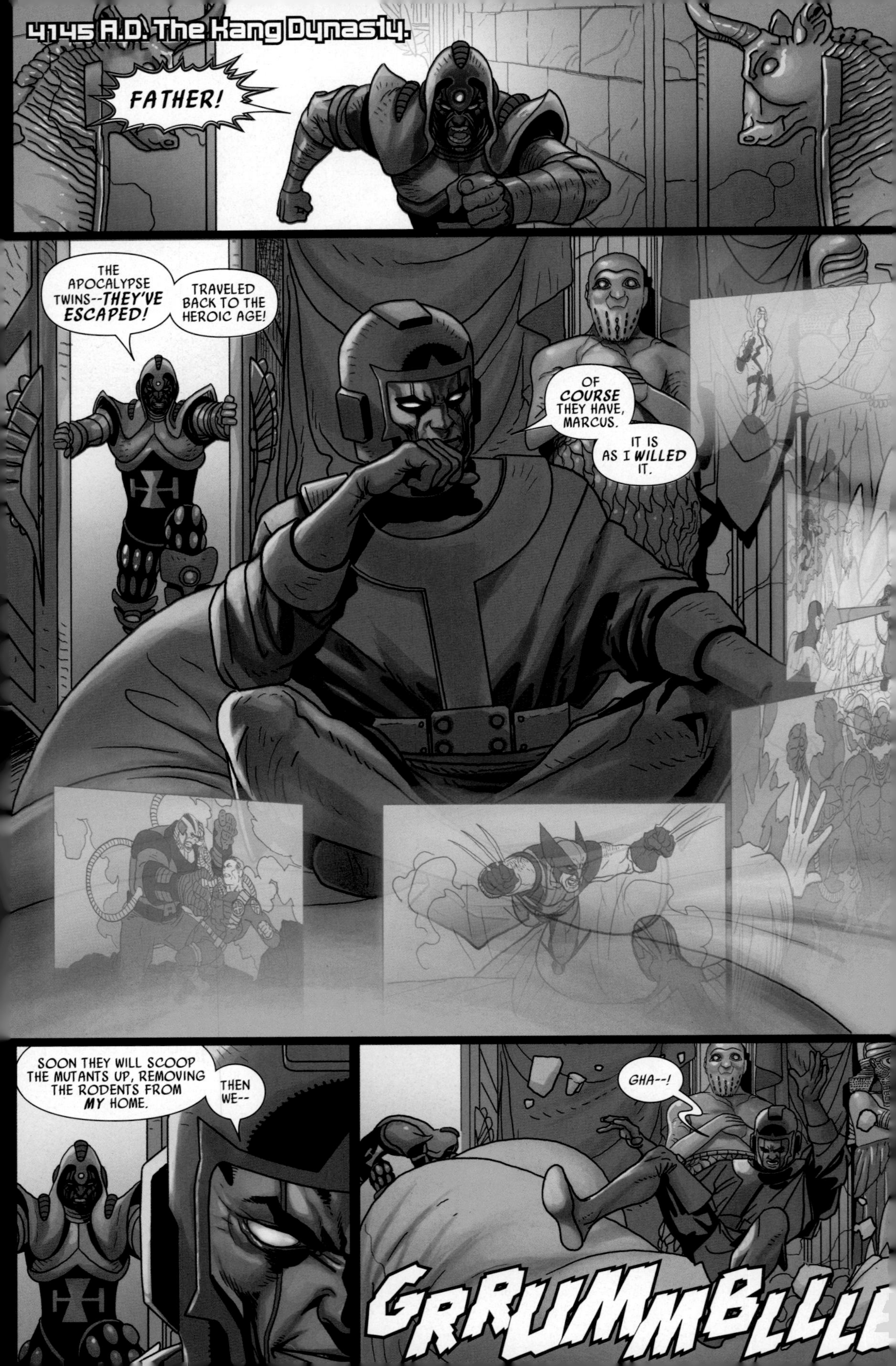
4145 A.D. The Kang Dynasty.
FATHER!
THE APOCALYPSE TWINS--THEY'VE ESCAPED!
TRAVELED BACK TO THE HEROIC AGE!
OF COURSE THEY HAVE, MARCUS.
IT IS AS I WILLED IT.
SOON THEY WILL SCOOP THE MUTANTS UP, REMOVING THE RODENTS FROM MY HOME.
THEN WE--
GHA--!
GRRUMMBLLLE

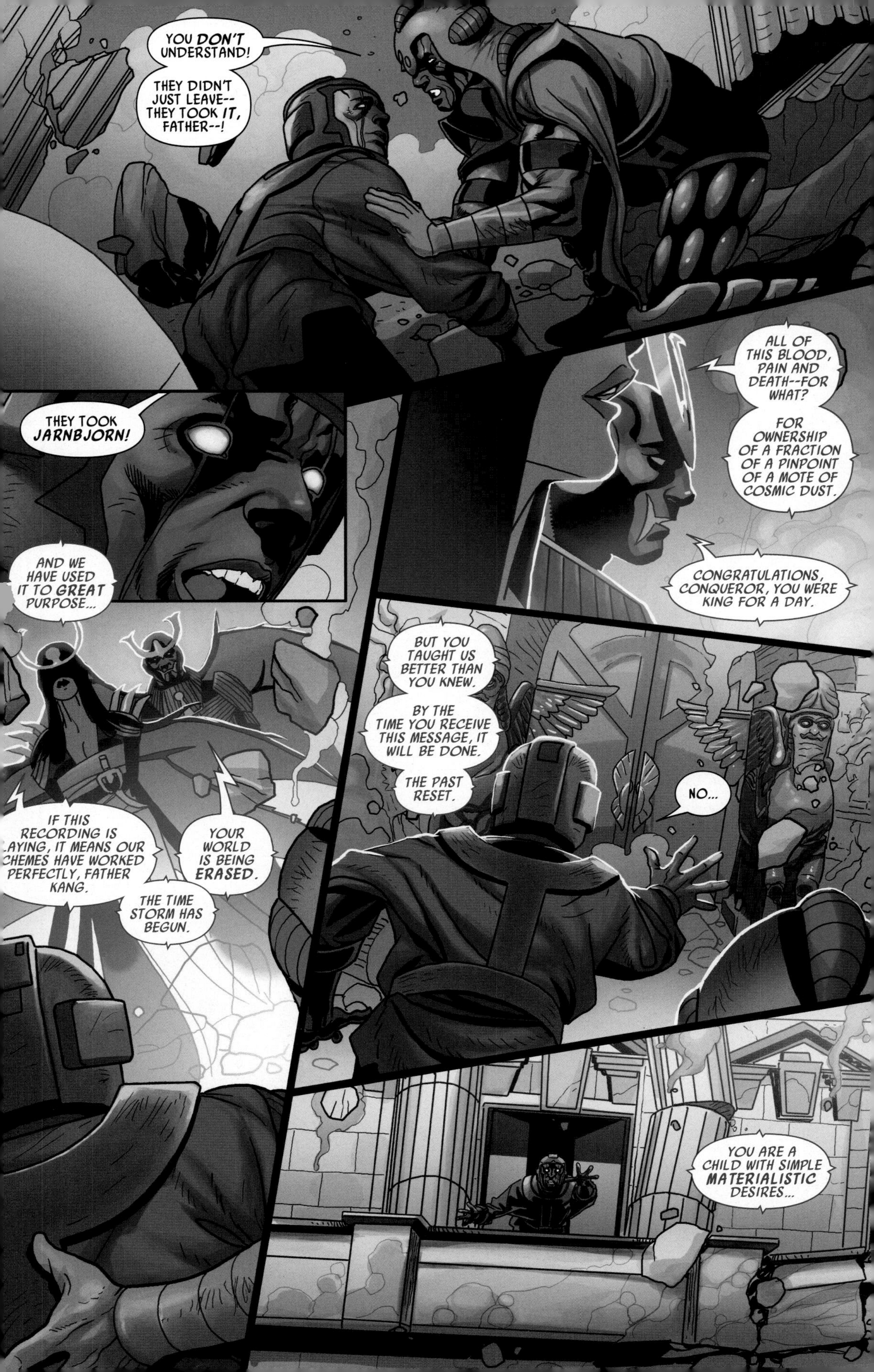

YOU **DON'T** UNDERSTAND!
THEY DIDN'T JUST LEAVE-- THEY TOOK *IT*, FATHER--!
THEY TOOK **JARNBJORN!**
ALL OF THIS BLOOD, PAIN AND DEATH--FOR WHAT?
FOR OWNERSHIP OF A FRACTION OF A PINPOINT OF A MOTE OF COSMIC DUST.
CONGRATULATIONS, CONQUEROR, YOU WERE KING FOR A DAY.
AND WE HAVE USED IT TO **GREAT** PURPOSE...
IF THIS RECORDING IS LAYING, IT MEANS OUR CHEMES HAVE WORKED PERFECTLY, FATHER KANG.
YOUR WORLD IS BEING **ERASED**.
THE TIME STORM HAS BEGUN.
BUT YOU TAUGHT US BETTER THAN YOU KNEW.
BY THE TIME YOU RECEIVE THIS MESSAGE, IT WILL BE DONE.
THE PAST RESET.
NO...
YOU ARE A CHILD WITH SIMPLE **MATERIALISTIC** DESIRES...

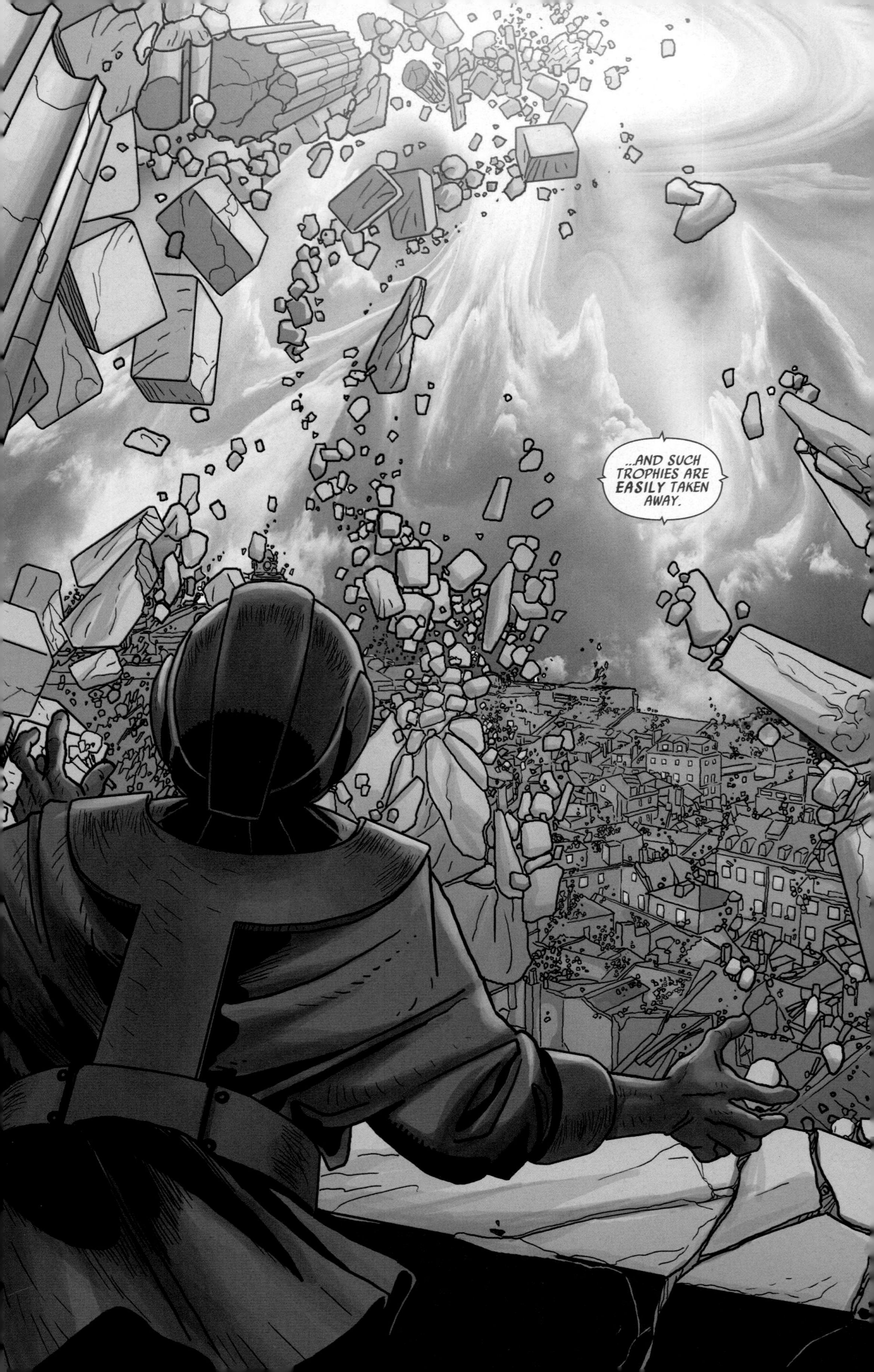
...AND SUCH TROPHIES ARE EASILY TAKEN AWAY.

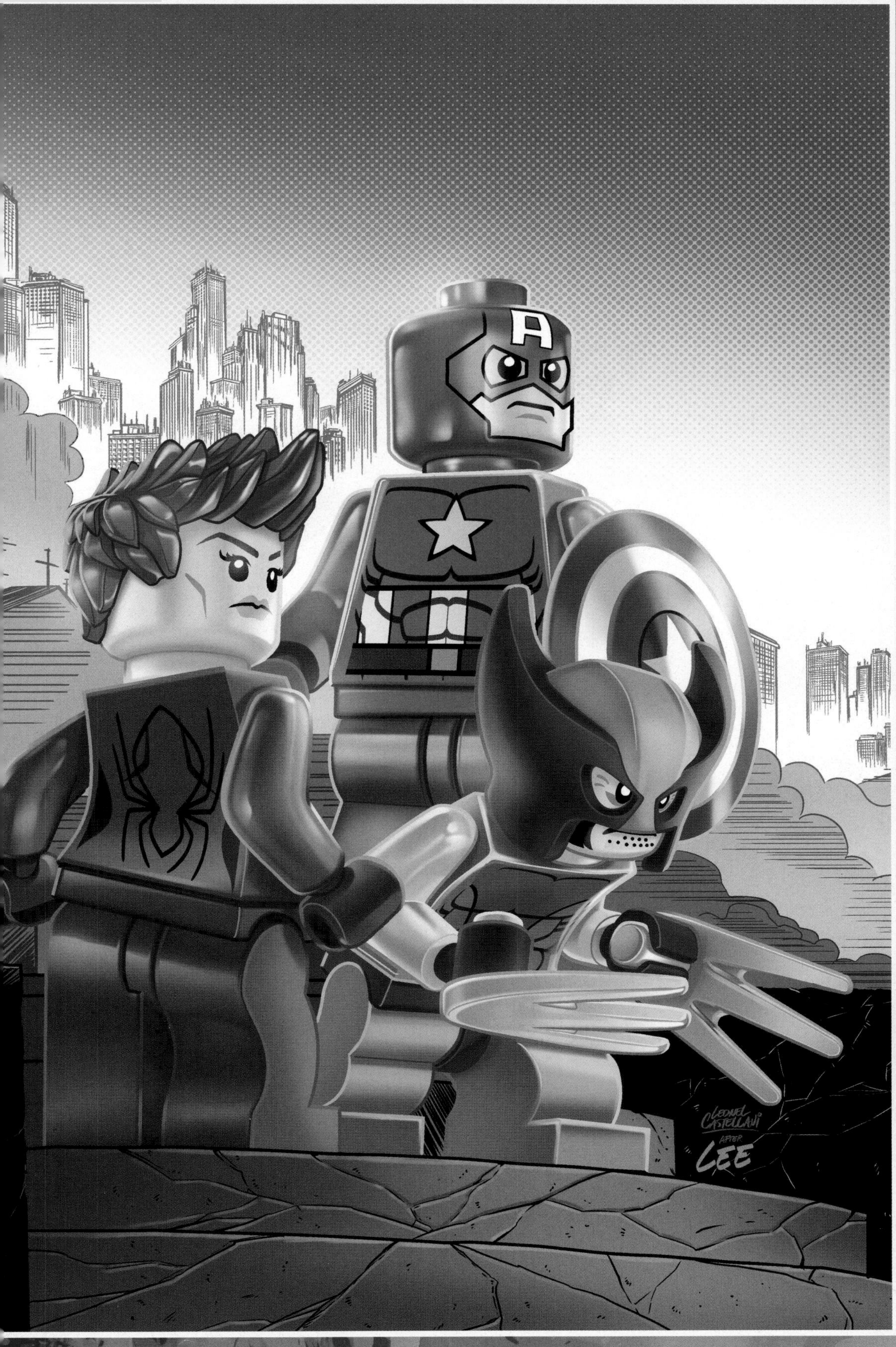
A
LEONEL CASTELLANI
AFTER
LEE

UNCANNY AVENGERS #13

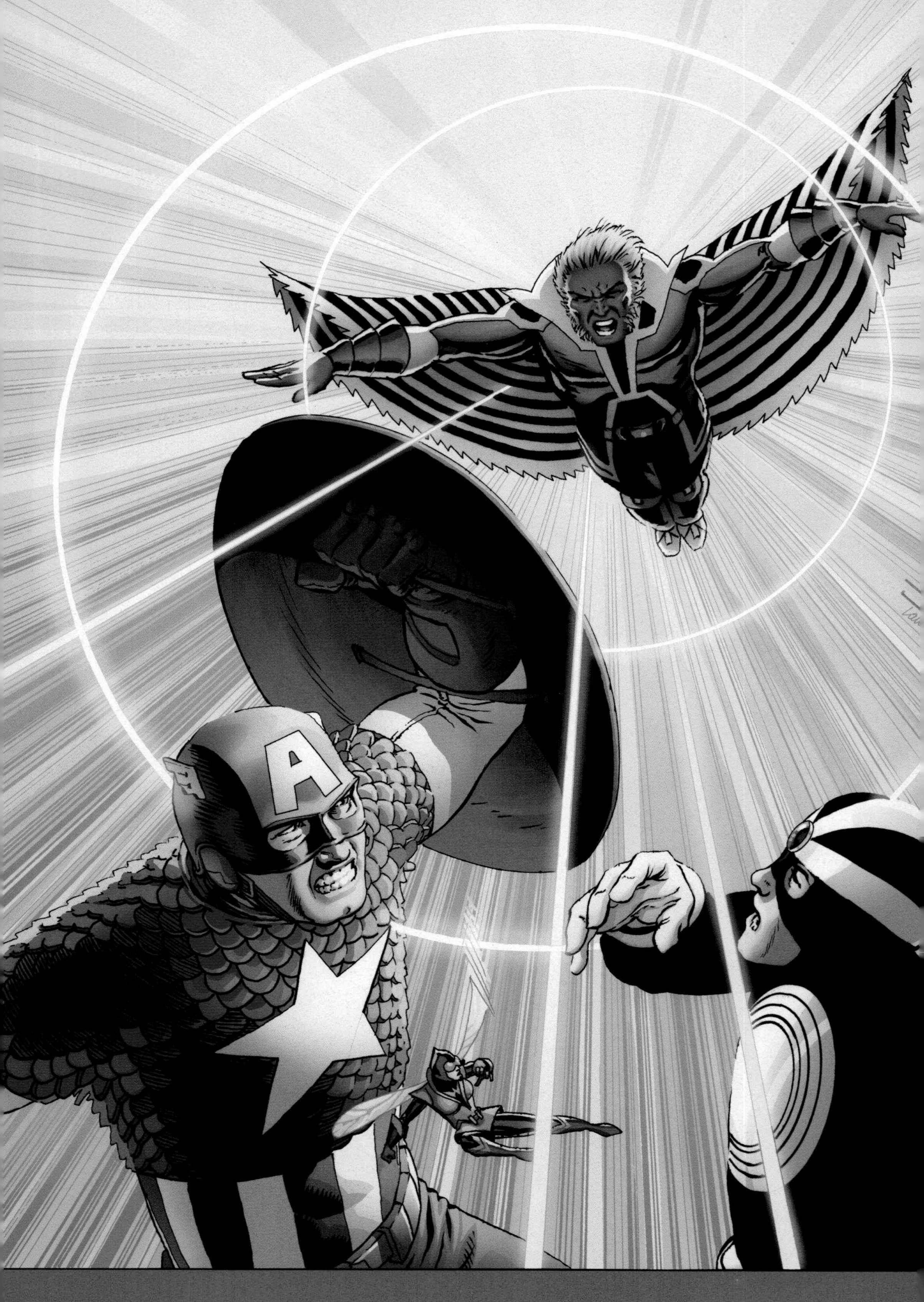

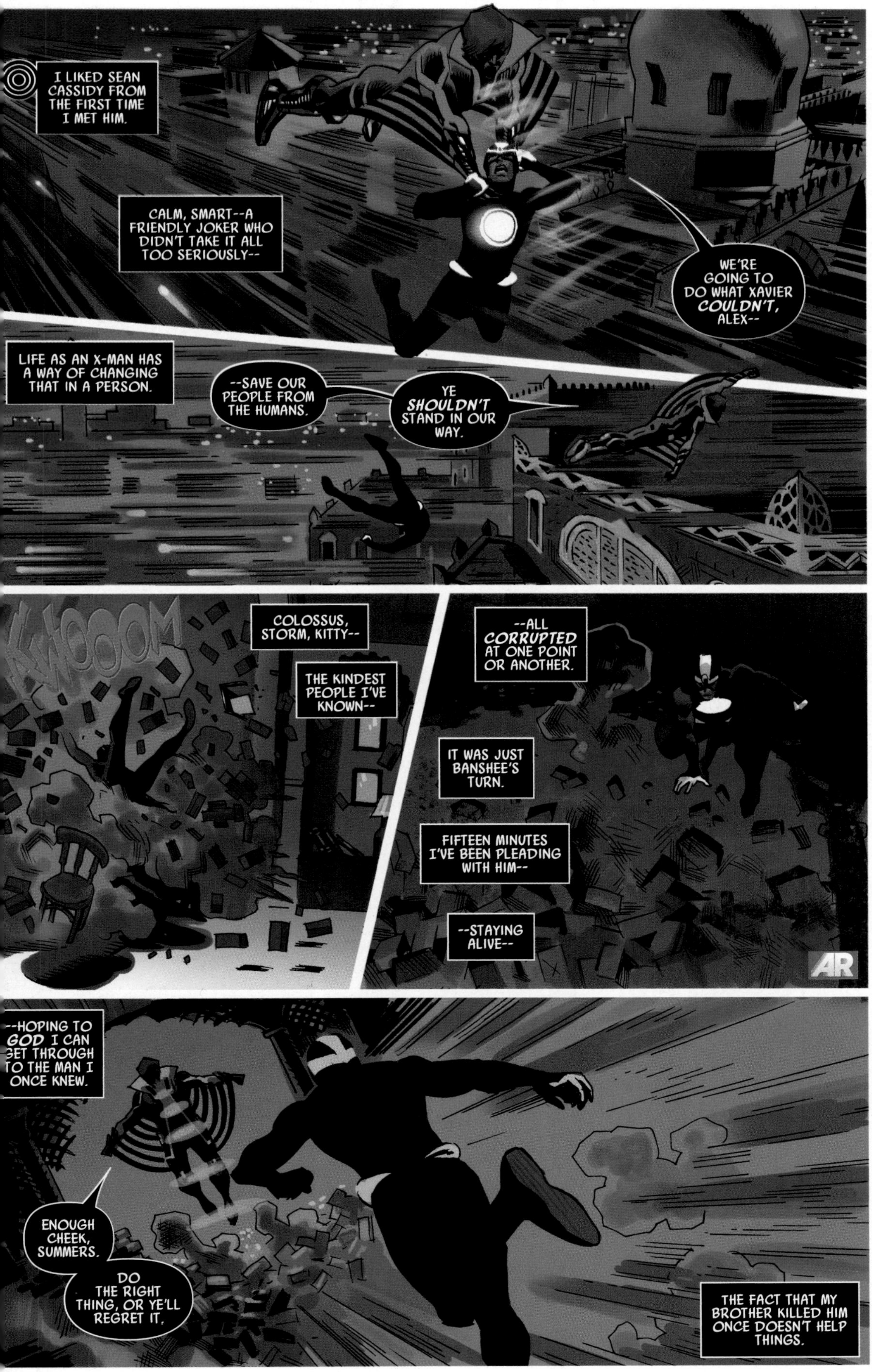
I LIKED SEAN CASSIDY FROM THE FIRST TIME I MET HIM.
CALM, SMART--A FRIENDLY JOKER WHO DIDN'T TAKE IT ALL TOO SERIOUSLY--
WE'RE GOING TO DO WHAT XAVIER COULDN'T, ALEX--
LIFE AS AN X-MAN HAS A WAY OF CHANGING THAT IN A PERSON.
--SAVE OUR PEOPLE FROM THE HUMANS.
YE SHOULDN'T STAND IN OUR WAY.
KWOOOM
COLOSSUS, STORM, KITTY--
THE KINDEST PEOPLE I'VE KNOWN--
--ALL CORRUPTED AT ONE POINT OR ANOTHER.
IT WAS JUST BANSHEE'S TURN.
FIFTEEN MINUTES I'VE BEEN PLEADING WITH HIM--
--STAYING ALIVE--
--HOPING TO GOD I CAN GET THROUGH TO THE MAN I ONCE KNEW.
ENOUGH CHEEK, SUMMERS.
DO THE RIGHT THING, OR YE'LL REGRET IT.
THE FACT THAT MY BROTHER KILLED HIM ONCE DOESN'T HELP THINGS.

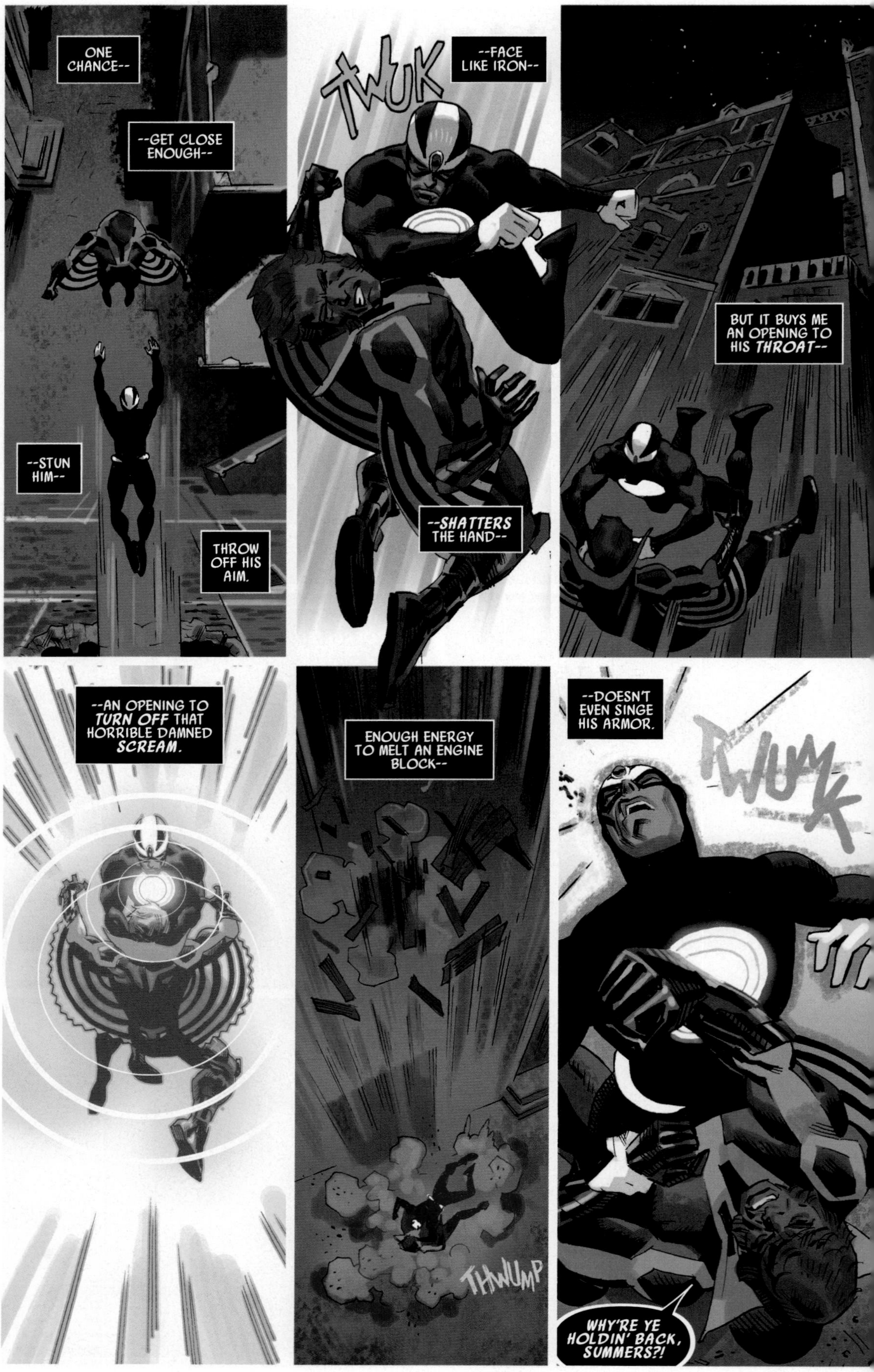
ONE CHANCE--
--GET CLOSE ENOUGH--
--STUN HIM--
THROW OFF HIS AIM.
TWUK
--FACE LIKE IRON--
--SHATTERS THE HAND--
BUT IT BUYS ME AN OPENING TO HIS THROAT--
--AN OPENING TO TURN OFF THAT HORRIBLE DAMNED SCREAM.
ENOUGH ENERGY TO MELT AN ENGINE BLOCK--
THWUMP
--DOESN'T EVEN SINGE HIS ARMOR.
WHY'RE YE HOLDIN' BACK, SUMMERS?!

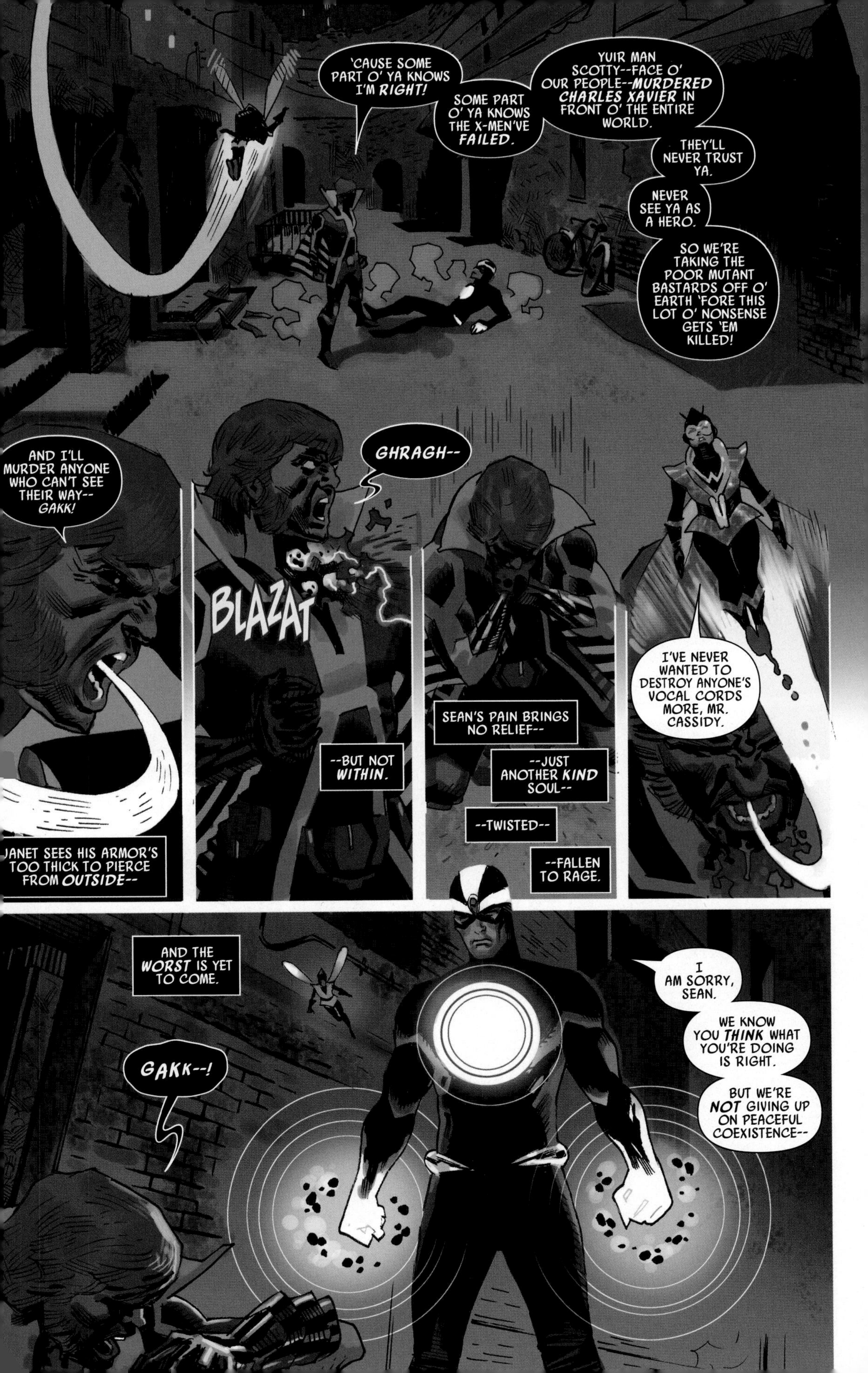
'CAUSE SOME PART O' YA KNOWS I'M RIGHT!
SOME PART O' YA KNOWS THE X-MEN'VE FAILED.
YUIR MAN SCOTTY--FACE O' OUR PEOPLE--MURDERED CHARLES XAVIER IN FRONT O' THE ENTIRE WORLD.
THEY'LL NEVER TRUST YA.
NEVER SEE YA AS A HERO.
SO WE'RE TAKING THE POOR MUTANT BASTARDS OFF O' EARTH 'FORE THIS LOT O' NONSENSE GETS 'EM KILLED!
AND I'LL MURDER ANYONE WHO CAN'T SEE THEIR WAY-- GAKK!
JANET SEES HIS ARMOR'S TOO THICK TO PIERCE FROM OUTSIDE--
GHRAGH--
BLAZAT
--BUT NOT WITHIN.
SEAN'S PAIN BRINGS NO RELIEF--
--JUST ANOTHER KIND SOUL--
--TWISTED--
--FALLEN TO RAGE.
I'VE NEVER WANTED TO DESTROY ANYONE'S VOCAL CORDS MORE, MR. CASSIDY.
AND THE WORST IS YET TO COME.
GAKK--!
I AM SORRY, SEAN.
WE KNOW YOU THINK WHAT YOU'RE DOING IS RIGHT.
BUT WE'RE NOT GIVING UP ON PEACEFUL COEXISTENCE--

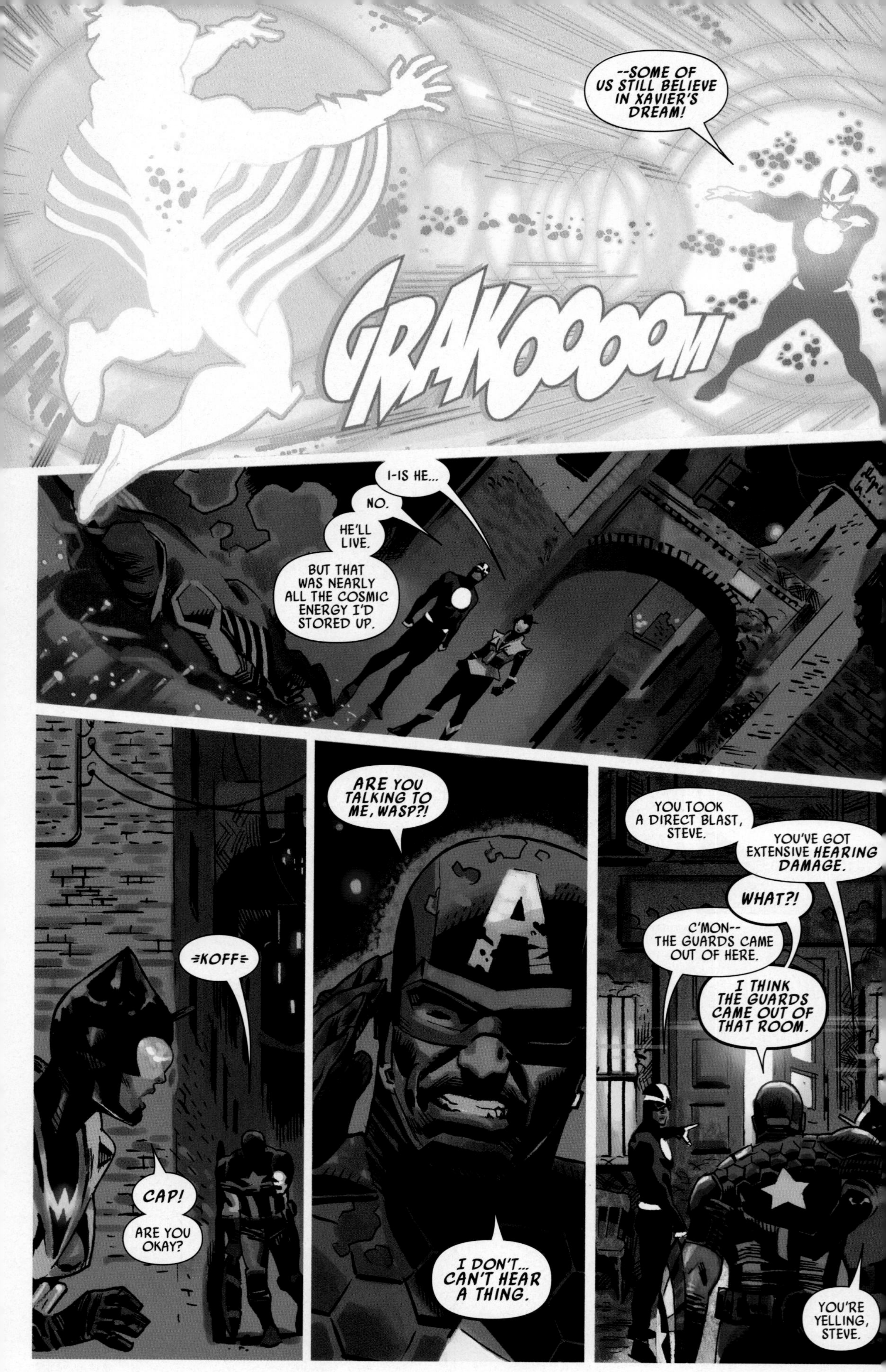
--SOME OF US STILL BELIEVE IN XAVIER'S DREAM!
GRAKOOOOM
I-IS HE...
NO.
HE'LL LIVE.
BUT THAT WAS NEARLY ALL THE COSMIC ENERGY I'D STORED UP.
=KOFF=
CAP!
ARE YOU OKAY?
ARE YOU TALKING TO ME, WASP?!
I DON'T... CAN'T HEAR A THING.
YOU TOOK A DIRECT BLAST, STEVE.
YOU'VE GOT EXTENSIVE HEARING DAMAGE.
WHAT?!
C'MON-- THE GUARDS CAME OUT OF HERE.
I THINK THE GUARDS CAME OUT OF THAT ROOM.
YOU'RE YELLING, STEVE.

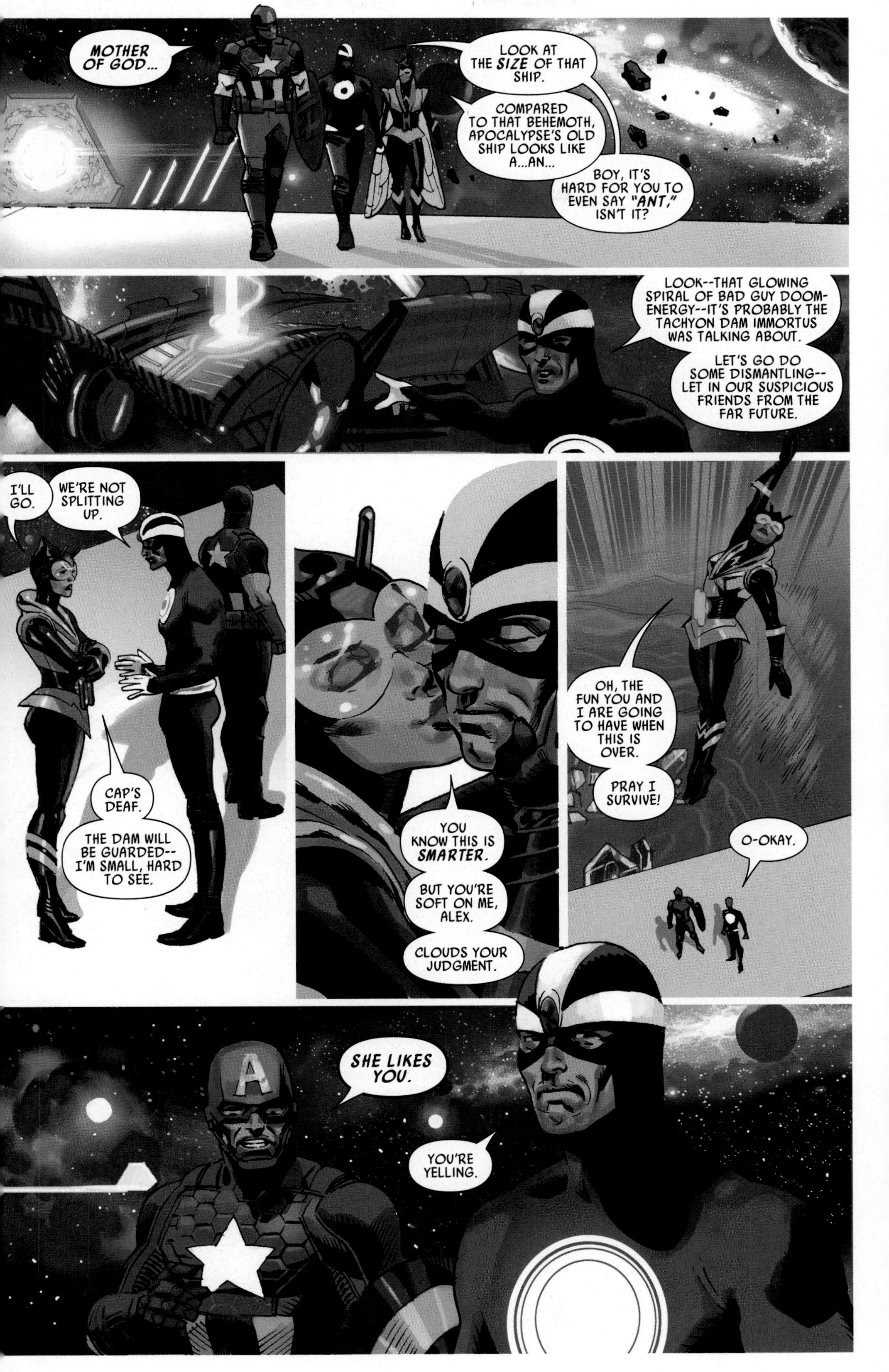
MOTHER OF GOD...
LOOK AT THE SIZE OF THAT SHIP.
COMPARED TO THAT BEHEMOTH, APOCALYPSE'S OLD SHIP LOOKS LIKE A...AN...
BOY, IT'S HARD FOR YOU TO EVEN SAY "ANT," ISN'T IT?
LOOK--THAT GLOWING SPIRAL OF BAD GUY DOOM-ENERGY--IT'S PROBABLY THE TACHYON DAM IMMORTUS WAS TALKING ABOUT.
LET'S GO DO SOME DISMANTLING--LET IN OUR SUSPICIOUS FRIENDS FROM THE FAR FUTURE.
I'LL GO.
WE'RE NOT SPLITTING UP.
CAP'S DEAF.
THE DAM WILL BE GUARDED--I'M SMALL, HARD TO SEE.
YOU KNOW THIS IS SMARTER.
BUT YOU'RE SOFT ON ME, ALEX.
CLOUDS YOUR JUDGMENT.
OH, THE FUN YOU AND I ARE GOING TO HAVE WHEN THIS IS OVER.
PRAY I SURVIVE!
O-OKAY.
SHE LIKES YOU.
YOU'RE YELLING.

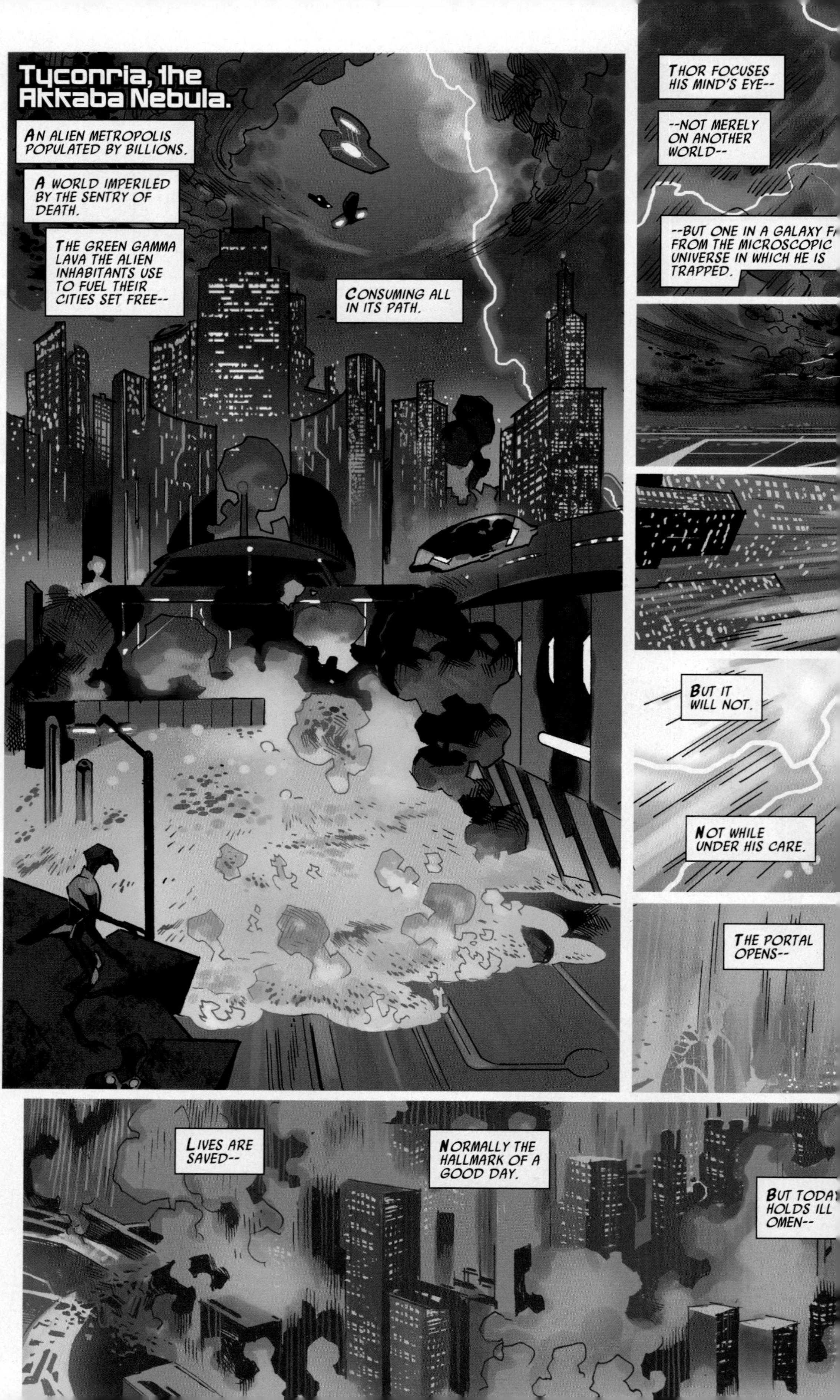
Tyconria, the Akkaba Nebula.
AN ALIEN METROPOLIS POPULATED BY BILLIONS.
A WORLD IMPERILED BY THE SENTRY OF DEATH.
THE GREEN GAMMA LAVA THE ALIEN INHABITANTS USE TO FUEL THEIR CITIES SET FREE--
CONSUMING ALL IN ITS PATH.
THOR FOCUSES HIS MIND'S EYE--
--NOT MERELY ON ANOTHER WORLD--
--BUT ONE IN A GALAXY F
FROM THE MICROSCOPIC UNIVERSE IN WHICH HE IS TRAPPED.
BUT IT WILL NOT.
NOT WHILE UNDER HIS CARE.
THE PORTAL OPENS--
LIVES ARE SAVED--
NORMALLY THE HALLMARK OF A GOOD DAY.
BUT TODAY HOLDS ILL OMEN--

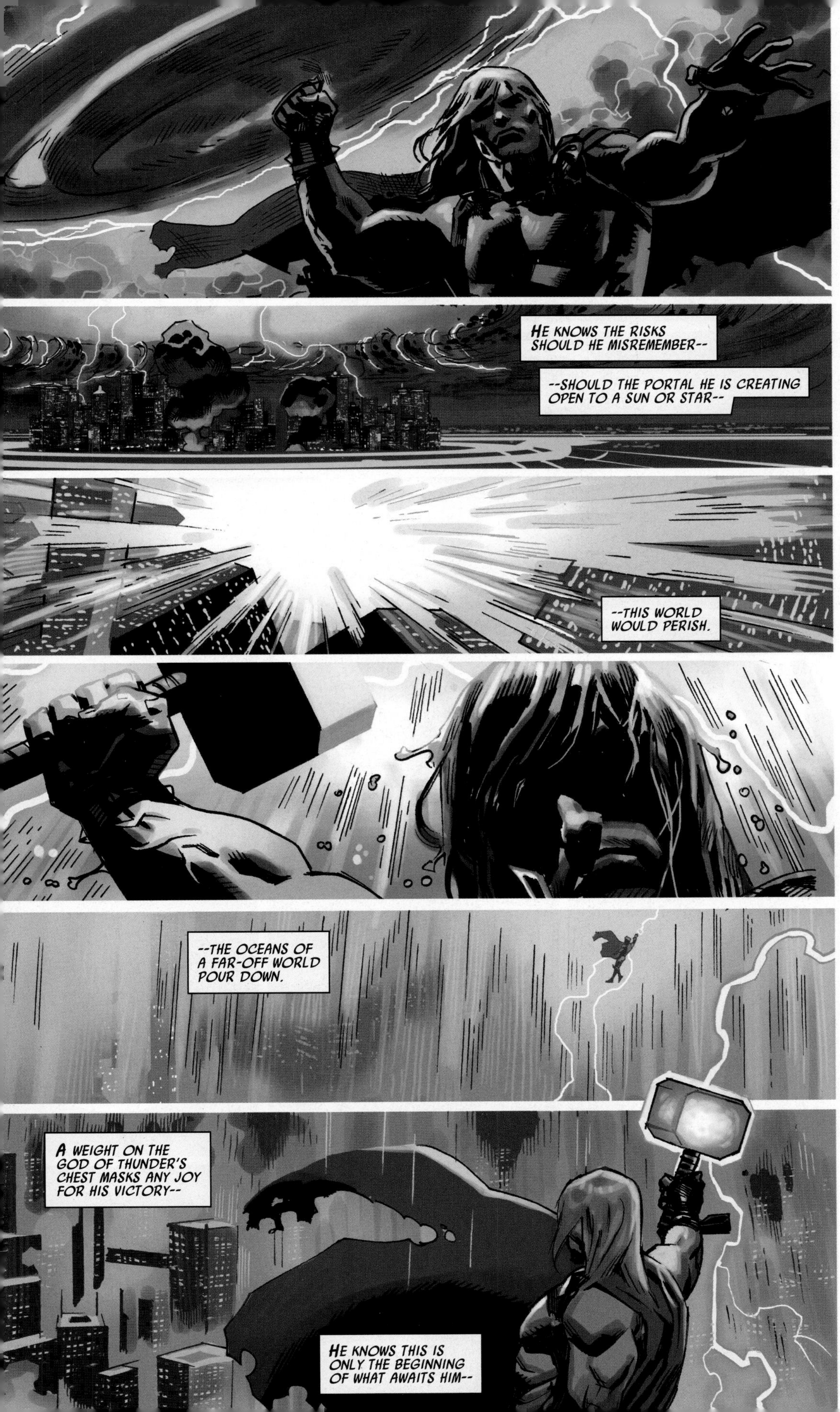
HE KNOWS THE RISKS SHOULD HE MISREMEMBER--
--SHOULD THE PORTAL HE IS CREATING OPEN TO A SUN OR STAR--
--THIS WORLD WOULD PERISH.
--THE OCEANS OF A FAR-OFF WORLD POUR DOWN.
A WEIGHT ON THE GOD OF THUNDER'S CHEST MASKS ANY JOY FOR HIS VICTORY--
HE KNOWS THIS IS ONLY THE BEGINNING OF WHAT AWAITS HIM--

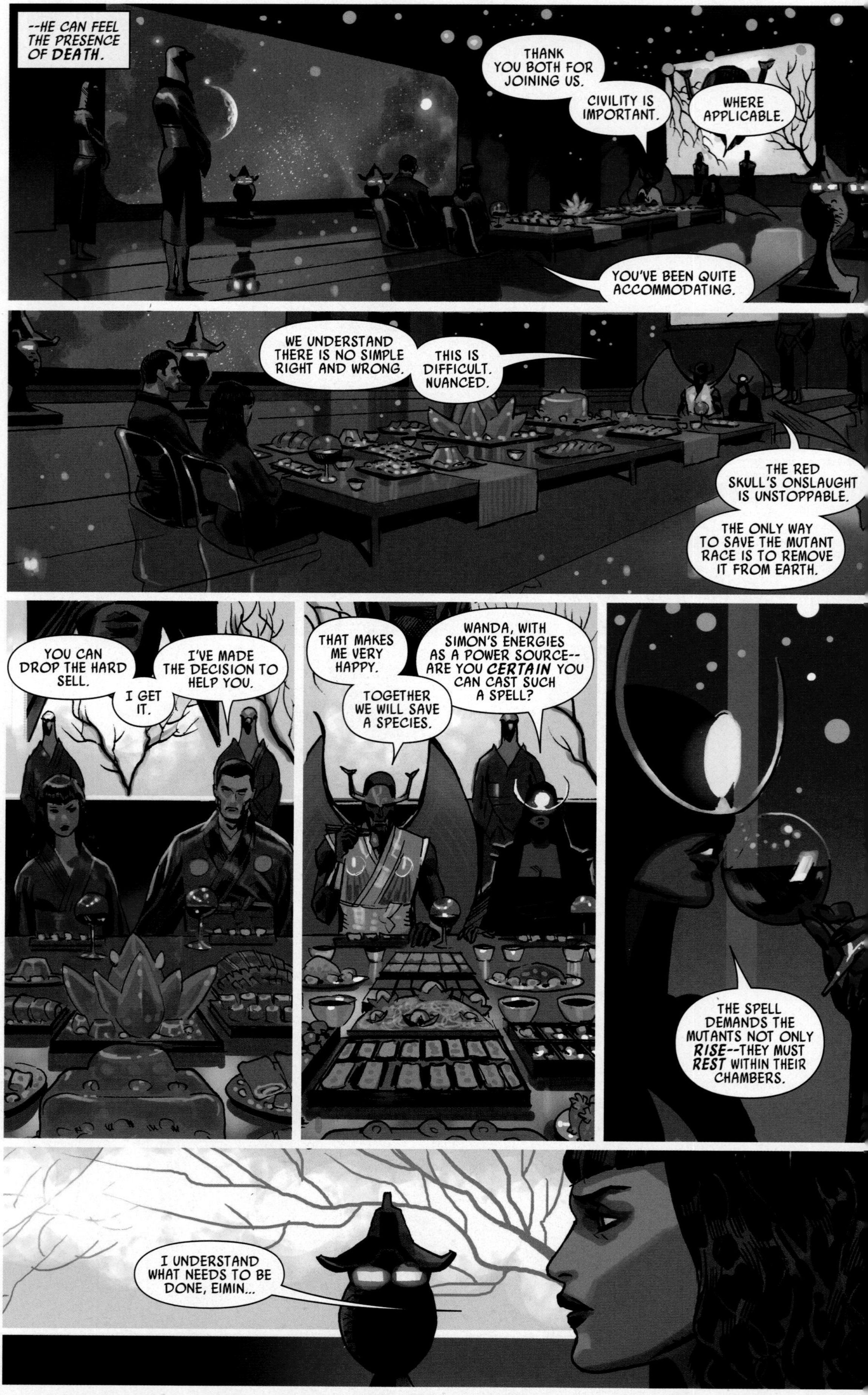
--HE CAN FEEL THE PRESENCE OF DEATH.
THANK YOU BOTH FOR JOINING US.
CIVILITY IS IMPORTANT.
WHERE APPLICABLE.
YOU'VE BEEN QUITE ACCOMMODATING.
WE UNDERSTAND THERE IS NO SIMPLE RIGHT AND WRONG.
THIS IS DIFFICULT. NUANCED.
THE RED SKULL'S ONSLAUGHT IS UNSTOPPABLE.
THE ONLY WAY TO SAVE THE MUTANT RACE IS TO REMOVE IT FROM EARTH.
YOU CAN DROP THE HARD SELL.
I GET IT.
I'VE MADE THE DECISION TO HELP YOU.
THAT MAKES ME VERY HAPPY.
TOGETHER WE WILL SAVE A SPECIES.
WANDA, WITH SIMON'S ENERGIES AS A POWER SOURCE--ARE YOU CERTAIN YOU CAN CAST SUCH A SPELL?
THE SPELL DEMANDS THE MUTANTS NOT ONLY RISE--THEY MUST REST WITHIN THEIR CHAMBERS.
I UNDERSTAND WHAT NEEDS TO BE DONE, EIMIN...

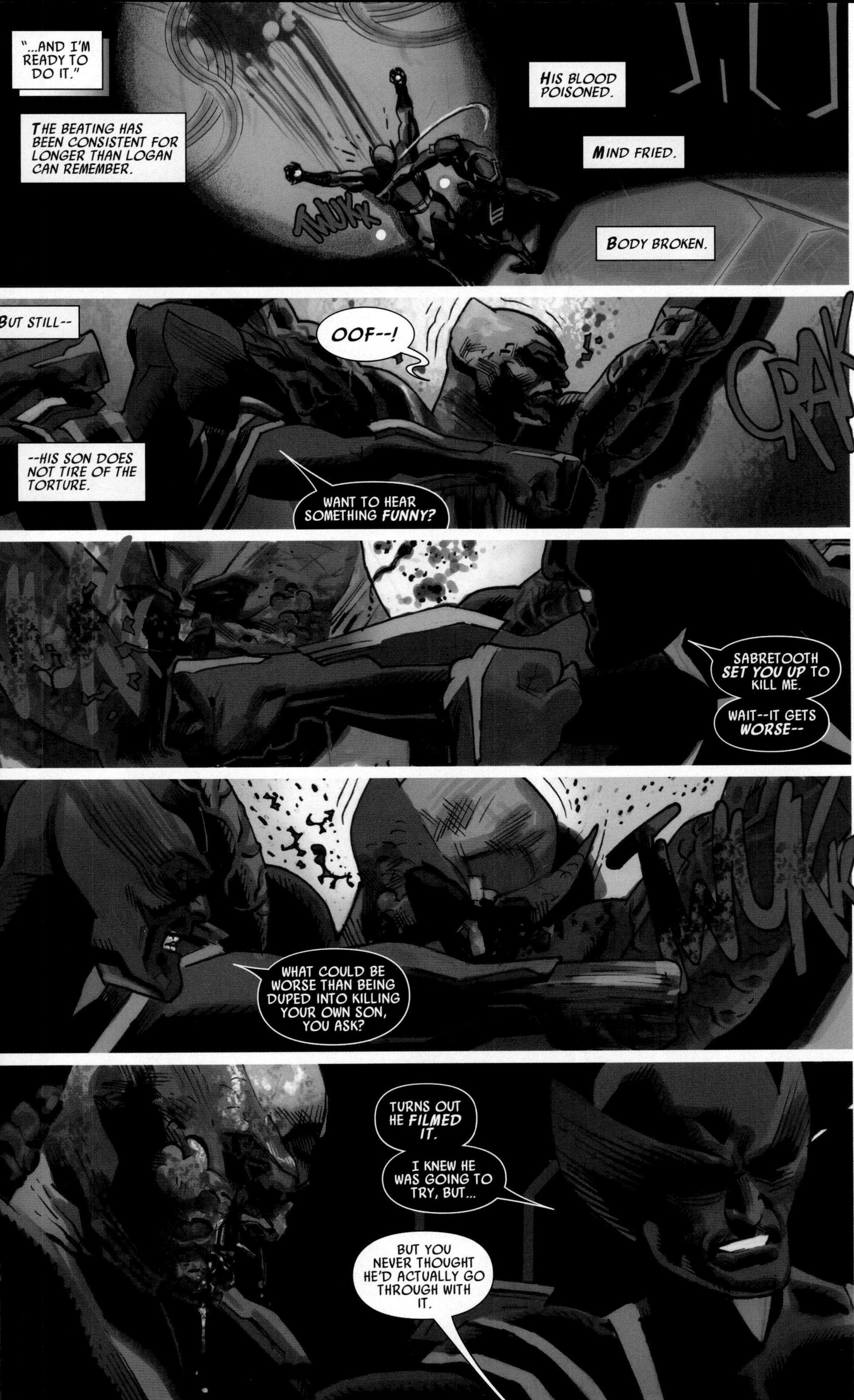
"...AND I'M READY TO DO IT."
THE BEATING HAS BEEN CONSISTENT FOR LONGER THAN LOGAN CAN REMEMBER.
THUKK
HIS BLOOD POISONED.
MIND FRIED.
BODY BROKEN.
BUT STILL--
OOF--!
CRAK
--HIS SON DOES NOT TIRE OF THE TORTURE.
WANT TO HEAR SOMETHING FUNNY?
SABRETOOTH SET YOU UP TO KILL ME.
WAIT--IT GETS WORSE--
THUKK
WHAT COULD BE WORSE THAN BEING DUPED INTO KILLING YOUR OWN SON, YOU ASK?
TURNS OUT HE FILMED IT.
I KNEW HE WAS GOING TO TRY, BUT...
BUT YOU NEVER THOUGHT HE'D ACTUALLY GO THROUGH WITH IT.

YOU *NEVER* BELIEVED YOUR FATHER WOULD ACTUALLY *MURDER* YOU.

SO YOU WENT ALONG WITH IT ALL, ASSUMING IT WOULD *BACKFIRE* IN SABRETOOTH'S FACE.

DAKEN DIED BETTING ON YOU, LOGAN.

SABRETOOTH'S VIDEO FOUND ITS WAY INTO THE HANDS OF *THE RED SKULL.*

DO THE *CONSEQUENCES* OF THIS SINK IN, YOU CALLOUSED SOCIOPATH?

THE SKULL WILL DISTRIBUTE COPIES OF IT TO *THE WORLD.*

WOLVERINE, THE AVENGER, *KILLING HIS OWN SON!*

WHAT *WILL* THEY SAY?

"THESE COSTUMED POLICE HAVE GONE *TOO* FAR."

"TAKEN THINGS INTO THEIR OWN HANDS."

"THE MUTANTS ARE *SAVAGES* WHO KILL THEIR OWN *CHILDREN.*"

I'VE SEEN IT.

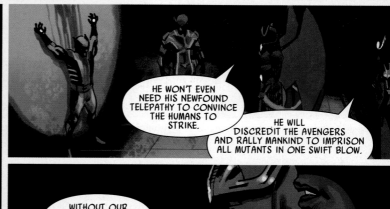

HE WON'T EVEN NEED HIS NEWFOUND TELEPATHY TO CONVINCE THE HUMANS TO STRIKE.

HE WILL DISCREDIT THE AVENGERS AND RALLY MANKIND TO IMPRISON ALL MUTANTS IN ONE SWIFT BLOW.

WITHOUT OUR INTERVENTION, THE SKULL'S ATTACK WOULD HAVE HAPPENED *TOMORROW.*

WITHIN A WEEK THEY BEGIN WORK ON THE CAMPS WE WERE RAISED IN.

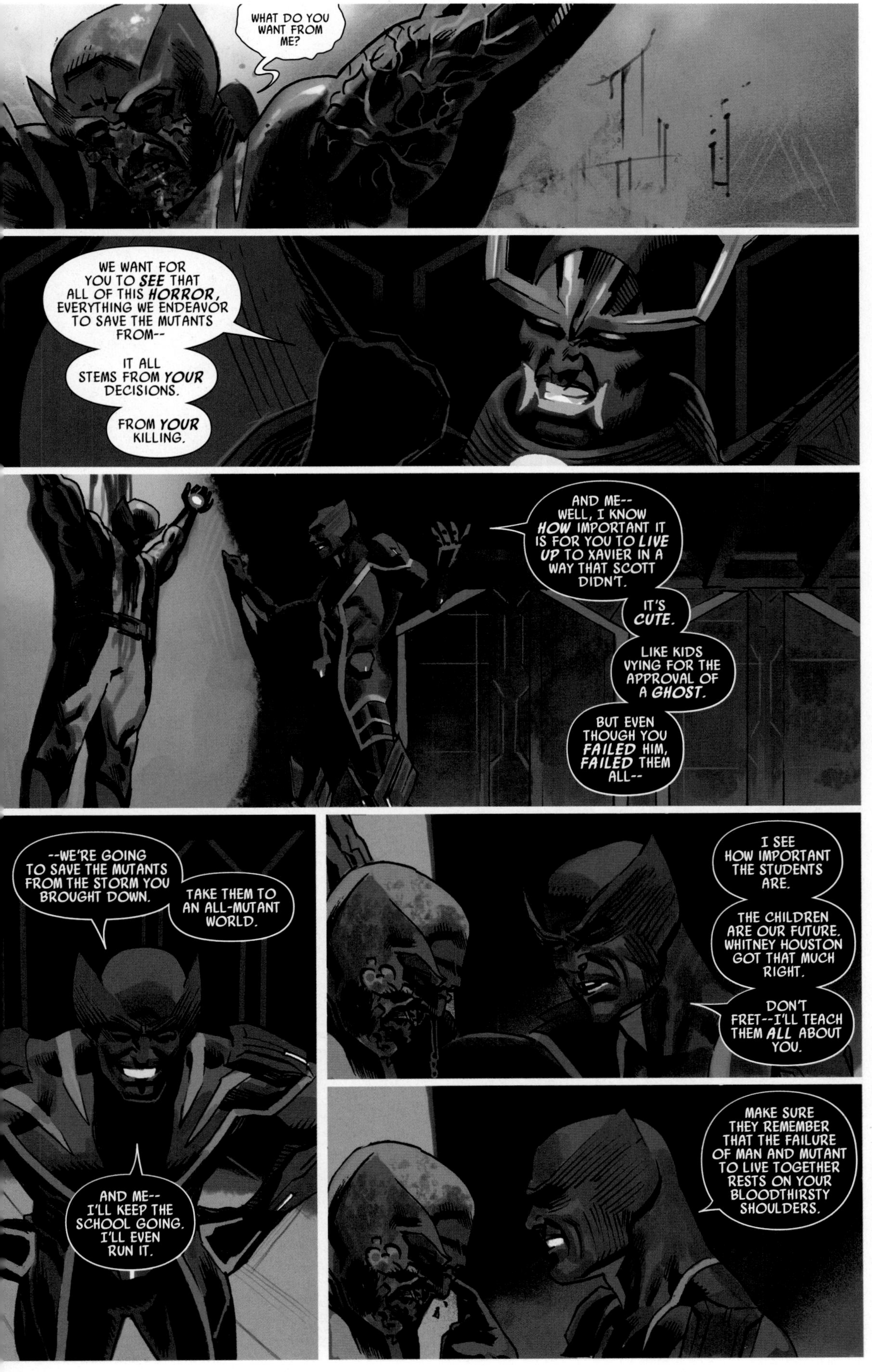
WHAT DO YOU WANT FROM ME?
WE WANT FOR YOU TO SEE THAT ALL OF THIS HORROR, EVERYTHING WE ENDEAVOR TO SAVE THE MUTANTS FROM--
IT ALL STEMS FROM YOUR DECISIONS.
FROM YOUR KILLING.
AND ME-- WELL, I KNOW HOW IMPORTANT IT IS FOR YOU TO LIVE UP TO XAVIER IN A WAY THAT SCOTT DIDN'T.
IT'S CUTE.
LIKE KIDS VYING FOR THE APPROVAL OF A GHOST.
BUT EVEN THOUGH YOU FAILED HIM, FAILED THEM ALL--
--WE'RE GOING TO SAVE THE MUTANTS FROM THE STORM YOU BROUGHT DOWN.
TAKE THEM TO AN ALL-MUTANT WORLD.
AND ME-- I'LL KEEP THE SCHOOL GOING. I'LL EVEN RUN IT.
I SEE HOW IMPORTANT THE STUDENTS ARE.
THE CHILDREN ARE OUR FUTURE. WHITNEY HOUSTON GOT THAT MUCH RIGHT.
DON'T FRET--I'LL TEACH THEM ALL ABOUT YOU.
MAKE SURE THEY REMEMBER THAT THE FAILURE OF MAN AND MUTANT TO LIVE TOGETHER RESTS ON YOUR BLOODTHIRSTY SHOULDERS.

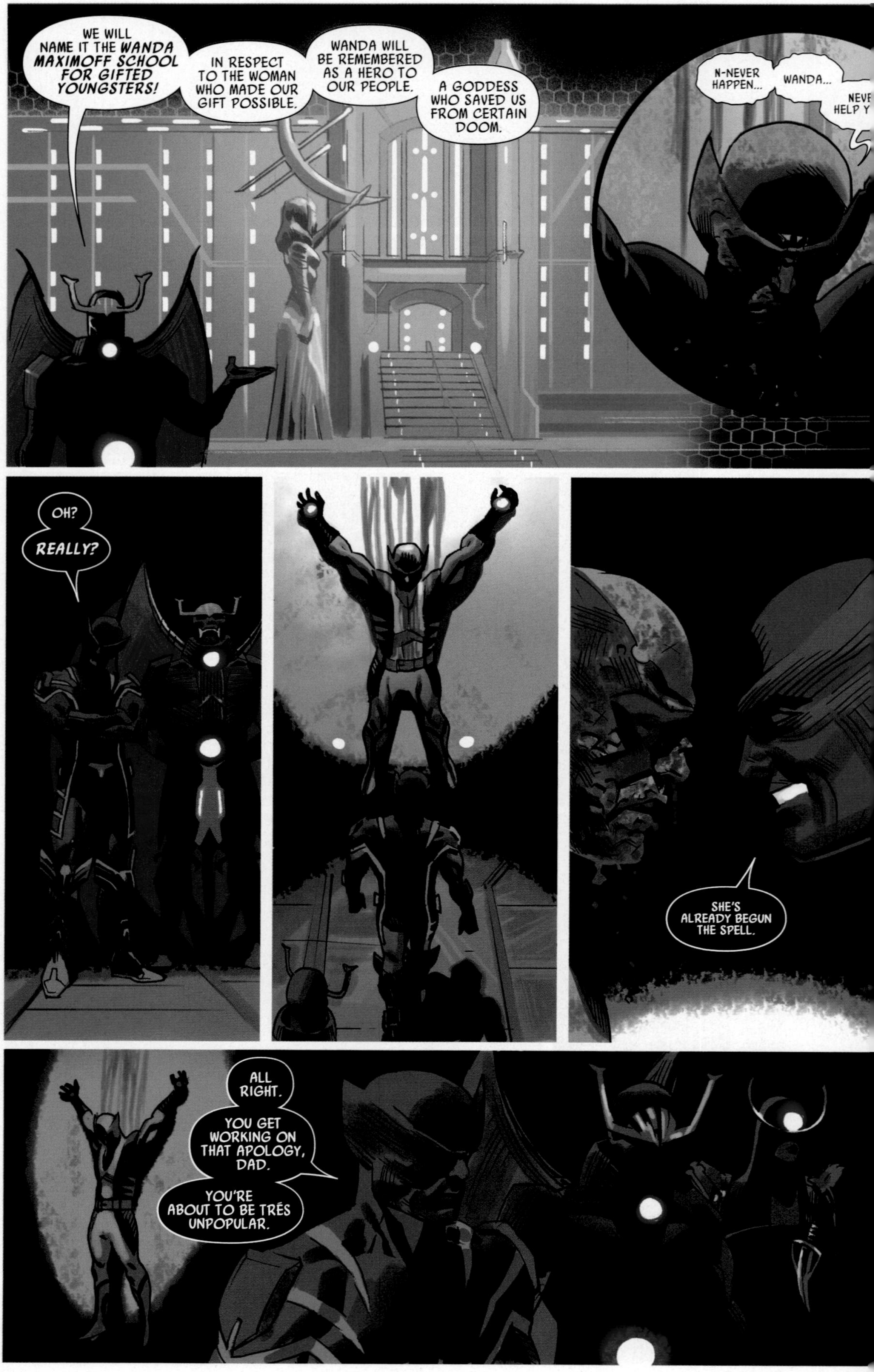
WE WILL NAME IT THE WANDA MAXIMOFF SCHOOL FOR GIFTED YOUNGSTERS!
IN RESPECT TO THE WOMAN WHO MADE OUR GIFT POSSIBLE.
WANDA WILL BE REMEMBERED AS A HERO TO OUR PEOPLE.
A GODDESS WHO SAVED US FROM CERTAIN DOOM.
N-NEVER HAPPEN...
WANDA...
OH?
REALLY?
SHE'S ALREADY BEGUN THE SPELL.
ALL RIGHT.
YOU GET WORKING ON THAT APOLOGY, DAD.
YOU'RE ABOUT TO BE TRÉS UNPOPULAR.

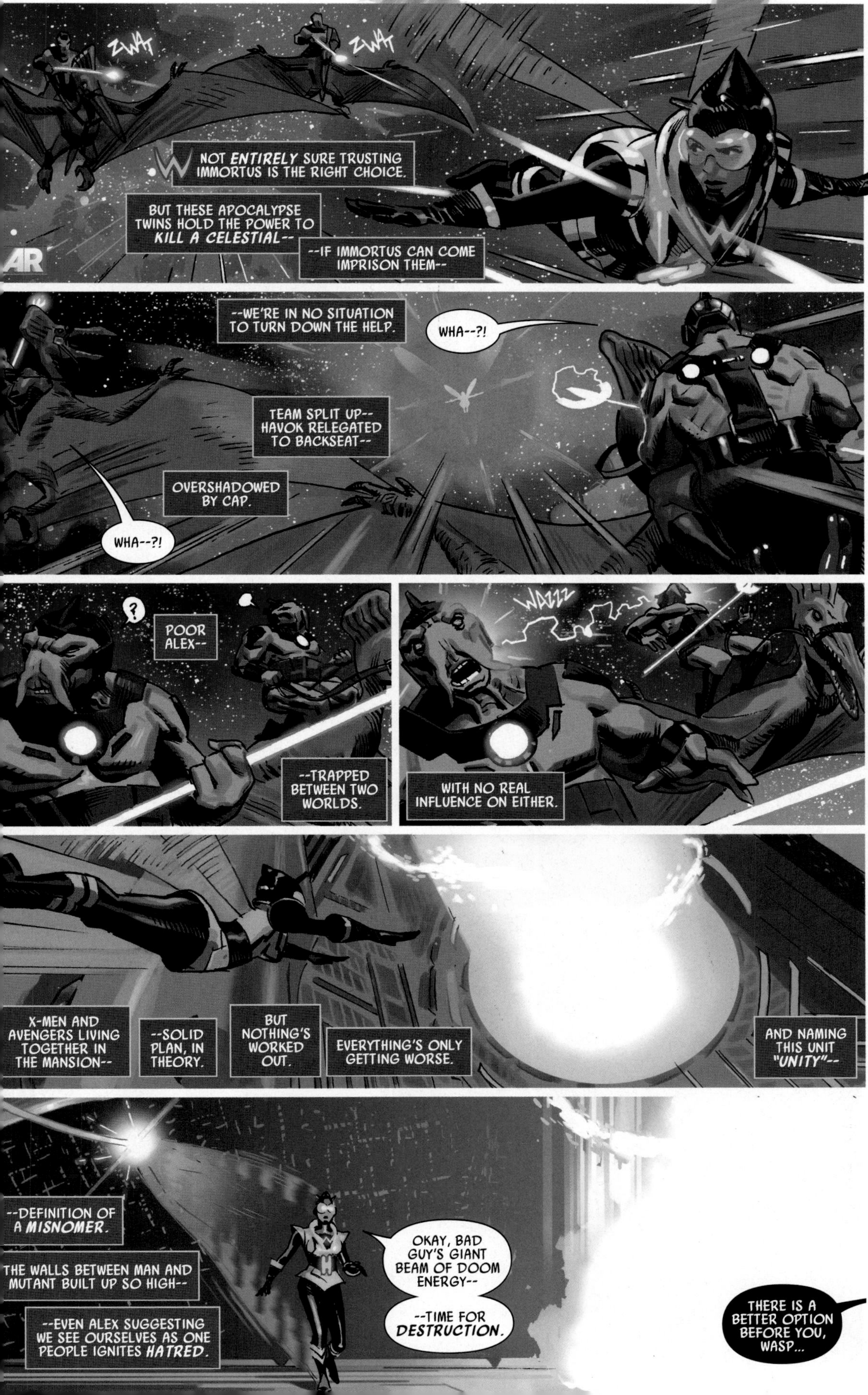
ZWAT
ZWAK
NOT ENTIRELY SURE TRUSTING IMMORTUS IS THE RIGHT CHOICE.
BUT THESE APOCALYPSE TWINS HOLD THE POWER TO KILL A CELESTIAL--
--IF IMMORTUS CAN COME IMPRISON THEM--
--WE'RE IN NO SITUATION TO TURN DOWN THE HELP.
WHA--?!
TEAM SPLIT UP--HAVOK RELEGATED TO BACKSEAT--
OVERSHADOWED BY CAP.
WHA--?!
?
POOR ALEX--
--TRAPPED BETWEEN TWO WORLDS.
WITH NO REAL INFLUENCE ON EITHER.
X-MEN AND AVENGERS LIVING TOGETHER IN THE MANSION--
--SOLID PLAN, IN THEORY.
BUT NOTHING'S WORKED OUT.
EVERYTHING'S ONLY GETTING WORSE.
AND NAMING THIS UNIT "UNITY"--
--DEFINITION OF A MISNOMER.
THE WALLS BETWEEN MAN AND MUTANT BUILT UP SO HIGH--
--EVEN ALEX SUGGESTING WE SEE OURSELVES AS ONE PEOPLE IGNITES HATRED.
OKAY, BAD GUY'S GIANT BEAM OF DOOM ENERGY--
--TIME FOR DESTRUCTION.
THERE IS A BETTER OPTION BEFORE YOU, WASP...

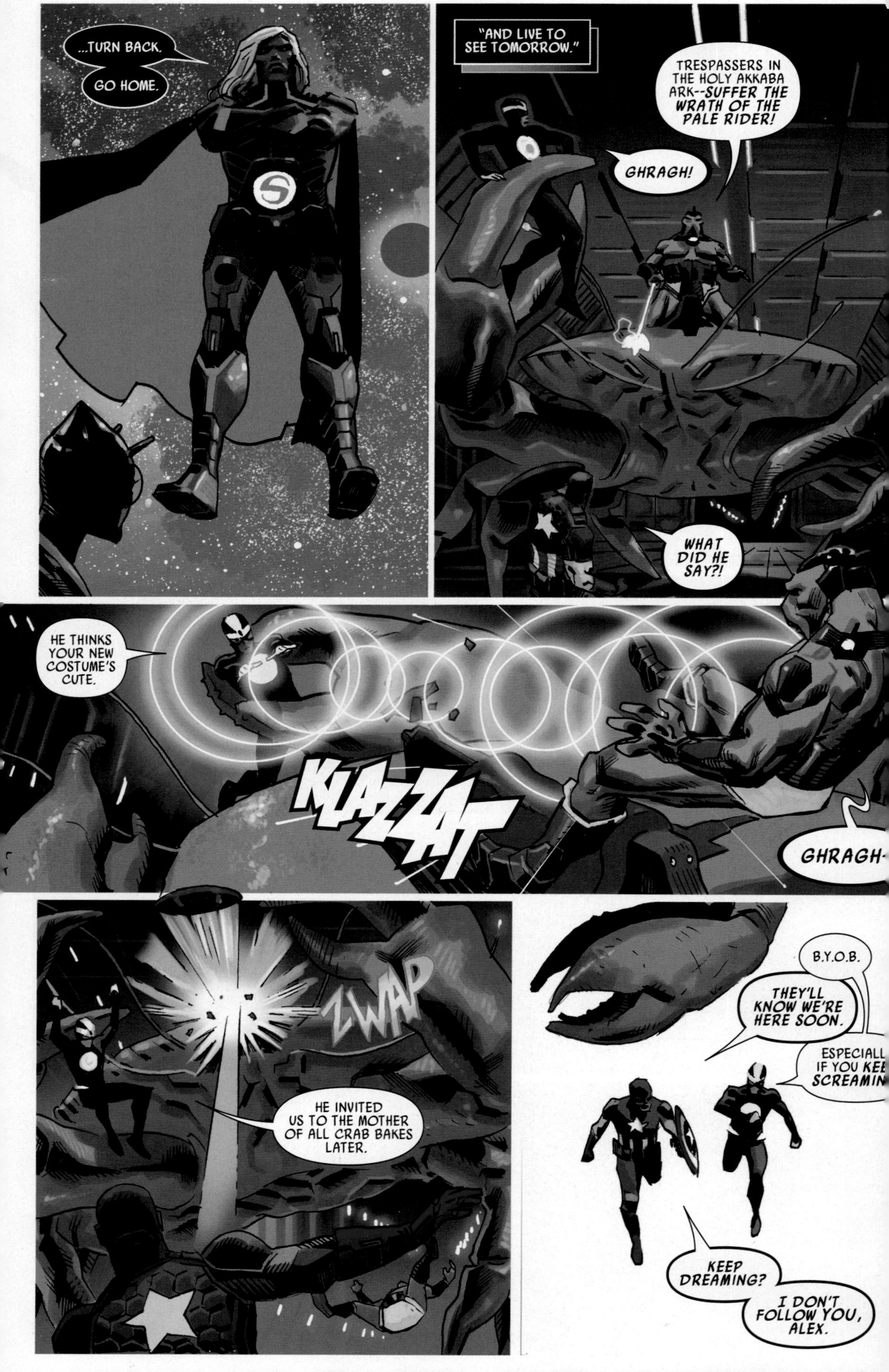
...TURN BACK.
GO HOME.
"AND LIVE TO SEE TOMORROW."
TRESPASSERS IN THE HOLY AKKABA ARK--SUFFER THE WRATH OF THE PALE RIDER!
GHRAGH!
WHAT DID HE SAY?!
HE THINKS YOUR NEW COSTUME'S CUTE.
KLAZZAT
GHRAGH-
ZWAP
HE INVITED US TO THE MOTHER OF ALL CRAB BAKES LATER.
B.Y.O.B.
THEY'LL KNOW WE'RE HERE SOON.
KEEP DREAMING?
I DON'T FOLLOW YOU, ALEX.

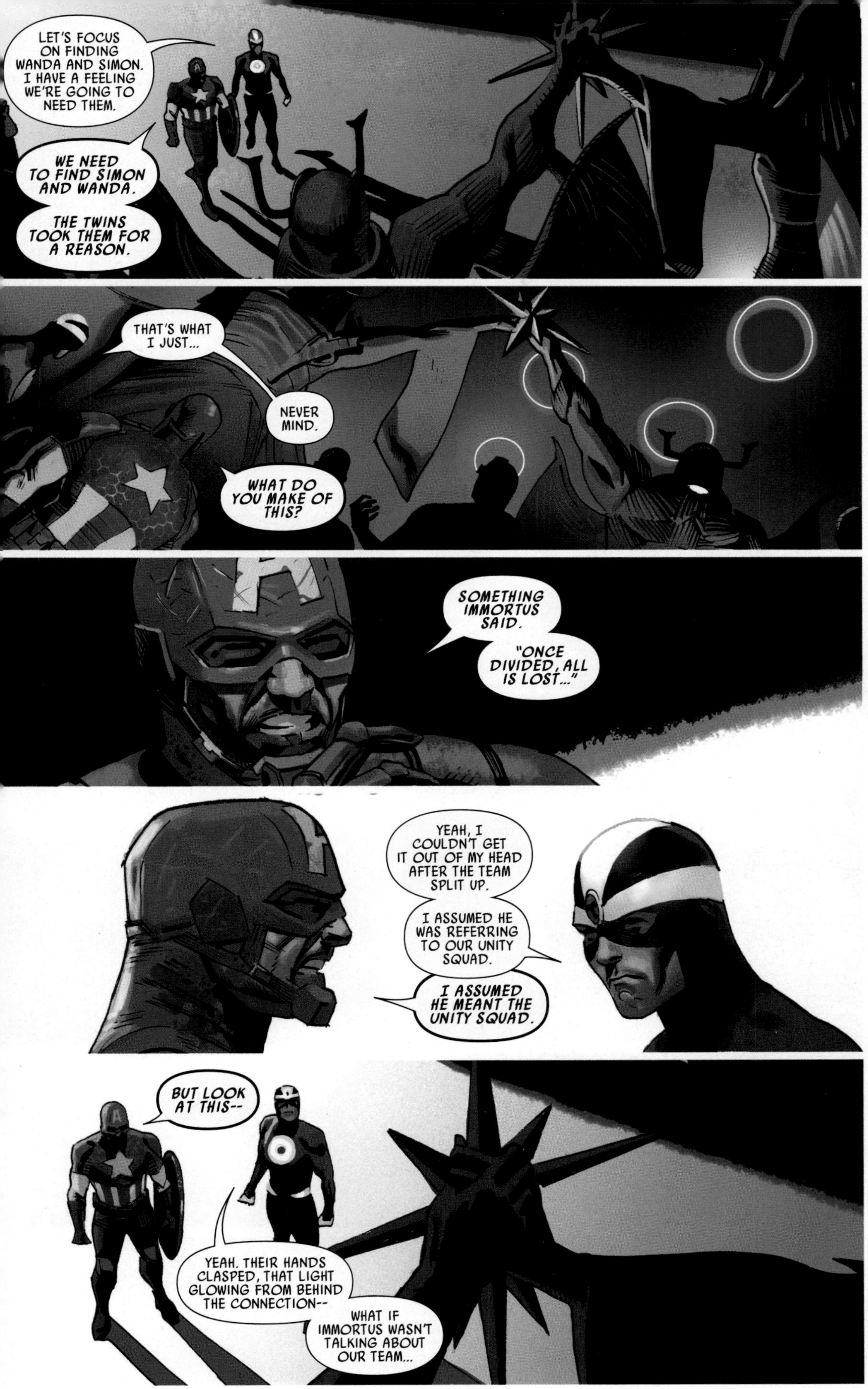
LET'S FOCUS ON FINDING WANDA AND SIMON. I HAVE A FEELING WE'RE GOING TO NEED THEM.
WE NEED TO FIND SIMON AND WANDA.
THE TWINS TOOK THEM FOR A REASON.
THAT'S WHAT I JUST...
NEVER MIND.
WHAT DO YOU MAKE OF THIS?
SOMETHING IMMORTUS SAID.
"ONCE DIVIDED, ALL IS LOST..."
YEAH, I COULDN'T GET IT OUT OF MY HEAD AFTER THE TEAM SPLIT UP.
I ASSUMED HE WAS REFERRING TO OUR UNITY SQUAD.
I ASSUMED HE MEANT THE UNITY SQUAD.
BUT LOOK AT THIS--
YEAH. THEIR HANDS CLASPED, THAT LIGHT GLOWING FROM BEHIND THE CONNECTION--
WHAT IF IMMORTUS WASN'T TALKING ABOUT OUR TEAM...

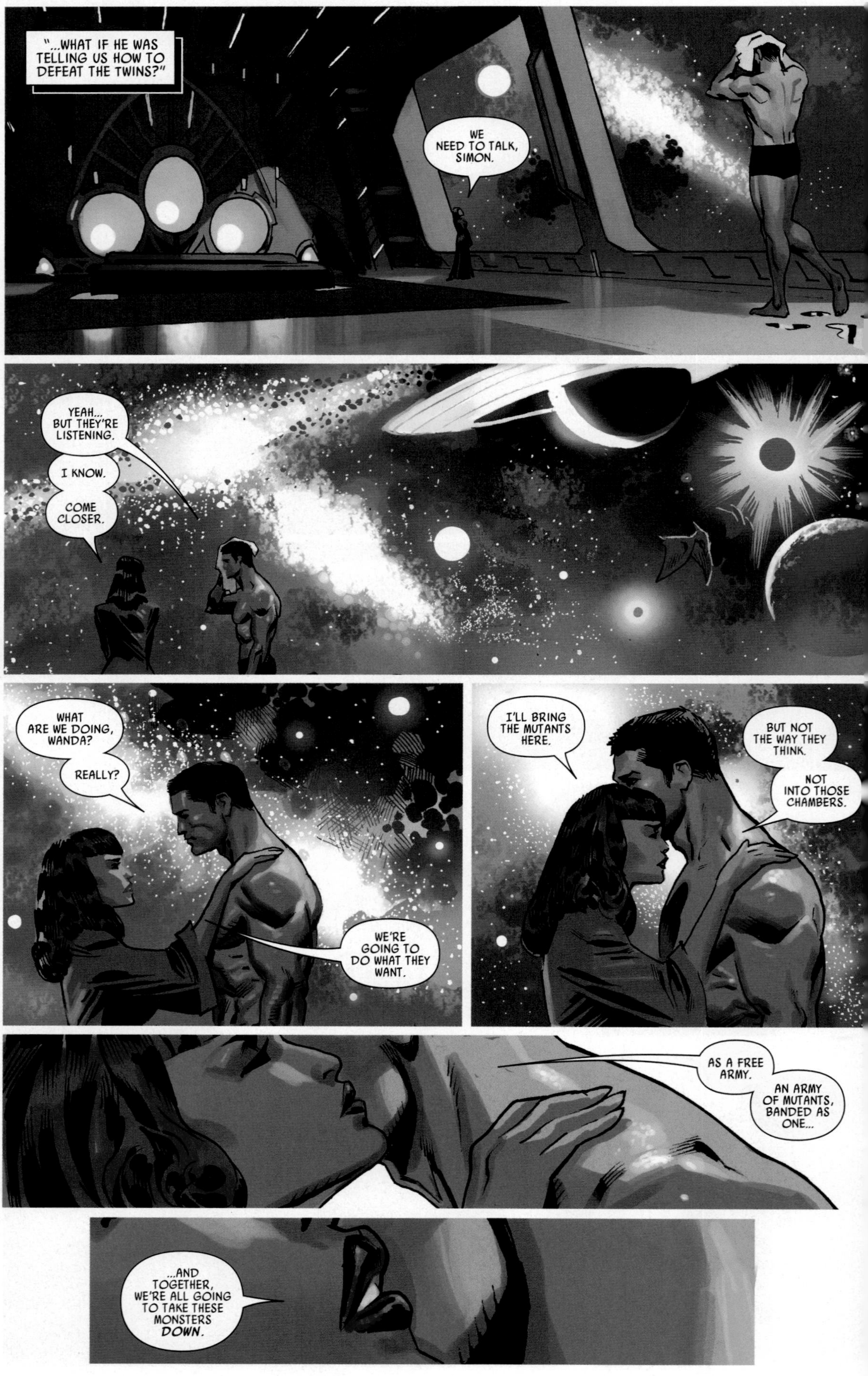
"...WHAT IF HE WAS TELLING US HOW TO DEFEAT THE TWINS?"
WE NEED TO TALK, SIMON.
YEAH... BUT THEY'RE LISTENING.
I KNOW.
COME CLOSER.
WHAT ARE WE DOING, WANDA?
REALLY?
WE'RE GOING TO DO WHAT THEY WANT.
I'LL BRING THE MUTANTS HERE.
BUT NOT THE WAY THEY THINK.
NOT INTO THOSE CHAMBERS.
AS A FREE ARMY.
AN ARMY OF MUTANTS, BANDED AS ONE...
...AND TOGETHER, WE'RE ALL GOING TO TAKE THESE MONSTERS DOWN.

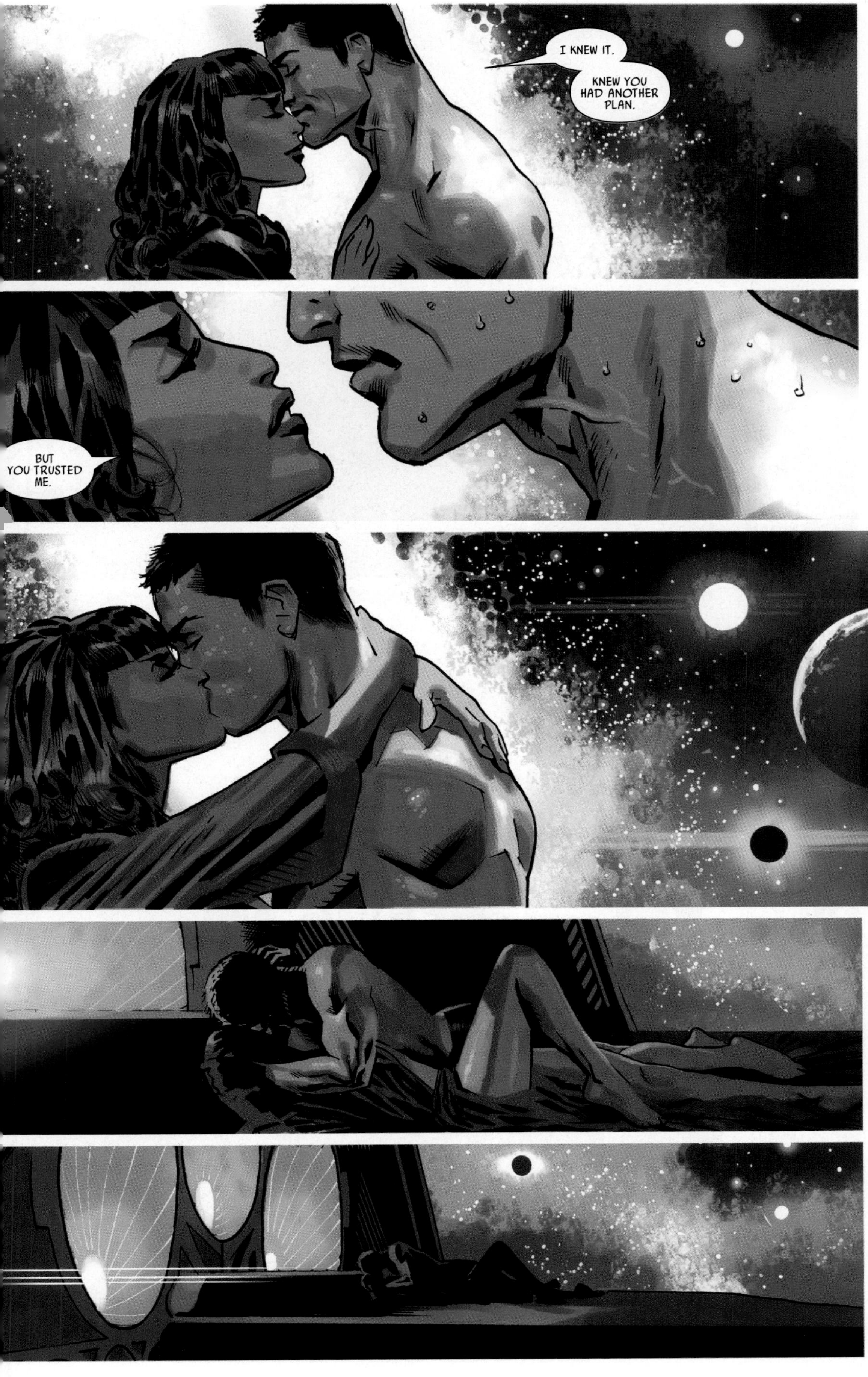
I KNEW IT.
KNEW YOU HAD ANOTHER PLAN.
BUT YOU TRUSTED ME.

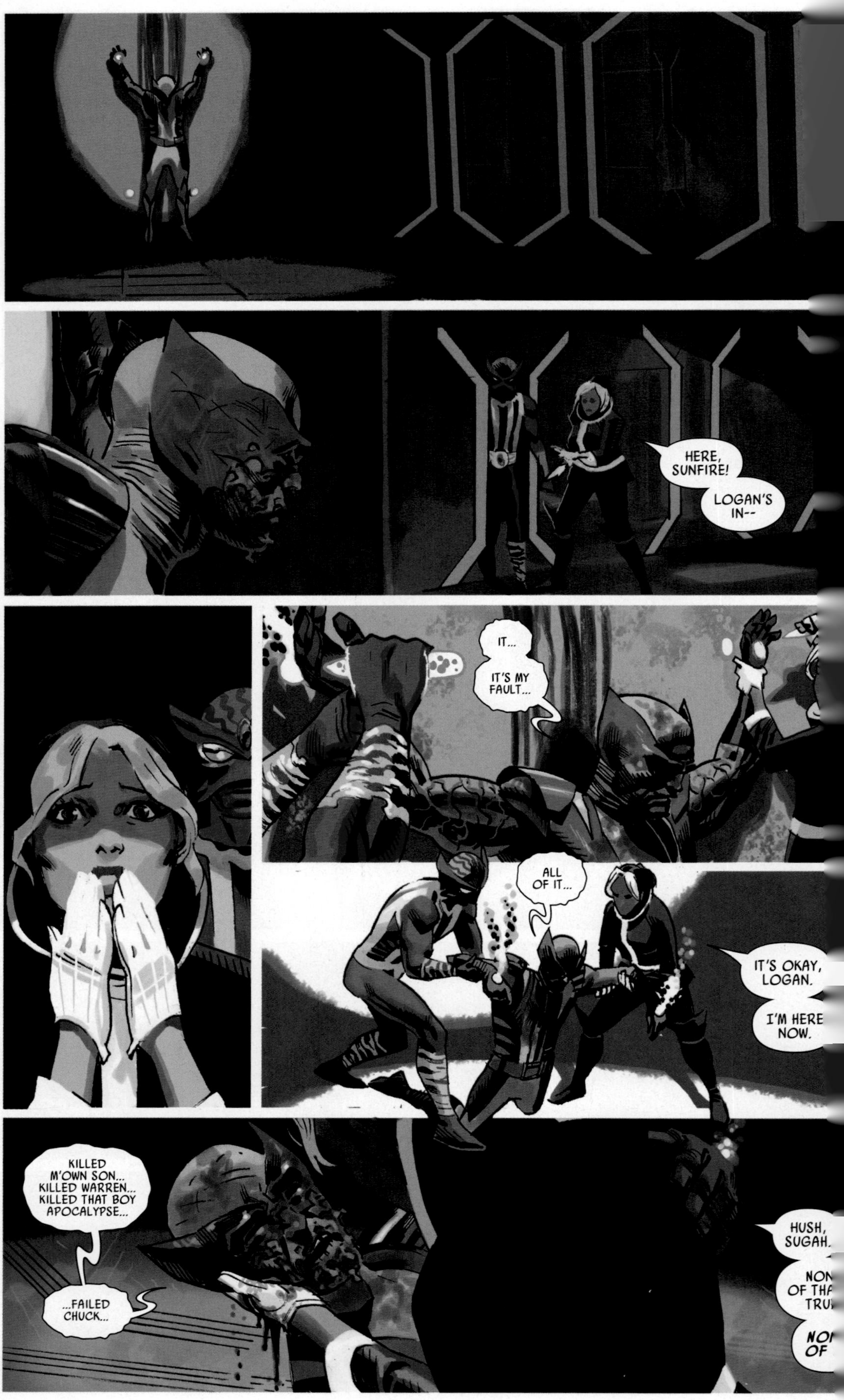
HERE, SUNFIRE!
LOGAN'S IN--
IT...
IT'S MY FAULT...
ALL OF IT...
IT'S OKAY, LOGAN.
I'M HERE NOW.
KILLED M'OWN SON... KILLED WARREN... KILLED THAT BOY APOCALYPSE...
...FAILED CHUCK...
HUSH, SUGAH.
NON OF THA TRU
NON OF

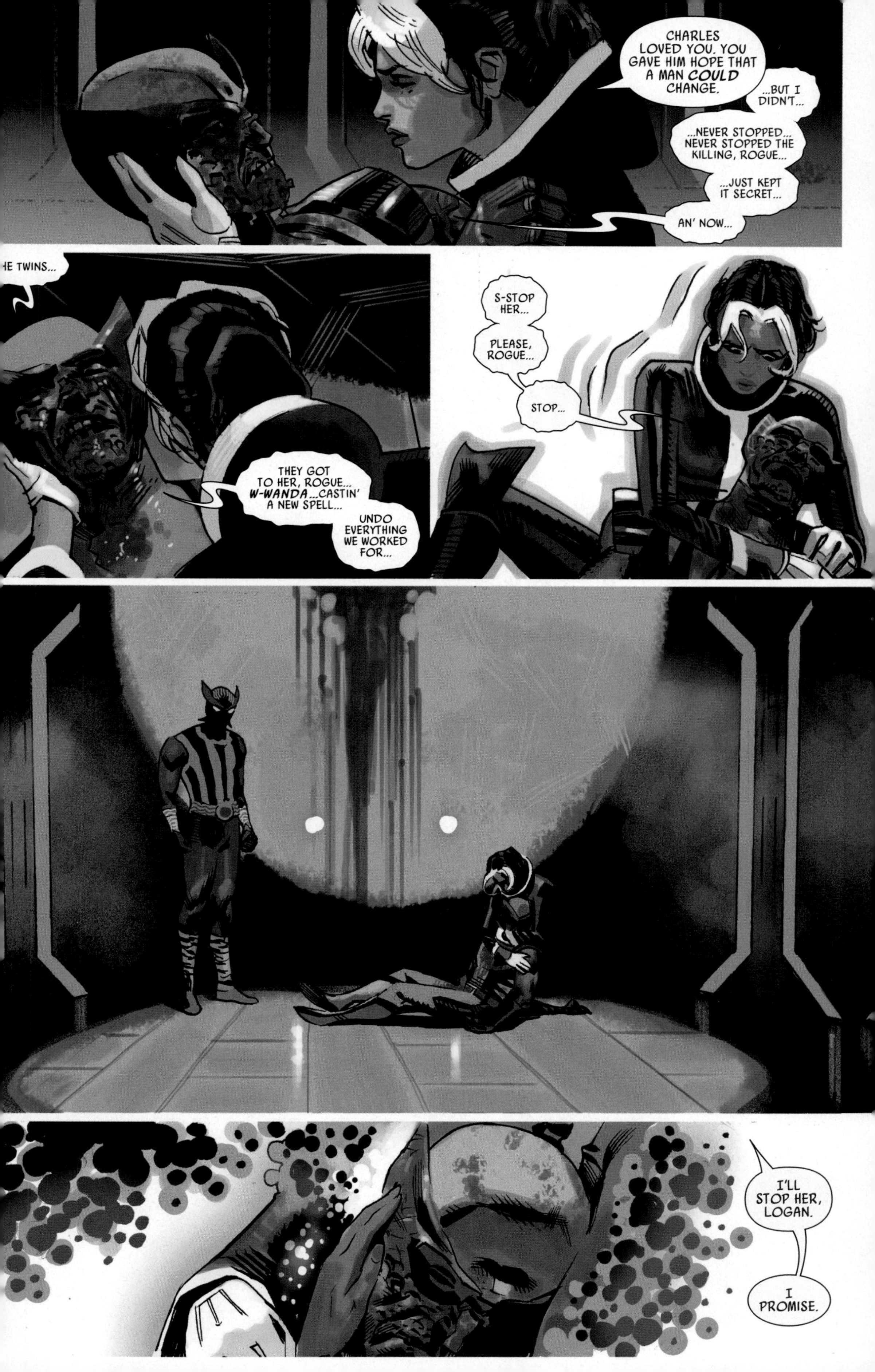

CHARLES LOVED YOU. YOU GAVE HIM HOPE THAT A MAN COULD CHANGE.
...BUT I DIDN'T...
...NEVER STOPPED... NEVER STOPPED THE KILLING, ROGUE...
...JUST KEPT IT SECRET...
AN' NOW...
HE TWINS...
THEY GOT TO HER, ROGUE... W-WANDA...CASTIN' A NEW SPELL...
UNDO EVERYTHING WE WORKED FOR...
S-STOP HER...
PLEASE, ROGUE...
STOP...
I'LL STOP HER, LOGAN.
I PROMISE.

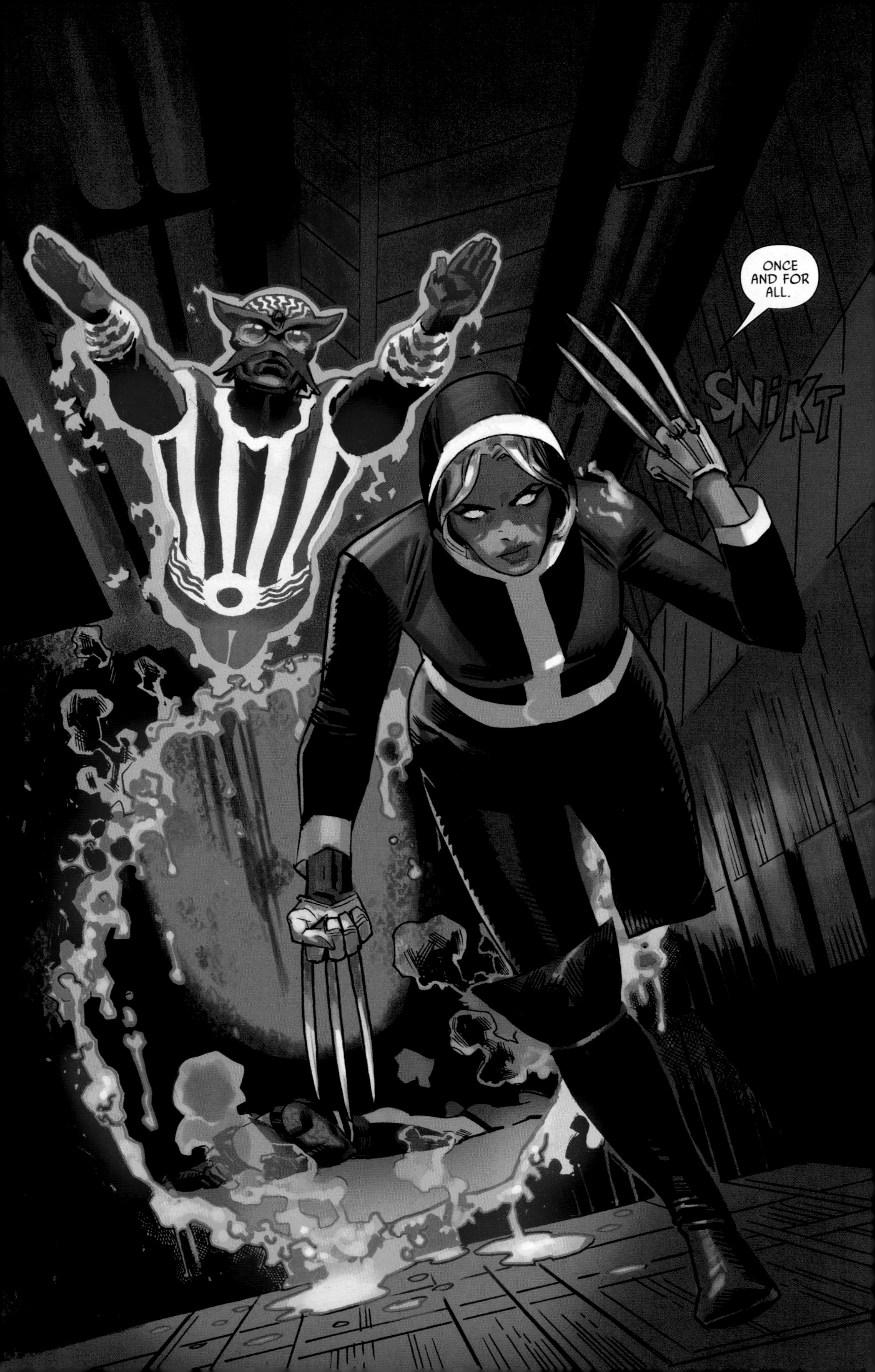
ONCE AND FOR ALL.
SNIKT

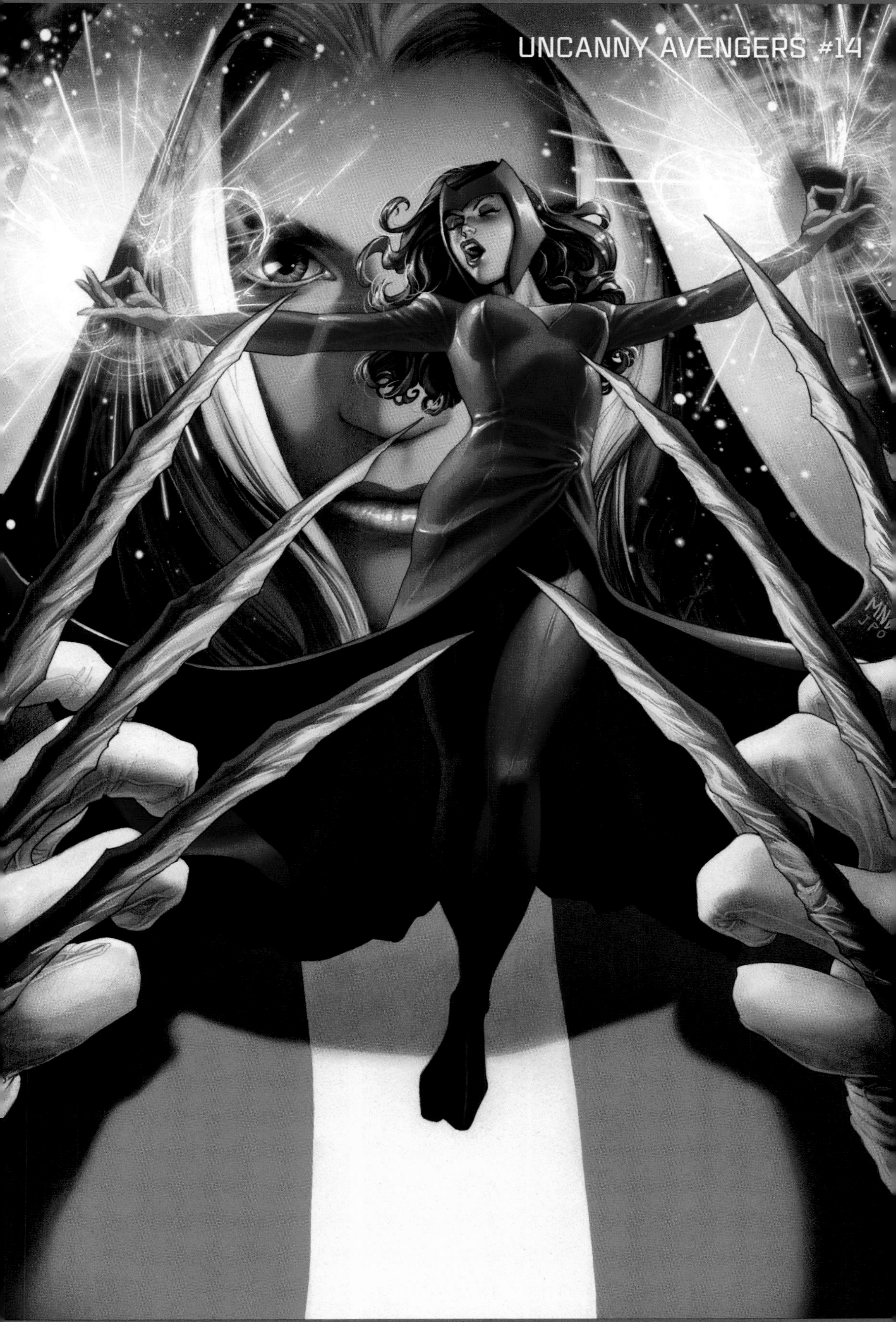
UNCANNY AVENGERS #14

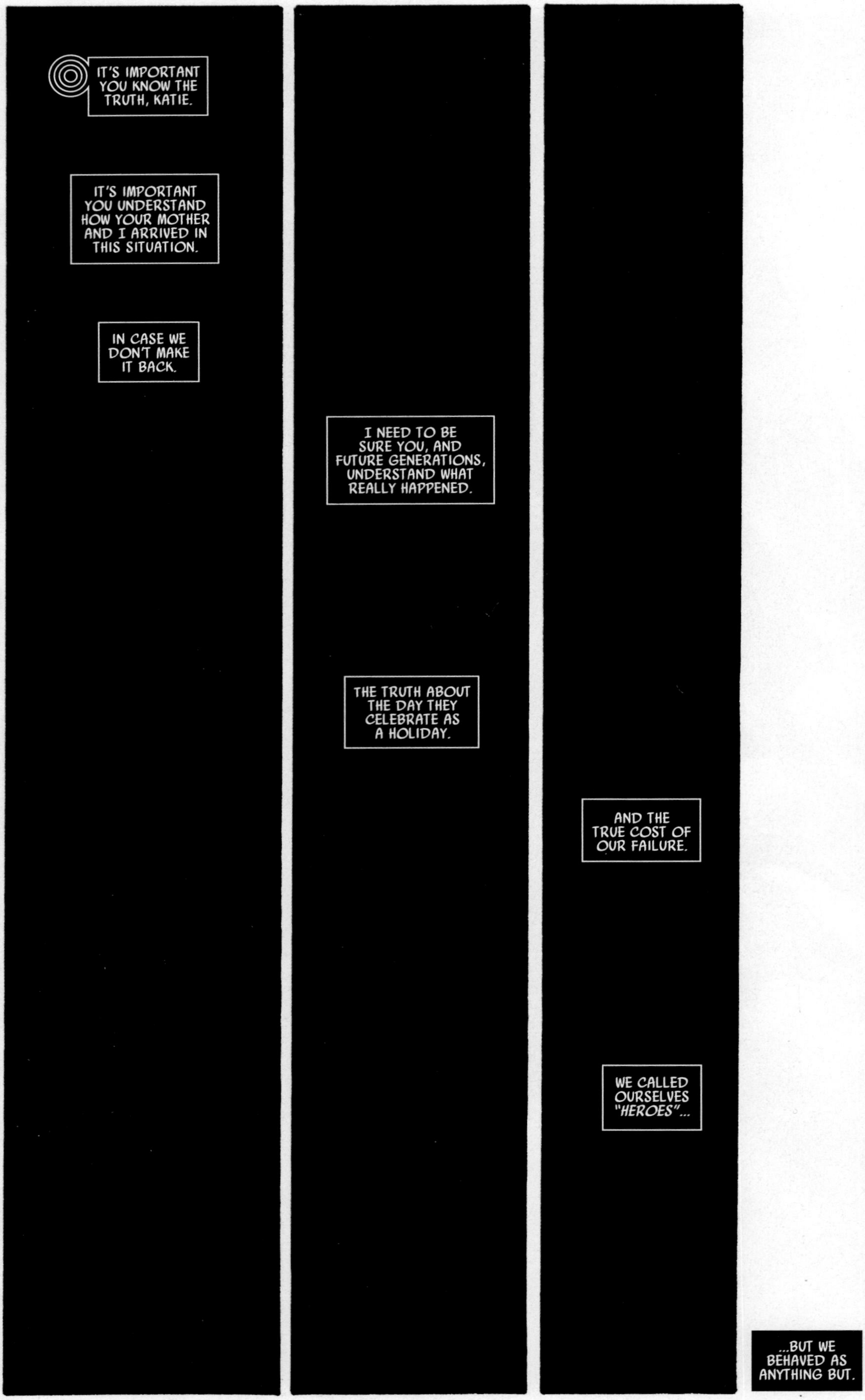
IT'S IMPORTANT YOU KNOW THE TRUTH, KATIE.
IT'S IMPORTANT YOU UNDERSTAND HOW YOUR MOTHER AND I ARRIVED IN THIS SITUATION.
IN CASE WE DON'T MAKE IT BACK.
I NEED TO BE SURE YOU, AND FUTURE GENERATIONS, UNDERSTAND WHAT REALLY HAPPENED.
THE TRUTH ABOUT THE DAY THEY CELEBRATE AS A HOLIDAY.
AND THE TRUE COST OF OUR FAILURE.
WE CALLED OURSELVES "*HEROES*"...
...BUT WE BEHAVED AS ANYTHING BUT.

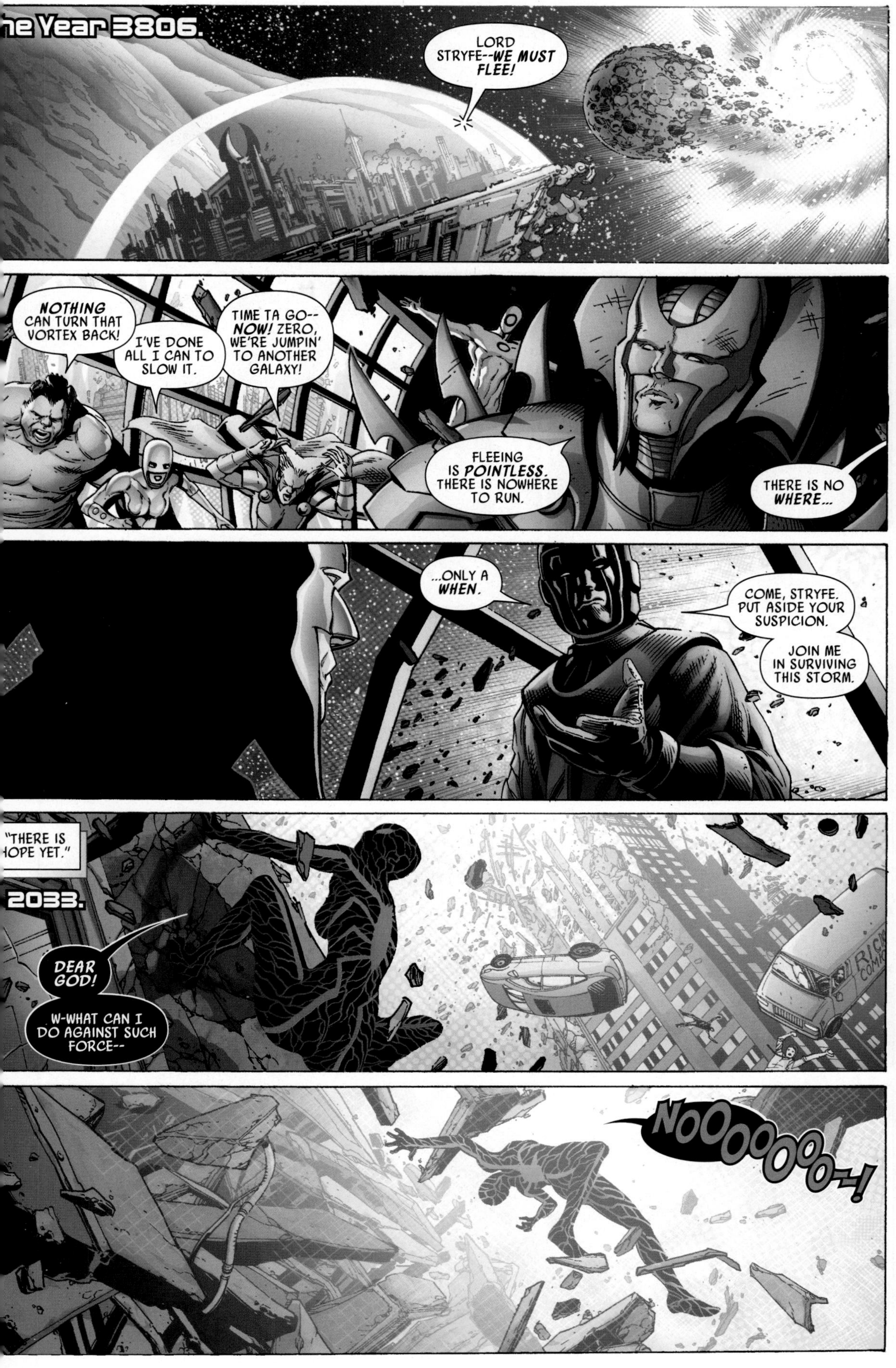
he Year 3806.
LORD STRYFE--WE MUST FLEE!
NOTHING CAN TURN THAT VORTEX BACK!
I'VE DONE ALL I CAN TO SLOW IT.
TIME TA GO--NOW! ZERO, WE'RE JUMPIN' TO ANOTHER GALAXY!
FLEEING IS POINTLESS. THERE IS NOWHERE TO RUN.
THERE IS NO WHERE...
...ONLY A WHEN.
COME, STRYFE. PUT ASIDE YOUR SUSPICION.
JOIN ME IN SURVIVING THIS STORM.
"THERE IS HOPE YET."
2033.
DEAR GOD!
W-WHAT CAN I DO AGAINST SUCH FORCE--
NOOOOOOO--!

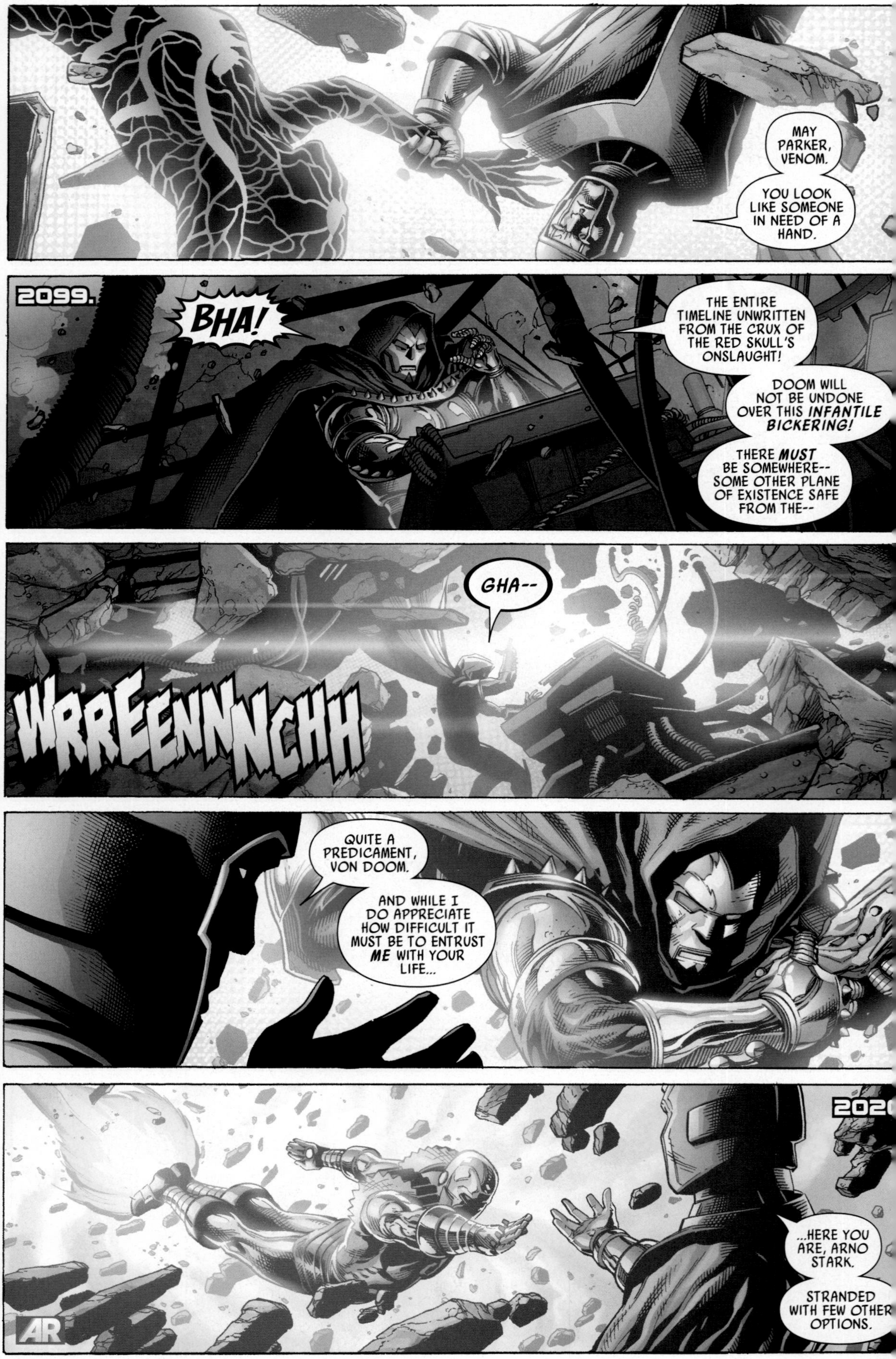
MAY PARKER, VENOM.
YOU LOOK LIKE SOMEONE IN NEED OF A HAND.
2099.
BHA!
THE ENTIRE TIMELINE UNWRITTEN FROM THE CRUX OF THE RED SKULL'S ONSLAUGHT!
DOOM WILL NOT BE UNDONE OVER THIS *INFANTILE BICKERING!*
THERE *MUST* BE SOMEWHERE-- SOME OTHER PLANE OF EXISTENCE SAFE FROM THE--
GHA--
WRREENNNCHH
QUITE A PREDICAMENT, VON DOOM.
AND WHILE I DO APPRECIATE HOW DIFFICULT IT MUST BE TO ENTRUST *ME* WITH YOUR LIFE...
...HERE YOU ARE, ARNO STARK.
STRANDED WITH FEW OTHER OPTIONS.

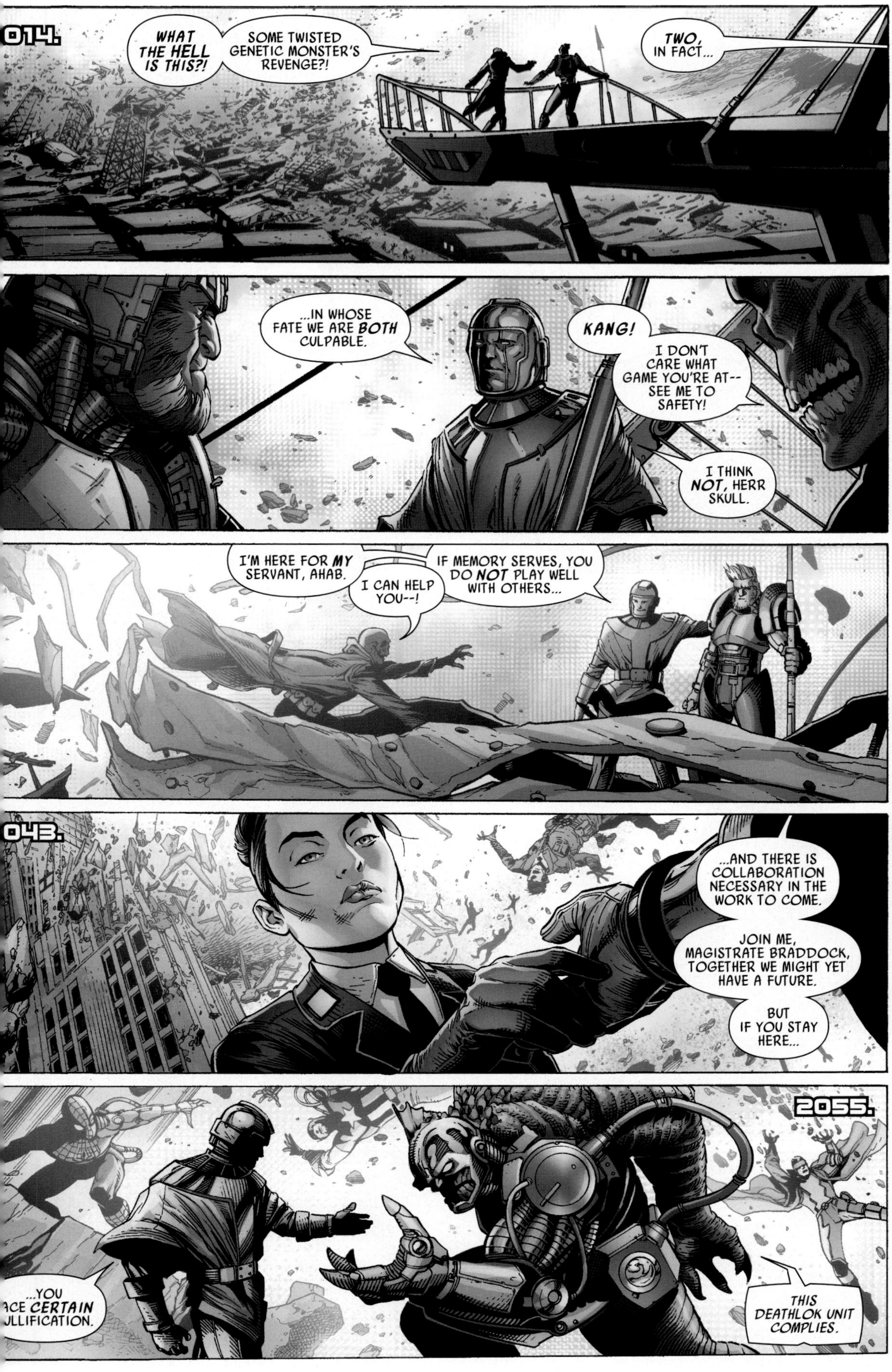

014.
WHAT THE HELL IS THIS?!
SOME TWISTED GENETIC MONSTER'S REVENGE?!
TWO, IN FACT...
...IN WHOSE FATE WE ARE BOTH CULPABLE.
KANG!
I DON'T CARE WHAT GAME YOU'RE AT-- SEE ME TO SAFETY!
I THINK NOT, HERR SKULL.
I'M HERE FOR MY SERVANT, AHAB.
I CAN HELP YOU--!
IF MEMORY SERVES, YOU DO NOT PLAY WELL WITH OTHERS...
043.
...AND THERE IS COLLABORATION NECESSARY IN THE WORK TO COME.
JOIN ME, MAGISTRATE BRADDOCK, TOGETHER WE MIGHT YET HAVE A FUTURE.
BUT IF YOU STAY HERE...
2055.
...YOU ACE CERTAIN ULLIFICATION.
THIS DEATHLOK UNIT COMPLIES.

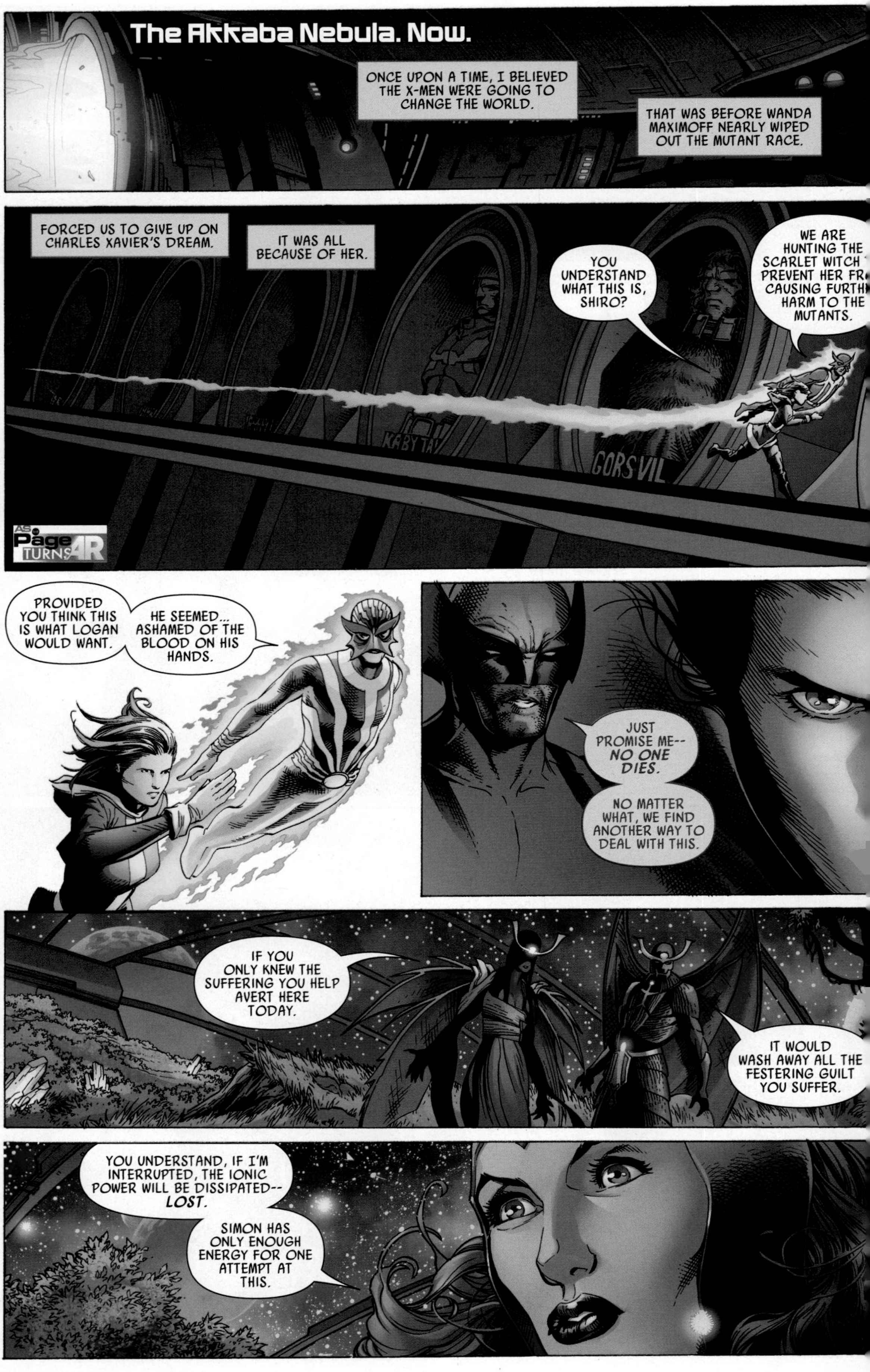
The Akkaba Nebula. Now.
ONCE UPON A TIME, I BELIEVED THE X-MEN WERE GOING TO CHANGE THE WORLD.
THAT WAS BEFORE WANDA MAXIMOFF NEARLY WIPED OUT THE MUTANT RACE.
FORCED US TO GIVE UP ON CHARLES XAVIER'S DREAM.
IT WAS ALL BECAUSE OF HER.
YOU UNDERSTAND WHAT THIS IS, SHIRO?
WE ARE HUNTING THE SCARLET WITCH
KABY TA
GORSVIL
PROVIDED YOU THINK THIS IS WHAT LOGAN WOULD WANT.
HE SEEMED... ASHAMED OF THE BLOOD ON HIS HANDS.
JUST PROMISE ME-- *NO ONE DIES.*
NO MATTER WHAT, WE FIND ANOTHER WAY TO DEAL WITH THIS.
IF YOU ONLY KNEW THE SUFFERING YOU HELP AVERT HERE TODAY.
IT WOULD WASH AWAY ALL THE FESTERING GUILT YOU SUFFER.
YOU UNDERSTAND, IF I'M INTERRUPTED, THE IONIC POWER WILL BE DISSIPATED-- *LOST.*
SIMON HAS ONLY ENOUGH ENERGY FOR ONE ATTEMPT AT THIS.

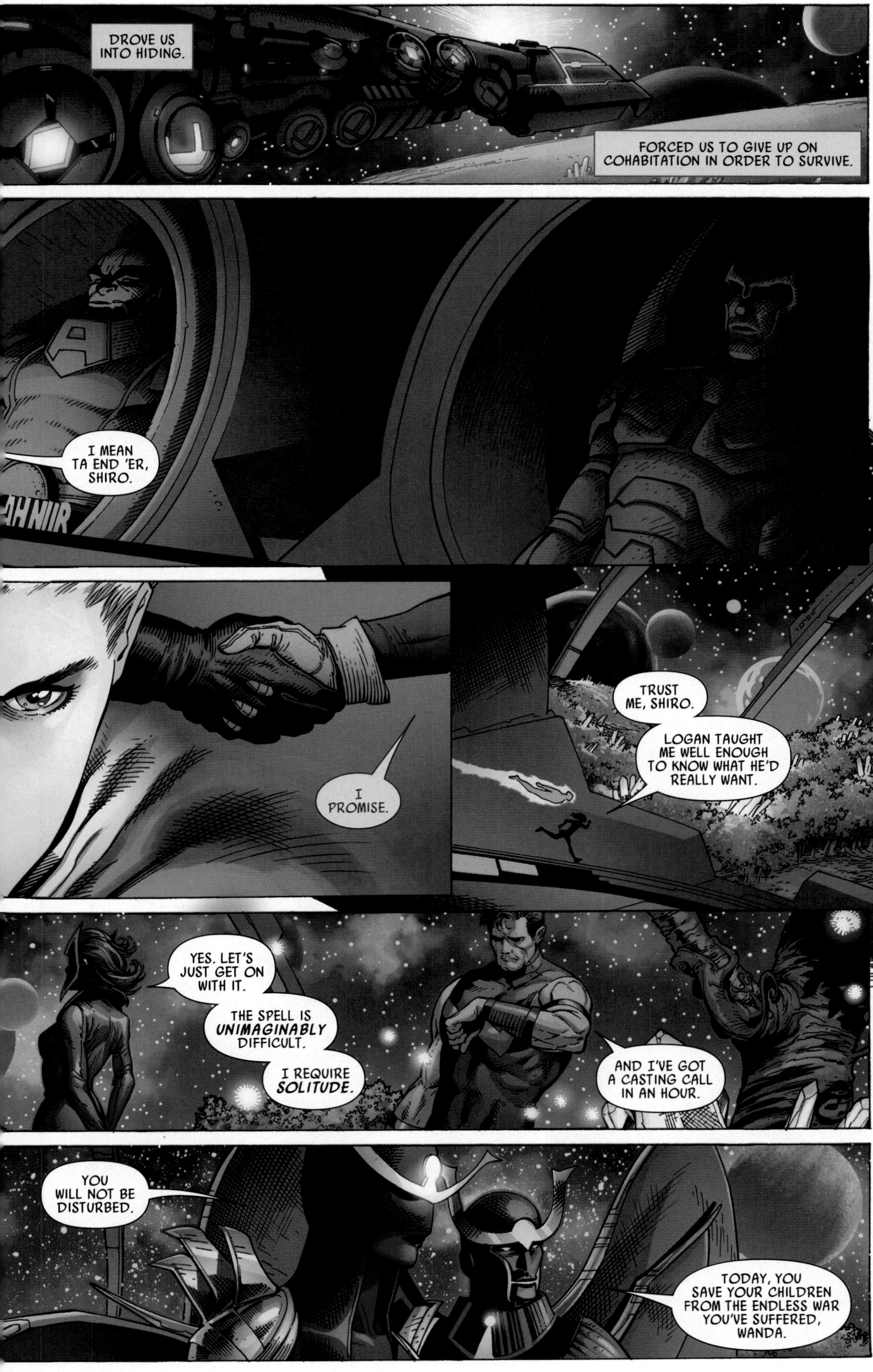
DROVE US INTO HIDING.
FORCED US TO GIVE UP ON COHABITATION IN ORDER TO SURVIVE.
I MEAN TA END 'ER, SHIRO.
I PROMISE.
TRUST ME, SHIRO.
LOGAN TAUGHT ME WELL ENOUGH TO KNOW WHAT HE'D REALLY WANT.
YES. LET'S JUST GET ON WITH IT.
THE SPELL IS *UNIMAGINABLY* DIFFICULT.
I REQUIRE *SOLITUDE.*
AND I'VE GOT A CASTING CALL IN AN HOUR.
YOU WILL NOT BE DISTURBED.
TODAY, YOU SAVE YOUR CHILDREN FROM THE ENDLESS WAR YOU'VE SUFFERED, WANDA.

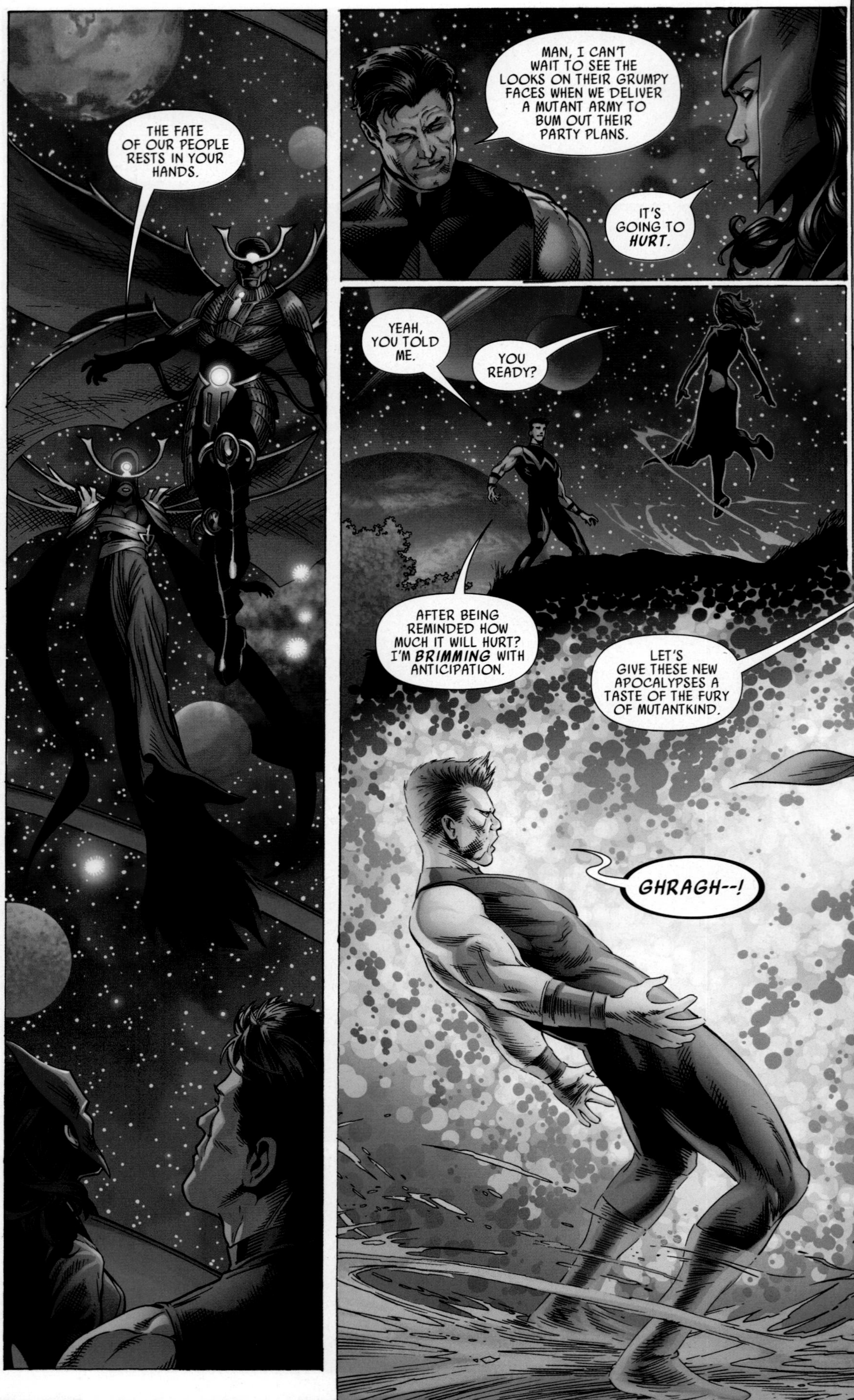
THE FATE OF OUR PEOPLE RESTS IN YOUR HANDS.
MAN, I CAN'T WAIT TO SEE THE LOOKS ON THEIR GRUMPY FACES WHEN WE DELIVER A MUTANT ARMY TO BUM OUT THEIR PARTY PLANS.
IT'S GOING TO HURT.
YEAH, YOU TOLD ME.
YOU READY?
AFTER BEING REMINDED HOW MUCH IT WILL HURT? I'M BRIMMING WITH ANTICIPATION.
LET'S GIVE THESE NEW APOCALYPSES A TASTE OF THE FURY OF MUTANTKIND.
GHRAGH--!

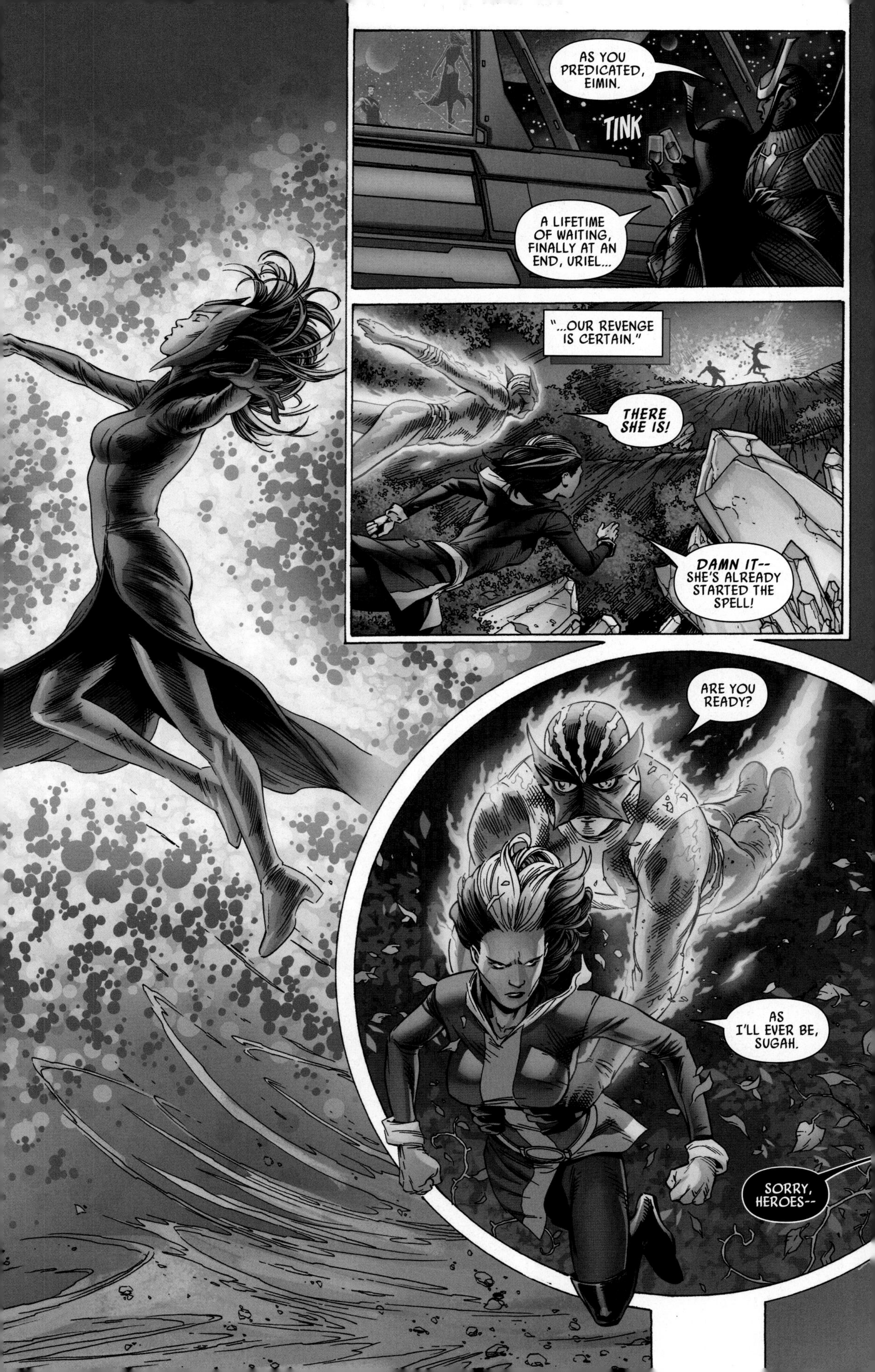
AS YOU PREDICATED, EIMIN.
TINK
A LIFETIME OF WAITING, FINALLY AT AN END, URIEL...
"...OUR REVENGE IS CERTAIN."
THERE SHE IS!
DAMN IT-- SHE'S ALREADY STARTED THE SPELL!
ARE YOU READY?
AS I'LL EVER BE, SUGAH.
SORRY, HEROES--

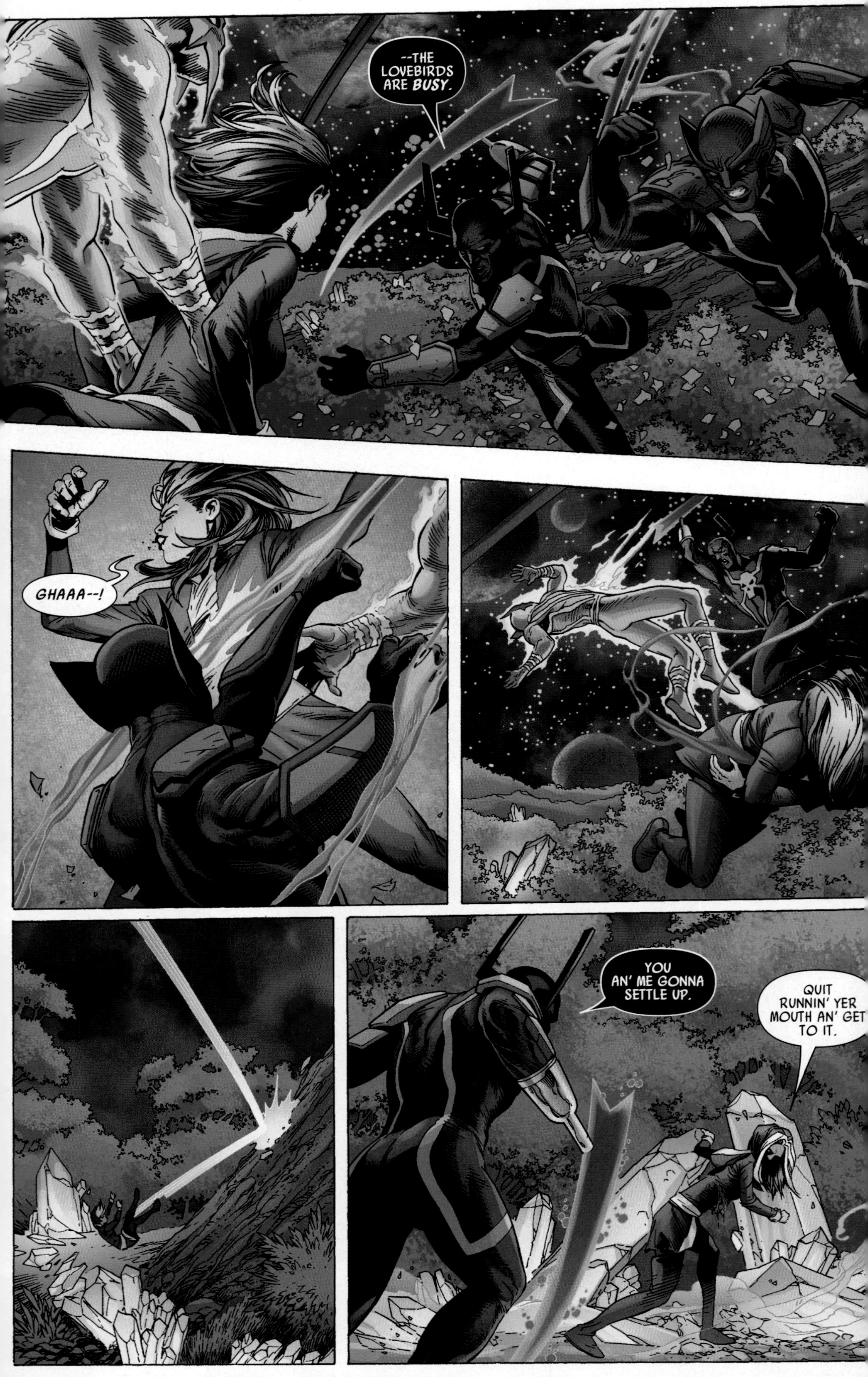
--THE LOVEBIRDS ARE BUSY.
GHAAA--!
YOU AN' ME GONNA SETTLE UP.
QUIT RUNNIN' YER MOUTH AN' GET TO IT.

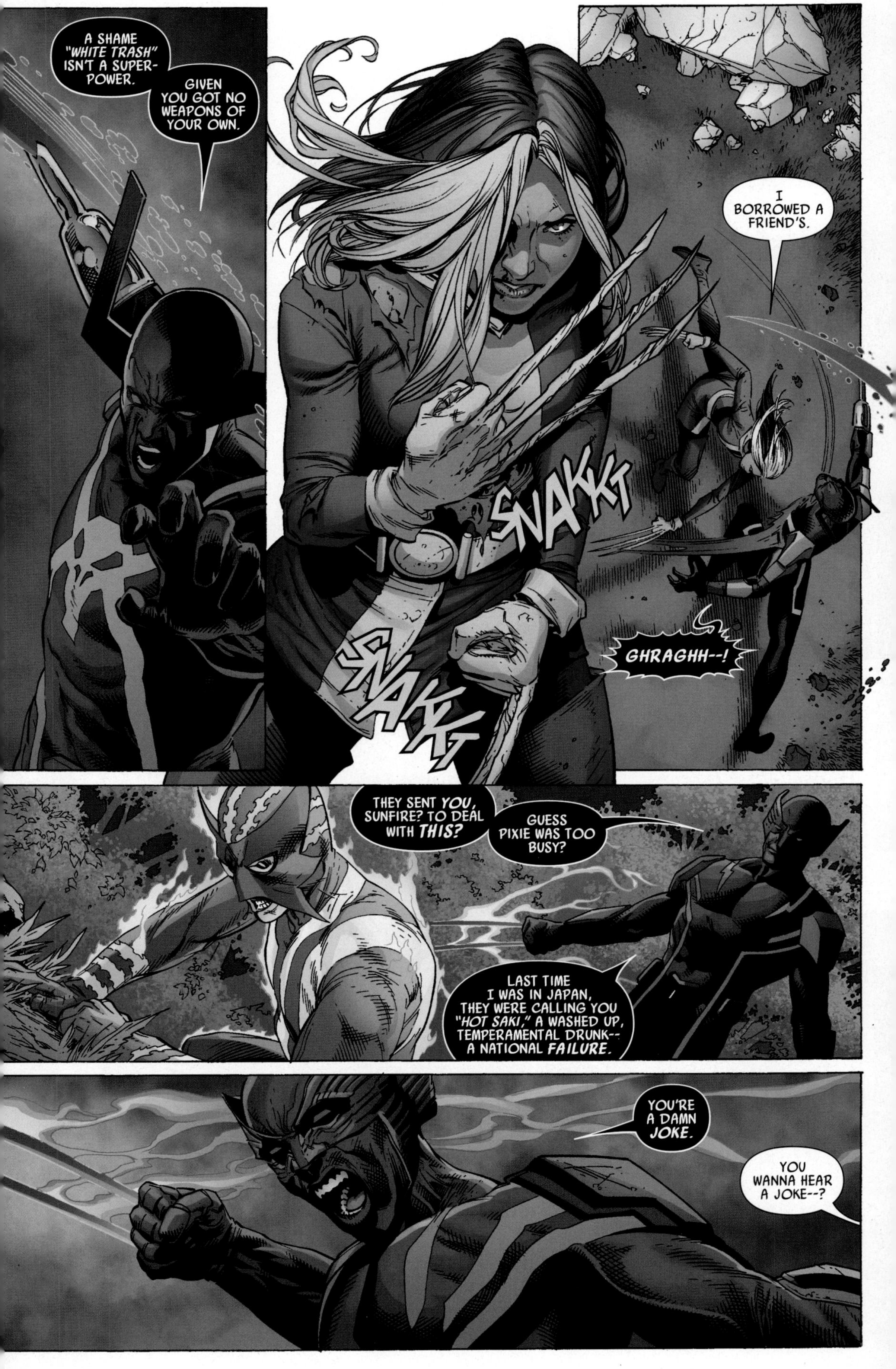
A SHAME "WHITE TRASH" ISN'T A SUPER-POWER.
GIVEN YOU GOT NO WEAPONS OF YOUR OWN.
SNAKKT
SNAKKT
I BORROWED A FRIEND'S.
GHRAGHH--!
THEY SENT YOU, SUNFIRE? TO DEAL WITH THIS?
GUESS PIXIE WAS TOO BUSY?
LAST TIME I WAS IN JAPAN, THEY WERE CALLING YOU "HOT SAKI," A WASHED UP, TEMPERAMENTAL DRUNK-- A NATIONAL FAILURE.
YOU'RE A DAMN JOKE.
YOU WANNA HEAR A JOKE--?

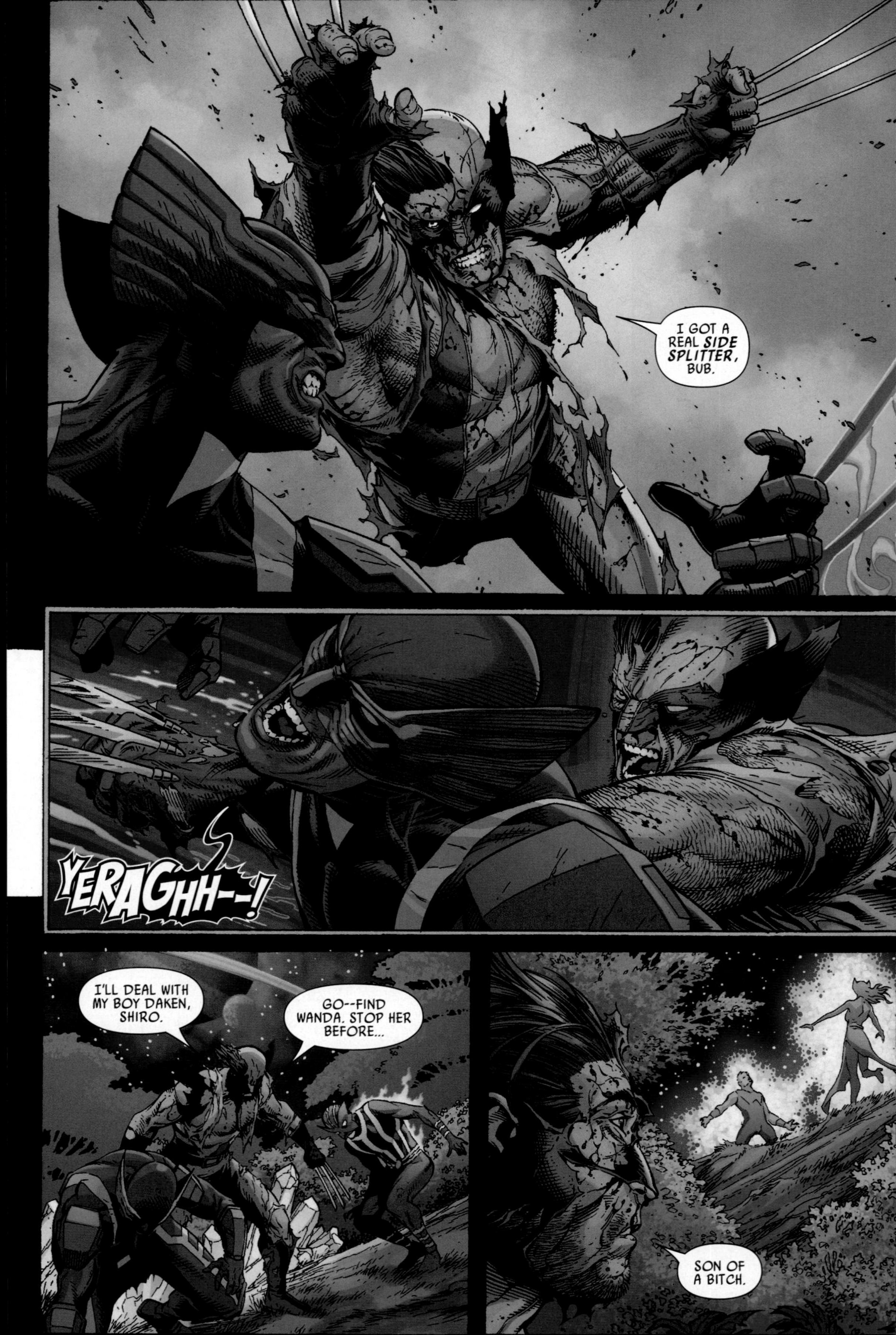
I GOT A REAL SIDE SPLITTER, BUB.
YERAGHH--!
I'LL DEAL WITH MY BOY DAKEN, SHIRO.
GO--FIND WANDA. STOP HER BEFORE...
SON OF A BITCH.

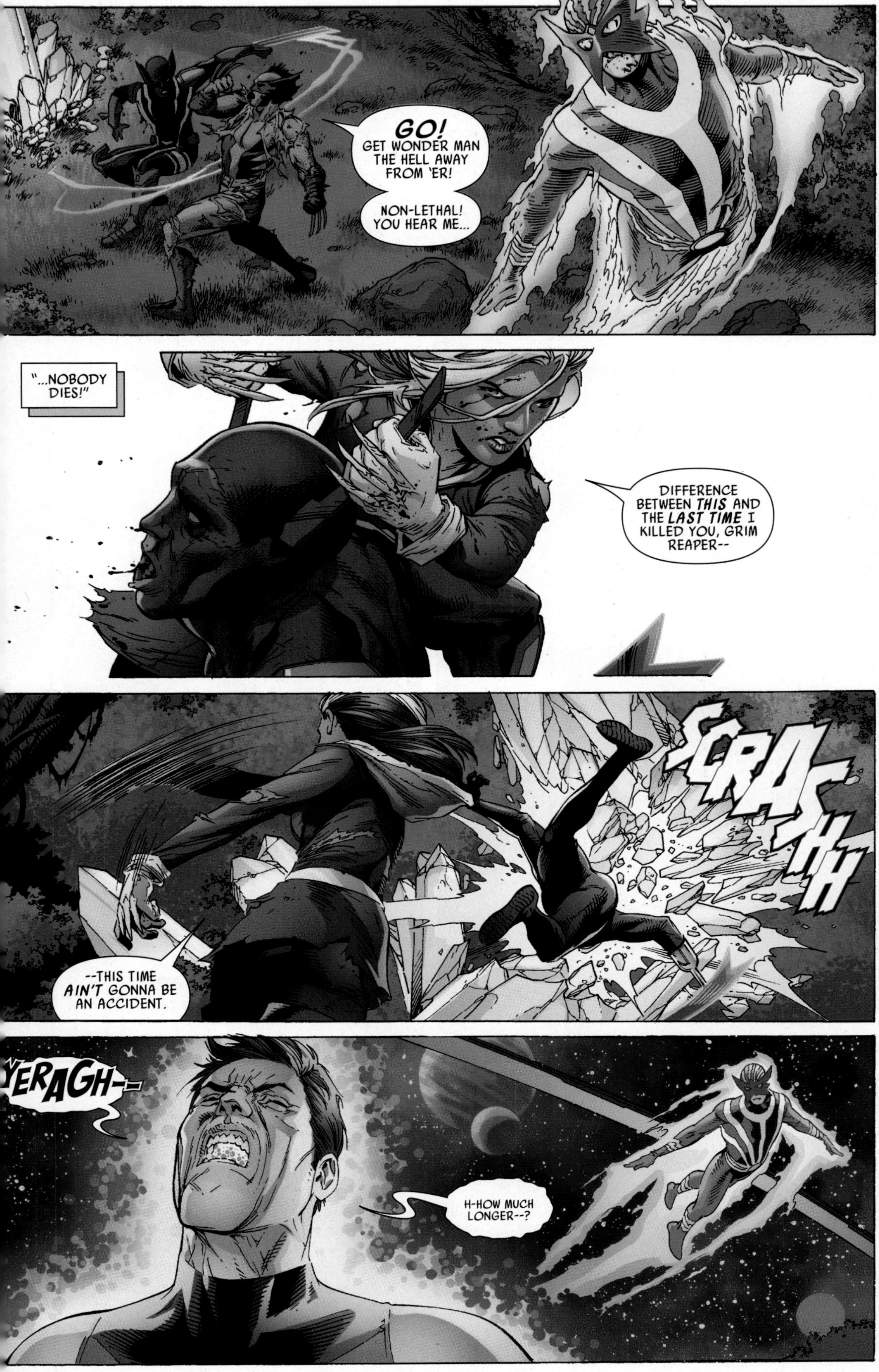
GO! GET WONDER MAN THE HELL AWAY FROM 'ER!
NON-LETHAL! YOU HEAR ME...
"...NOBODY DIES!"
DIFFERENCE BETWEEN THIS AND THE LAST TIME I KILLED YOU, GRIM REAPER--
SCRASHH
--THIS TIME AIN'T GONNA BE AN ACCIDENT.
YERAGH--
H-HOW MUCH LONGER--?

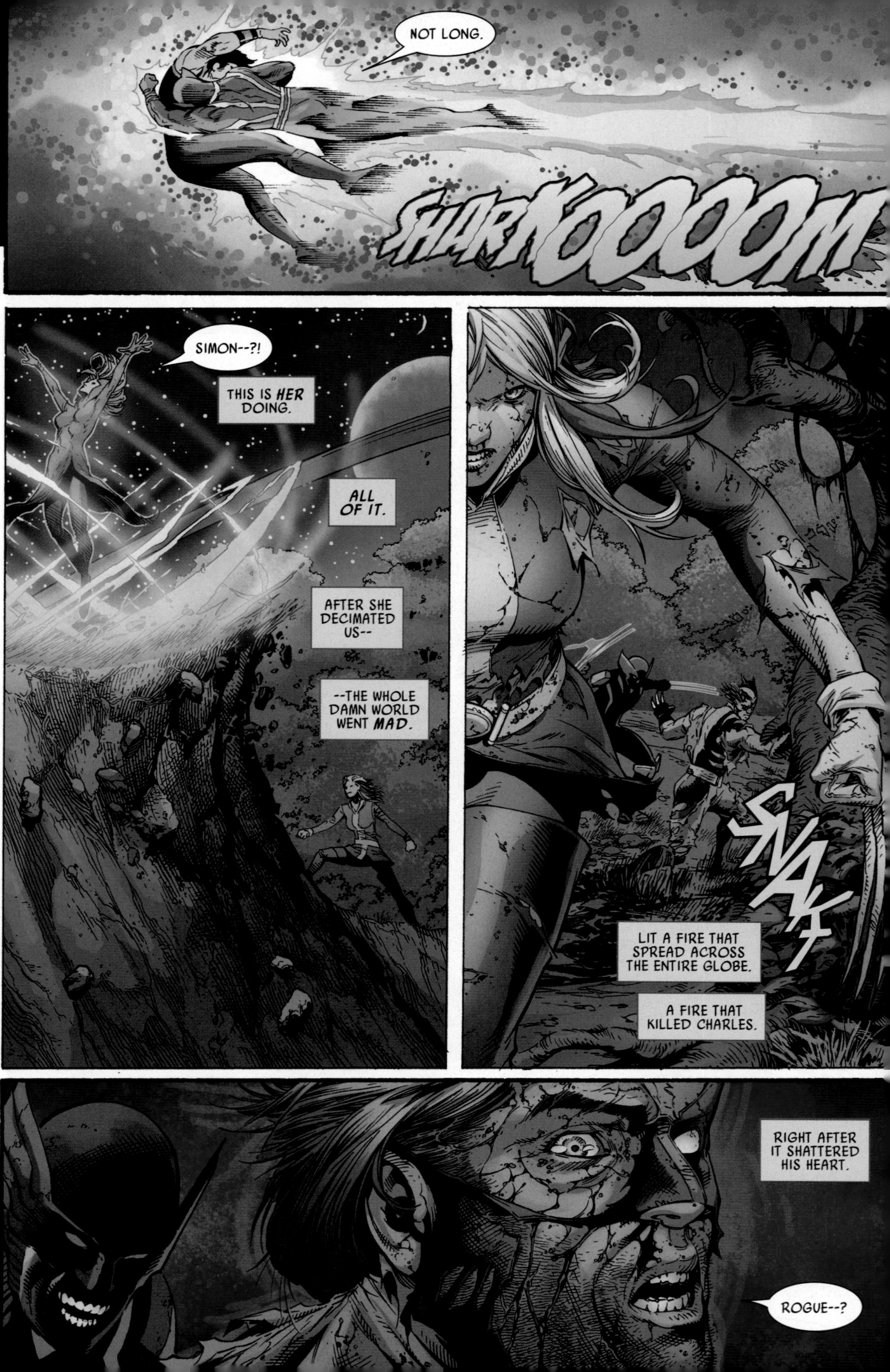
NOT LONG.
SHARKOOOOM
SIMON--?!
THIS IS HER DOING.
ALL OF IT.
AFTER SHE DECIMATED US--
--THE WHOLE DAMN WORLD WENT MAD.
SNAKT
LIT A FIRE THAT SPREAD ACROSS THE ENTIRE GLOBE.
A FIRE THAT KILLED CHARLES.
RIGHT AFTER IT SHATTERED HIS HEART.
ROGUE--?

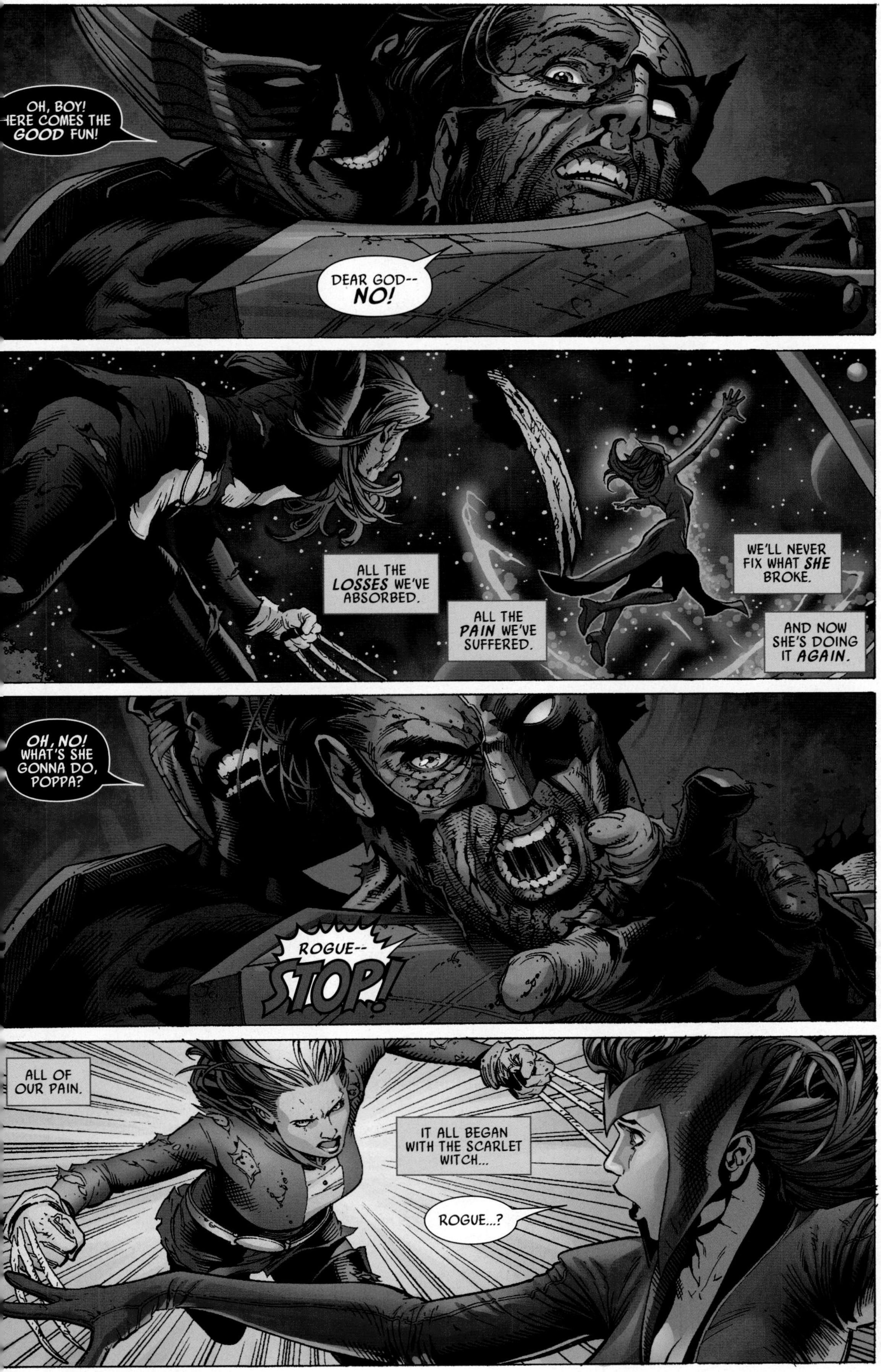
OH, BOY! HERE COMES THE GOOD FUN!
DEAR GOD-- NO!
ALL THE LOSSES WE'VE ABSORBED.
ALL THE PAIN WE'VE SUFFERED.
WE'LL NEVER FIX WHAT SHE BROKE.
AND NOW SHE'S DOING IT AGAIN.
OH, NO! WHAT'S SHE GONNA DO, POPPA?
ROGUE-- STOP!
ALL OF OUR PAIN.
IT ALL BEGAN WITH THE SCARLET WITCH...
ROGUE...?

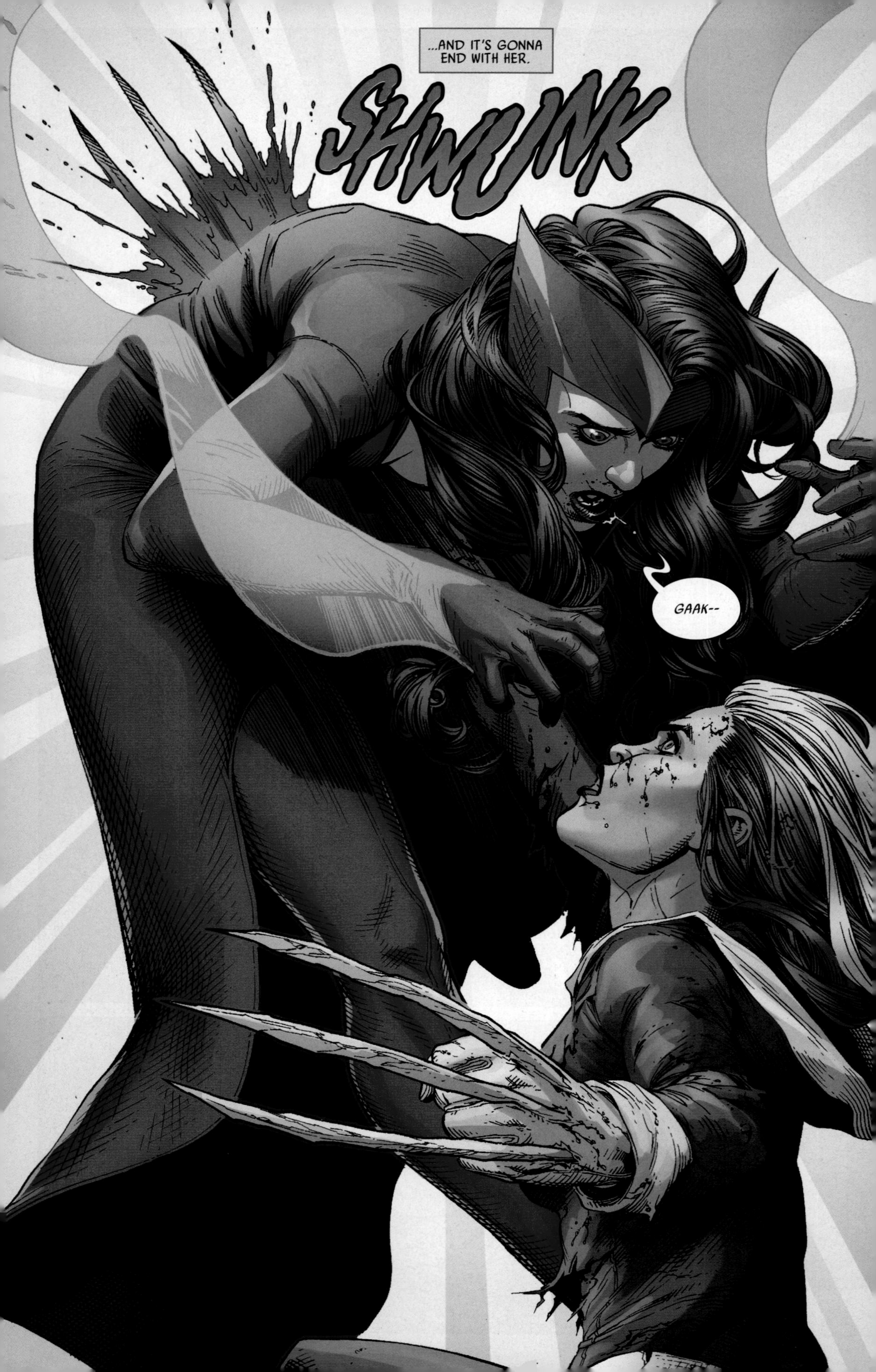
...AND IT'S GONNA END WITH HER.
SHWUNK
GAAK--

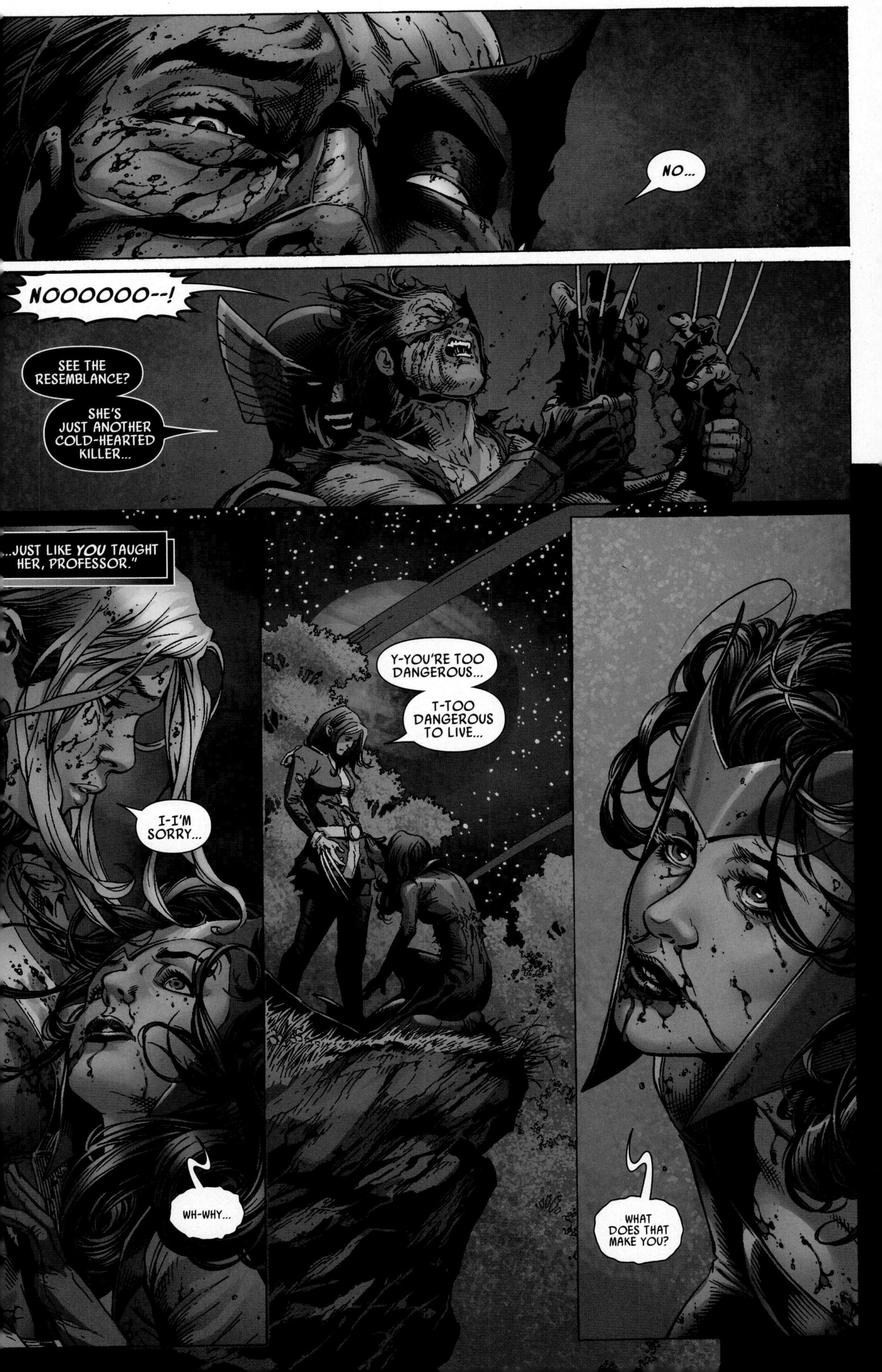
NO...
NOOOOOO--!
SEE THE RESEMBLANCE?
SHE'S JUST ANOTHER COLD-HEARTED KILLER...
...JUST LIKE YOU TAUGHT HER, PROFESSOR."
I-I'M SORRY...
WH-WHY...
Y-YOU'RE TOO DANGEROUS...
T-TOO DANGEROUS TO LIVE...
WHAT DOES THAT MAKE YOU?

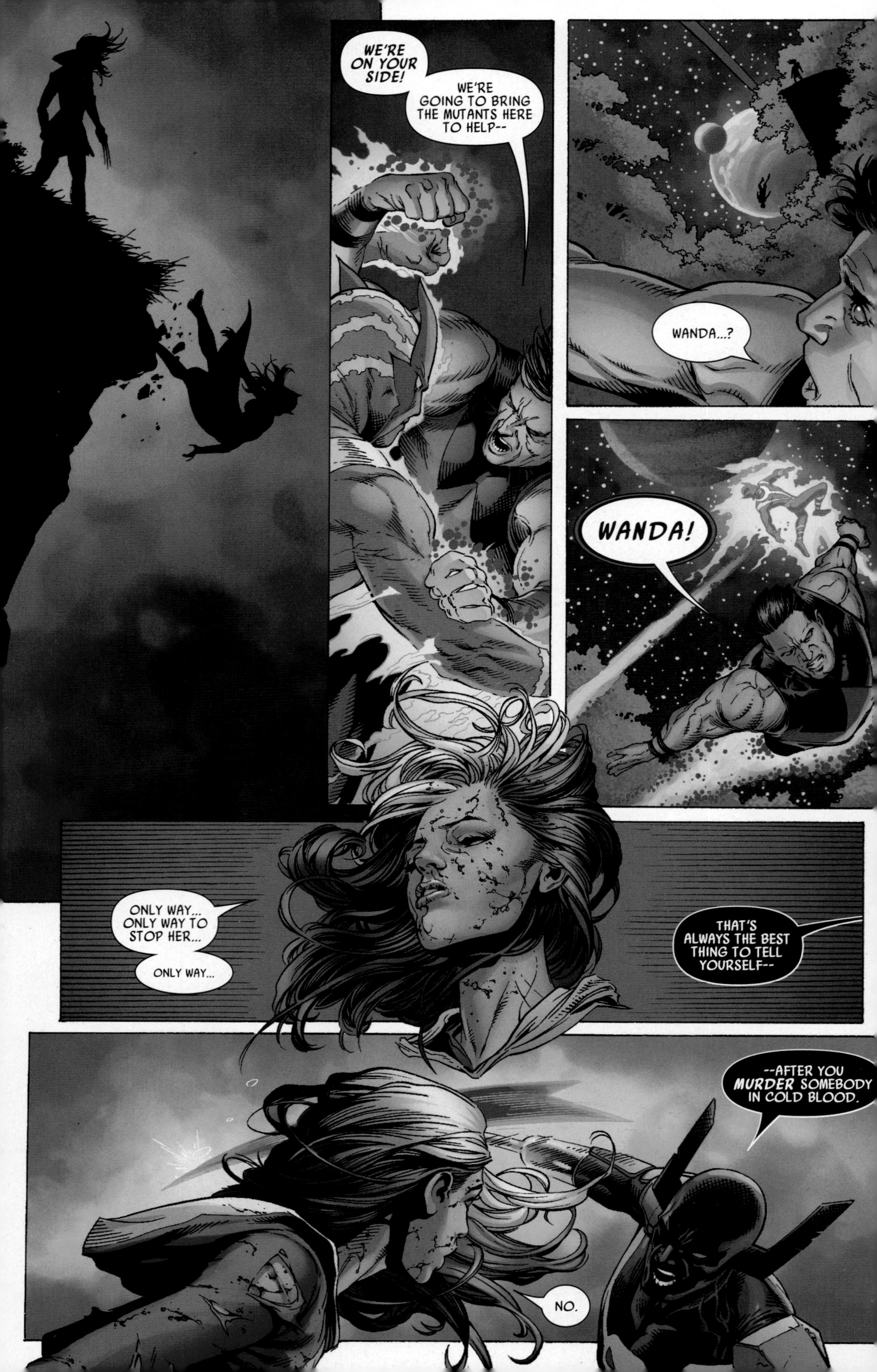
WE'RE ON YOUR SIDE!
WE'RE GOING TO BRING THE MUTANTS HERE TO HELP--
WANDA...?
WANDA!
ONLY WAY... ONLY WAY TO STOP HER...
ONLY WAY...
THAT'S ALWAYS THE BEST THING TO TELL YOURSELF--
--AFTER YOU MURDER SOMEBODY IN COLD BLOOD.
NO.

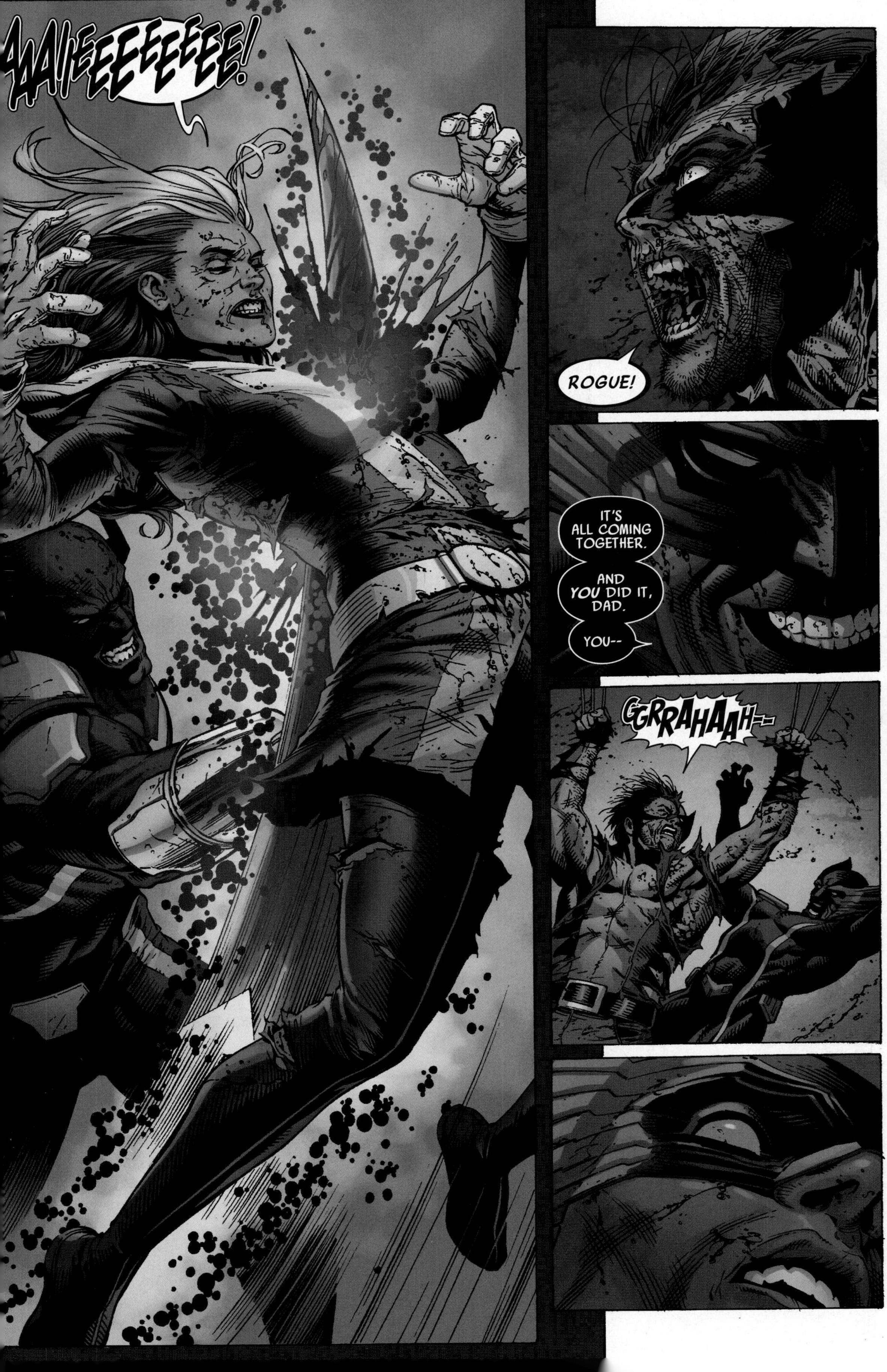
AAAIIEEEEEEEE!
ROGUE!
IT'S ALL COMING TOGETHER.
AND YOU DID IT, DAD.
YOU--
GGRRAHAAH--

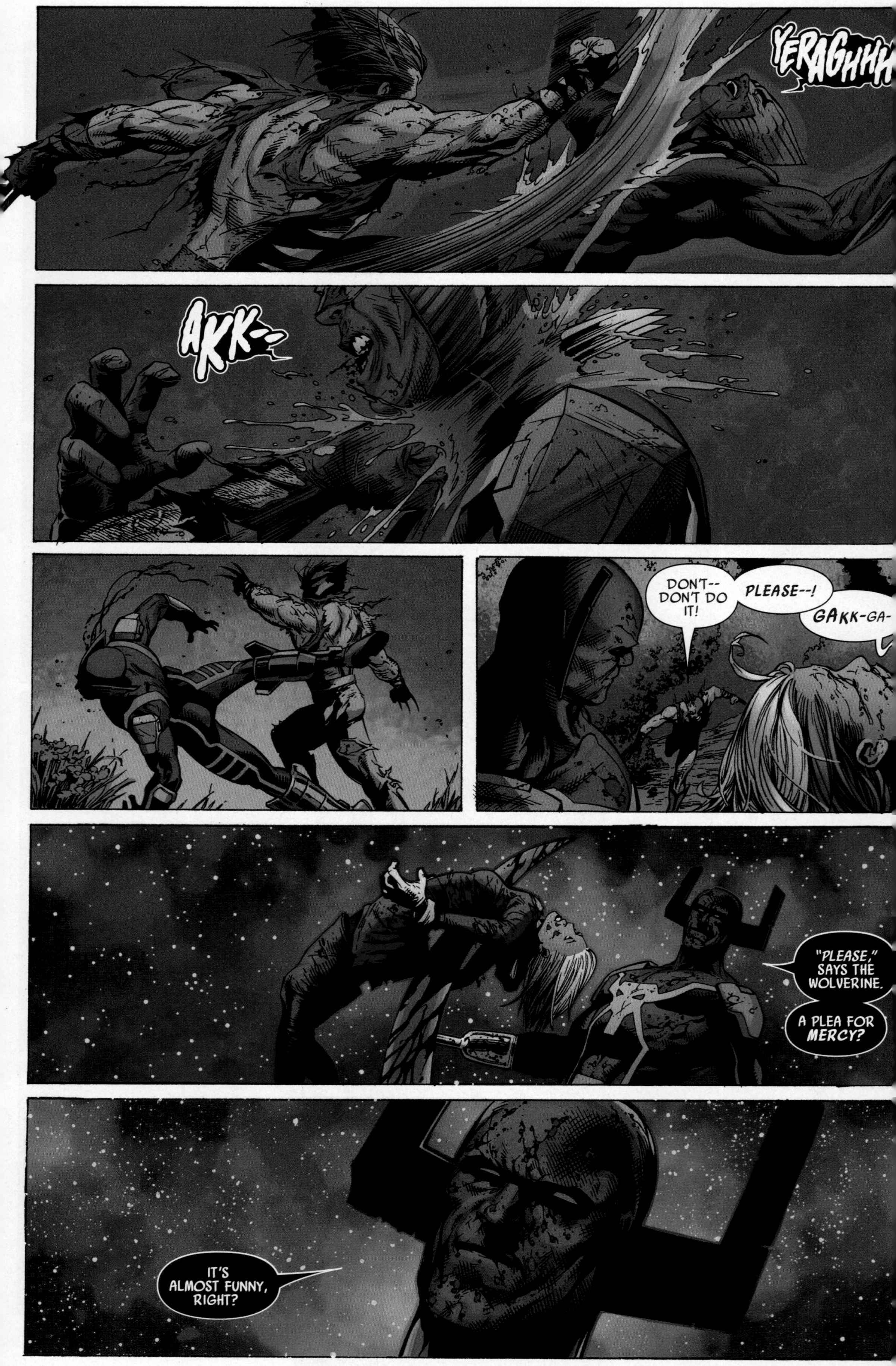
YERAGHHH
AKK--
DON'T-- DON'T DO IT!
PLEASE--!
GAKK-GA-
"PLEASE," SAYS THE WOLVERINE.
A PLEA FOR MERCY?
IT'S ALMOST FUNNY, RIGHT?

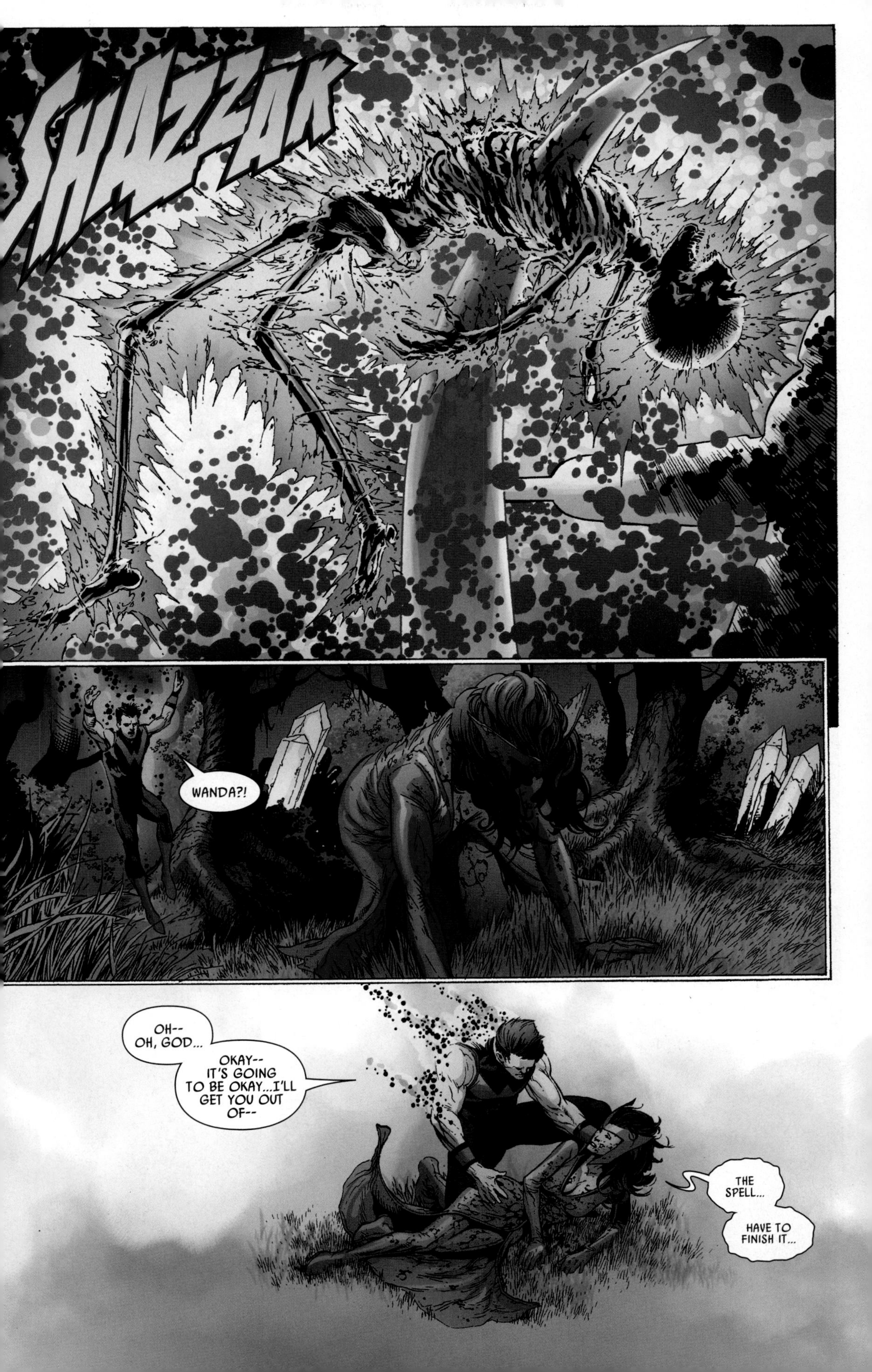
SHAZAK
WANDA?!
OH-- OH, GOD...
OKAY-- IT'S GOING TO BE OKAY...I'LL GET YOU OUT OF--
THE SPELL...
HAVE TO FINISH IT...

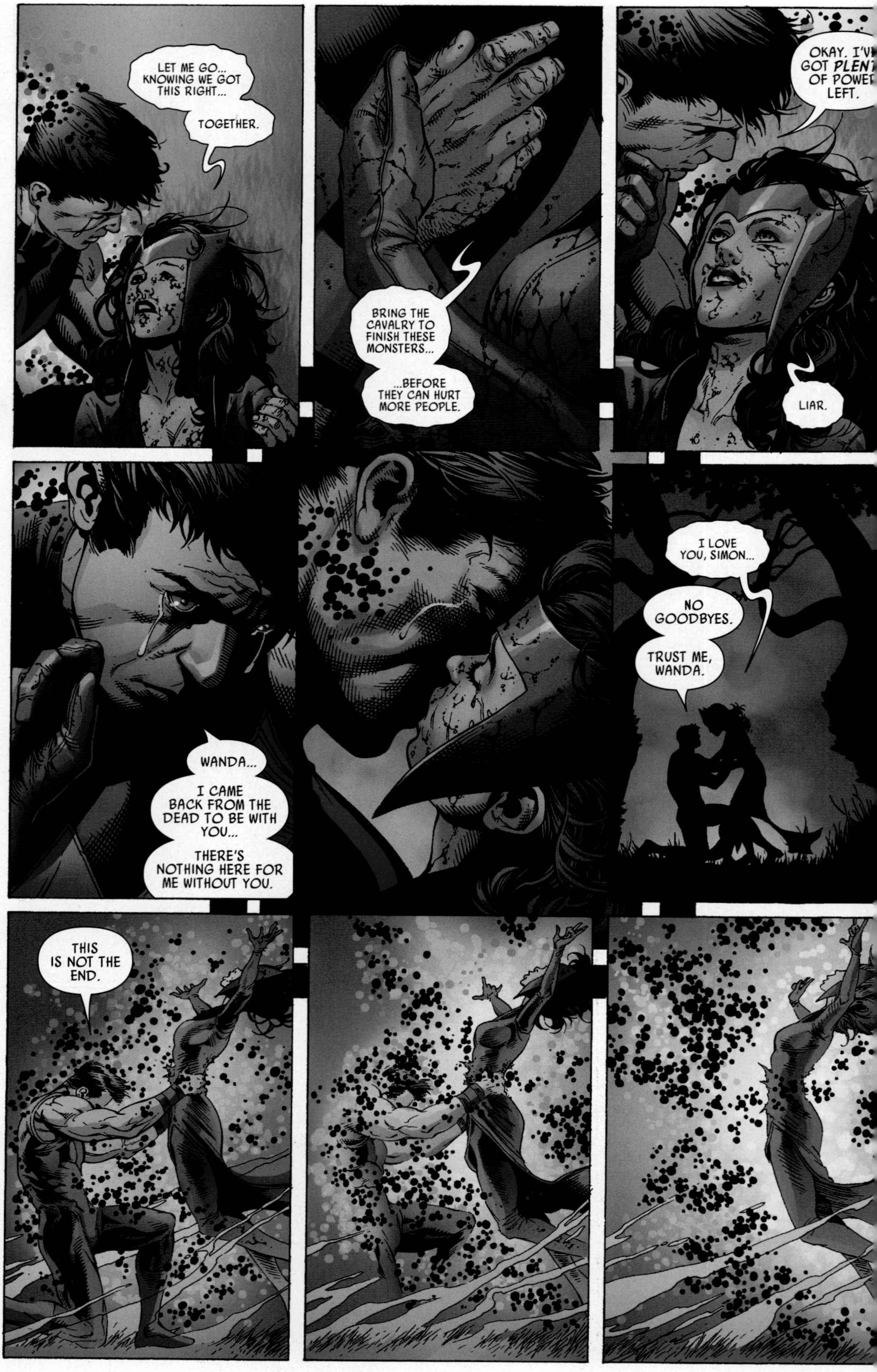
LET ME GO... KNOWING WE GOT THIS RIGHT...
TOGETHER.
BRING THE CAVALRY TO FINISH THESE MONSTERS...
...BEFORE THEY CAN HURT MORE PEOPLE.
OKAY. I'VE GOT PLENTY OF POWER LEFT.
LIAR.
WANDA...
I CAME BACK FROM THE DEAD TO BE WITH YOU...
THERE'S NOTHING HERE FOR ME WITHOUT YOU.
I LOVE YOU, SIMON...
NO GOODBYES.
TRUST ME, WANDA.
THIS IS NOT THE END.

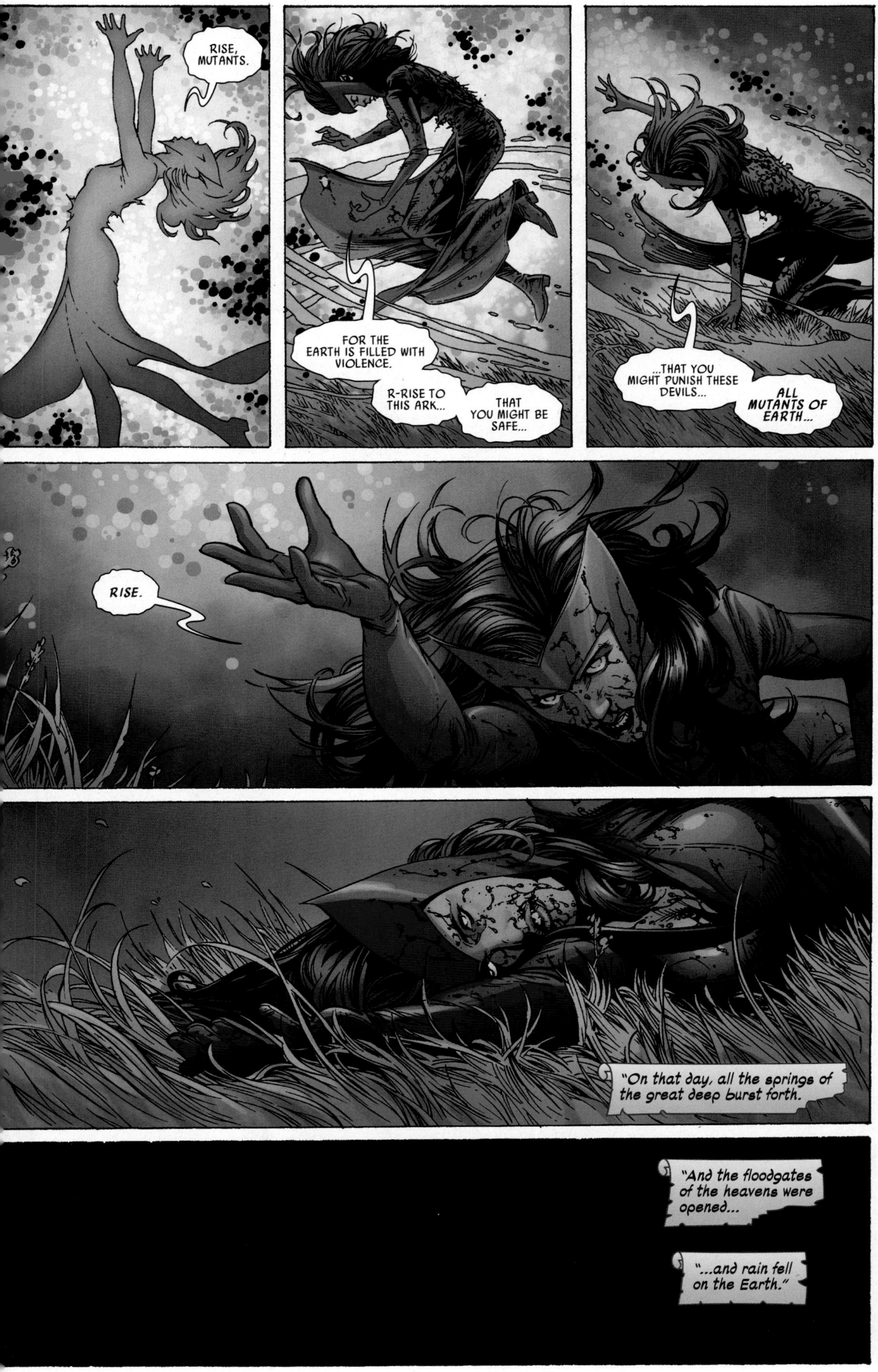
RISE, MUTANTS.
FOR THE EARTH IS FILLED WITH VIOLENCE.
R-RISE TO THIS ARK...
THAT YOU MIGHT BE SAFE...
...THAT YOU MIGHT PUNISH THESE DEVILS...
ALL MUTANTS OF EARTH...
RISE.
"On that day, all the springs of the great deep burst forth.
"And the floodgates of the heavens were opened...
"...and rain fell on the Earth."

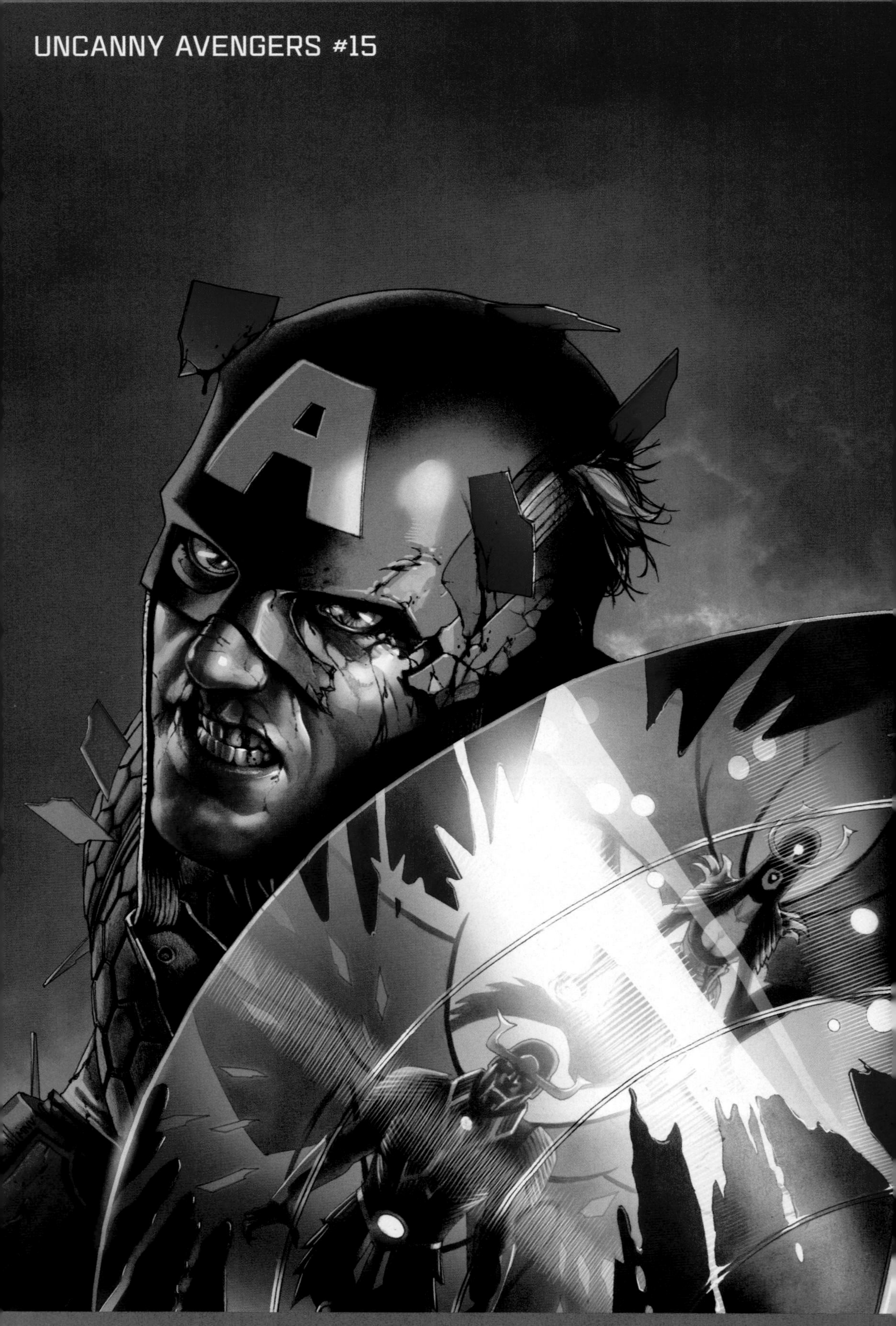
UNCANNY AVENGERS #15

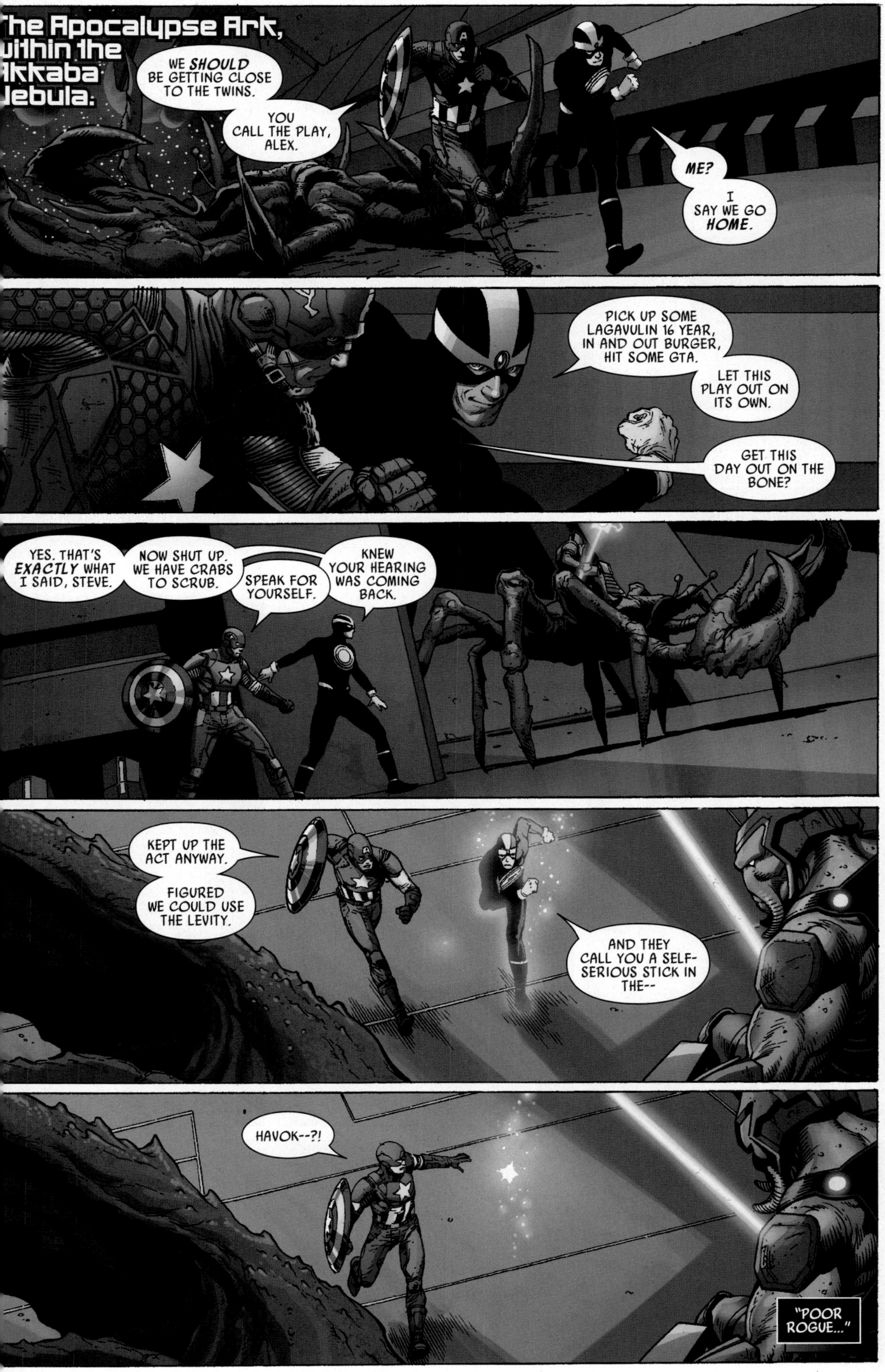
The Apocalypse Ark, within the Akkaba Nebula.
WE SHOULD BE GETTING CLOSE TO THE TWINS.
YOU CALL THE PLAY, ALEX.
ME?
I SAY WE GO HOME.
PICK UP SOME LAGAVULIN 16 YEAR, IN AND OUT BURGER, HIT SOME GTA.
LET THIS PLAY OUT ON ITS OWN.
GET THIS DAY OUT ON THE BONE?
YES. THAT'S EXACTLY WHAT I SAID, STEVE.
NOW SHUT UP. WE HAVE CRABS TO SCRUB.
SPEAK FOR YOURSELF.
KNEW YOUR HEARING WAS COMING BACK.
KEPT UP THE ACT ANYWAY.
FIGURED WE COULD USE THE LEVITY.
AND THEY CALL YOU A SELF-SERIOUS STICK IN THE--
HAVOK--?!
"POOR ROGUE..."

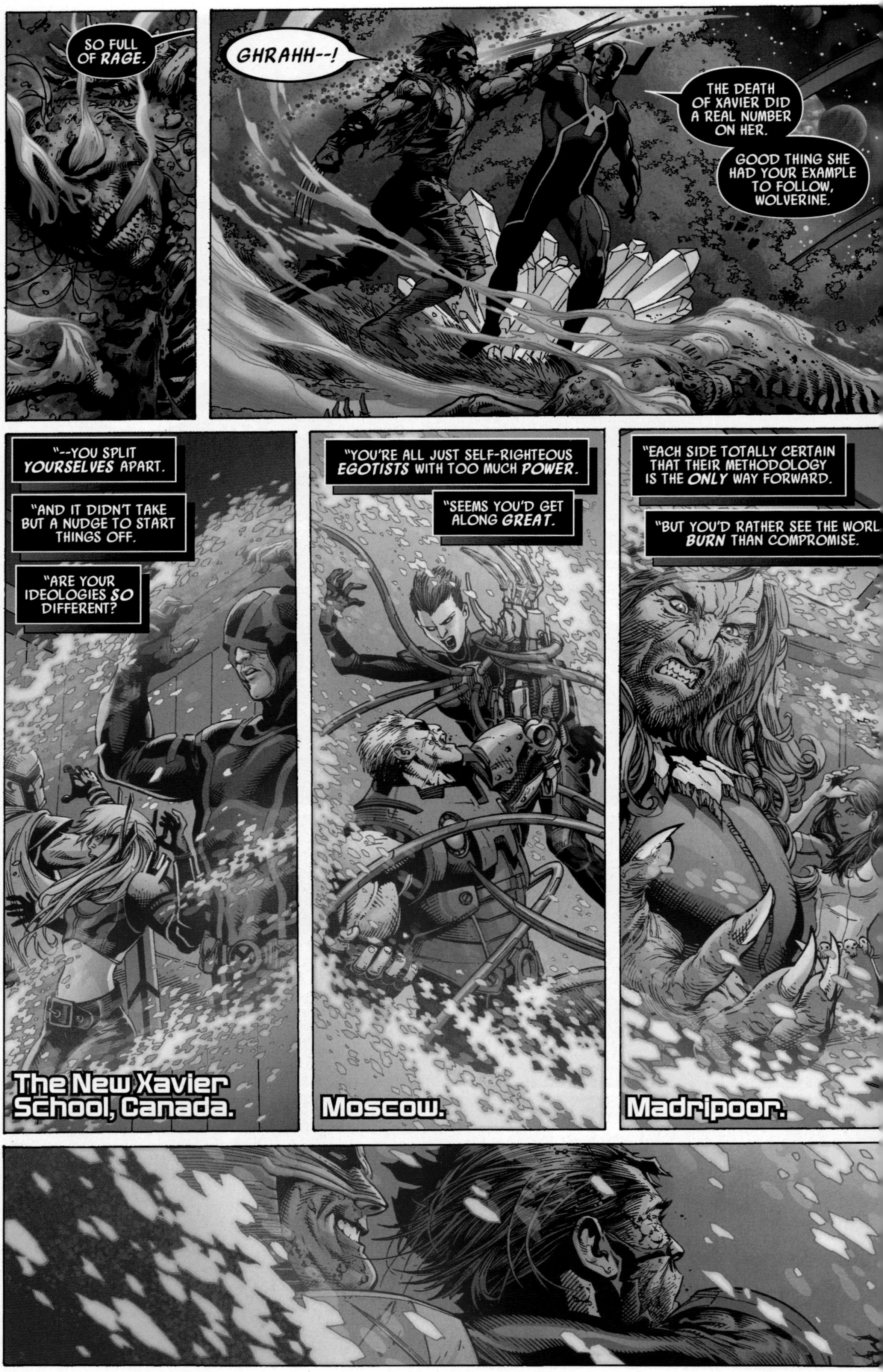
SO FULL OF RAGE.
GHRAHH--!
THE DEATH OF XAVIER DID A REAL NUMBER ON HER.
GOOD THING SHE HAD YOUR EXAMPLE TO FOLLOW, WOLVERINE.
"--YOU SPLIT YOURSELVES APART.
"AND IT DIDN'T TAKE BUT A NUDGE TO START THINGS OFF.
"ARE YOUR IDEOLOGIES SO DIFFERENT?
The New Xavier School, Canada.
"YOU'RE ALL JUST SELF-RIGHTEOUS EGOTISTS WITH TOO MUCH POWER.
"SEEMS YOU'D GET ALONG GREAT.
Moscow.
"EACH SIDE TOTALLY CERTAIN THAT THEIR METHODOLOGY IS THE ONLY WAY FORWARD.
"BUT YOU'D RATHER SEE THE WORL BURN THAN COMPROMISE.
Madripoor.

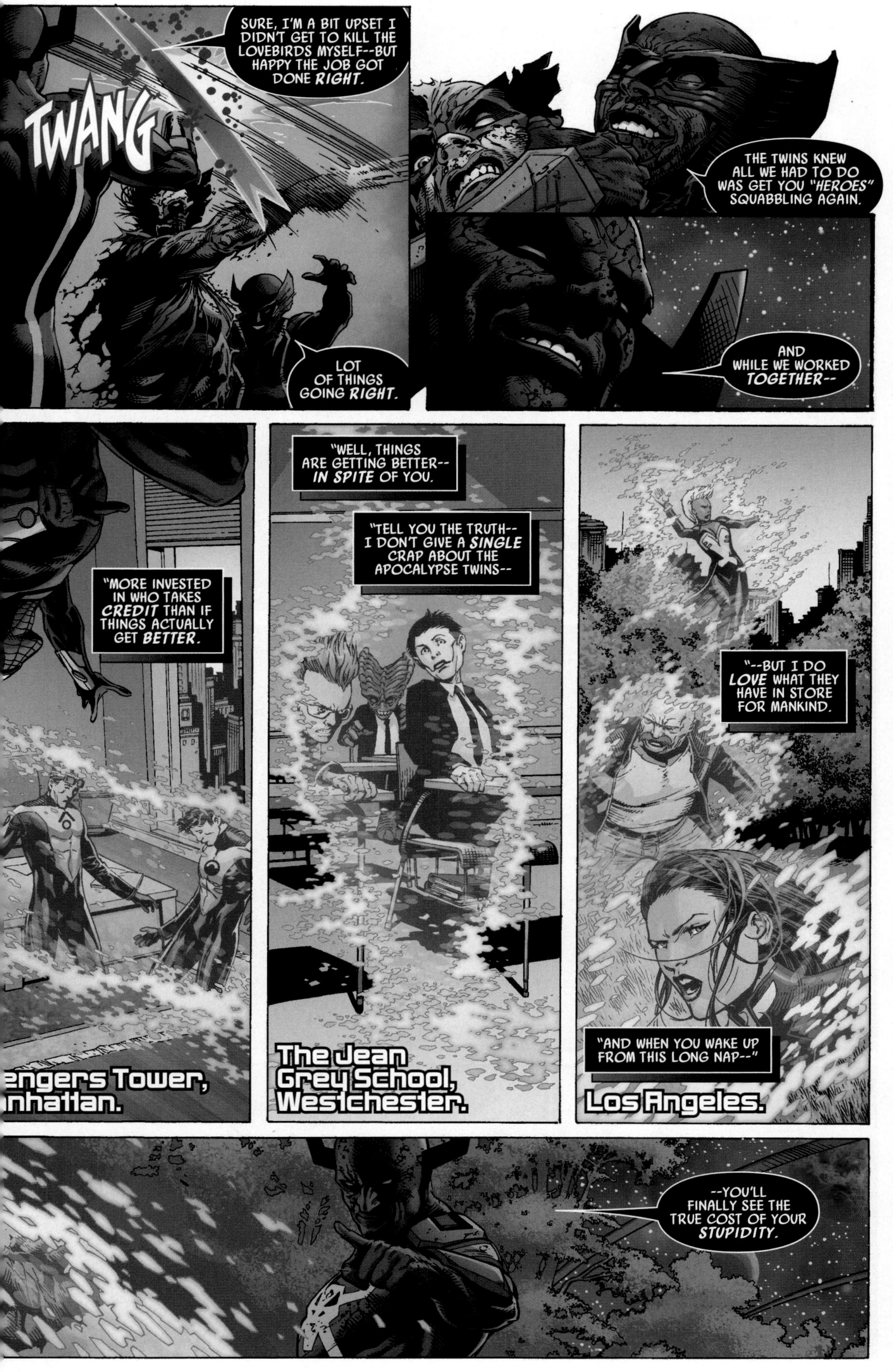

SURE, I'M A BIT UPSET I DIDN'T GET TO KILL THE LOVEBIRDS MYSELF--BUT HAPPY THE JOB GOT DONE RIGHT.
TWANG
LOT OF THINGS GOING RIGHT.
THE TWINS KNEW ALL WE HAD TO DO WAS GET YOU "HEROES" SQUABBLING AGAIN.
AND WHILE WE WORKED TOGETHER--
"MORE INVESTED IN WHO TAKES CREDIT THAN IF THINGS ACTUALLY GET BETTER.
engers Tower, nhattan.
"WELL, THINGS ARE GETTING BETTER-- IN SPITE OF YOU.
"TELL YOU THE TRUTH-- I DON'T GIVE A SINGLE CRAP ABOUT THE APOCALYPSE TWINS--
The Jean Grey School, Westchester.
"--BUT I DO LOVE WHAT THEY HAVE IN STORE FOR MANKIND.
"AND WHEN YOU WAKE UP FROM THIS LONG NAP--"
Los Angeles.
--YOU'LL FINALLY SEE THE TRUE COST OF YOUR STUPIDITY.

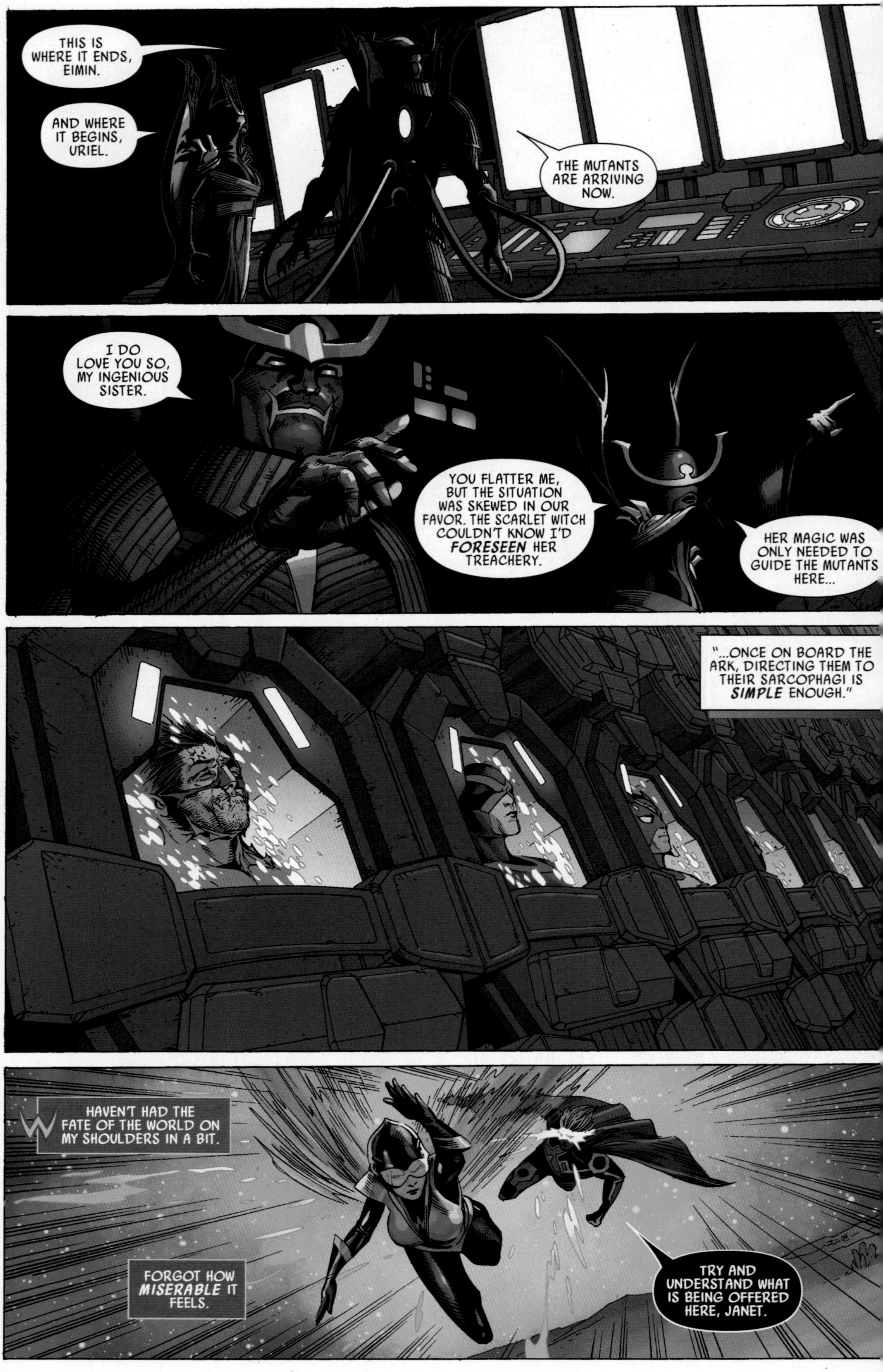
THIS IS WHERE IT ENDS, EIMIN.
AND WHERE IT BEGINS, URIEL.
THE MUTANTS ARE ARRIVING NOW.
I DO LOVE YOU SO, MY INGENIOUS SISTER.
YOU FLATTER ME, BUT THE SITUATION WAS SKEWED IN OUR FAVOR. THE SCARLET WITCH COULDN'T KNOW I'D FORESEEN HER TREACHERY.
HER MAGIC WAS ONLY NEEDED TO GUIDE THE MUTANTS HERE...
"...ONCE ON BOARD THE ARK, DIRECTING THEM TO THEIR SARCOPHAGI IS SIMPLE ENOUGH."
HAVEN'T HAD THE FATE OF THE WORLD ON MY SHOULDERS IN A BIT.
FORGOT HOW MISERABLE IT FEELS.
TRY AND UNDERSTAND WHAT IS BEING OFFERED HERE, JANET.

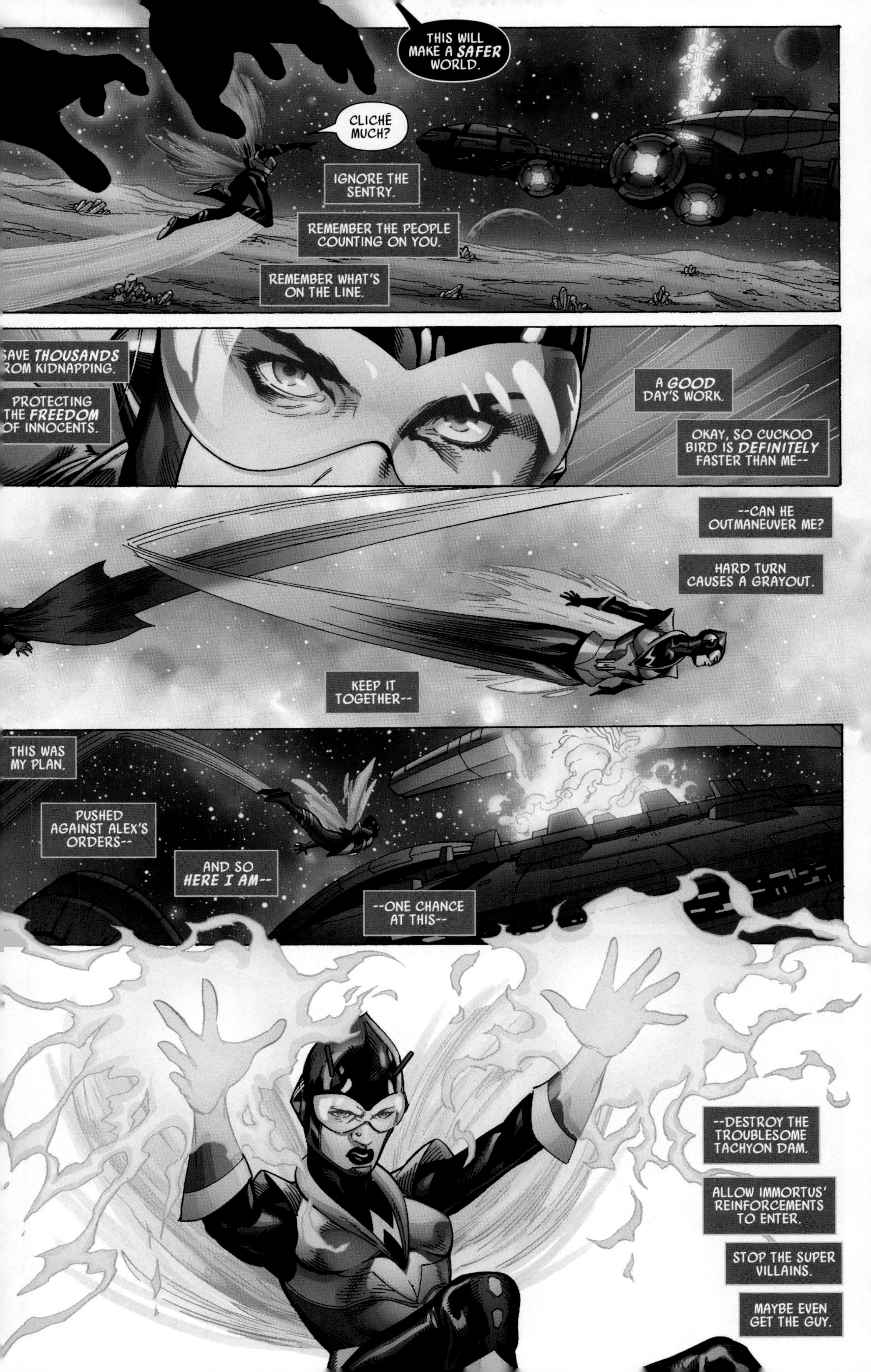
THIS WILL MAKE A SAFER WORLD.
CLICHÉ MUCH?
IGNORE THE SENTRY.
REMEMBER THE PEOPLE COUNTING ON YOU.
REMEMBER WHAT'S ON THE LINE.
SAVE THOUSANDS FROM KIDNAPPING.
PROTECTING THE FREEDOM OF INNOCENTS.
A GOOD DAY'S WORK.
OKAY, SO CUCKOO BIRD IS DEFINITELY FASTER THAN ME--
--CAN HE OUTMANEUVER ME?
HARD TURN CAUSES A GRAYOUT.
KEEP IT TOGETHER--
THIS WAS MY PLAN.
PUSHED AGAINST ALEX'S ORDERS--
AND SO HERE I AM--
--ONE CHANCE AT THIS--
--DESTROY THE TROUBLESOME TACHYON DAM.
ALLOW IMMORTUS' REINFORCEMENTS TO ENTER.
STOP THE SUPER VILLAINS.
MAYBE EVEN GET THE GUY.

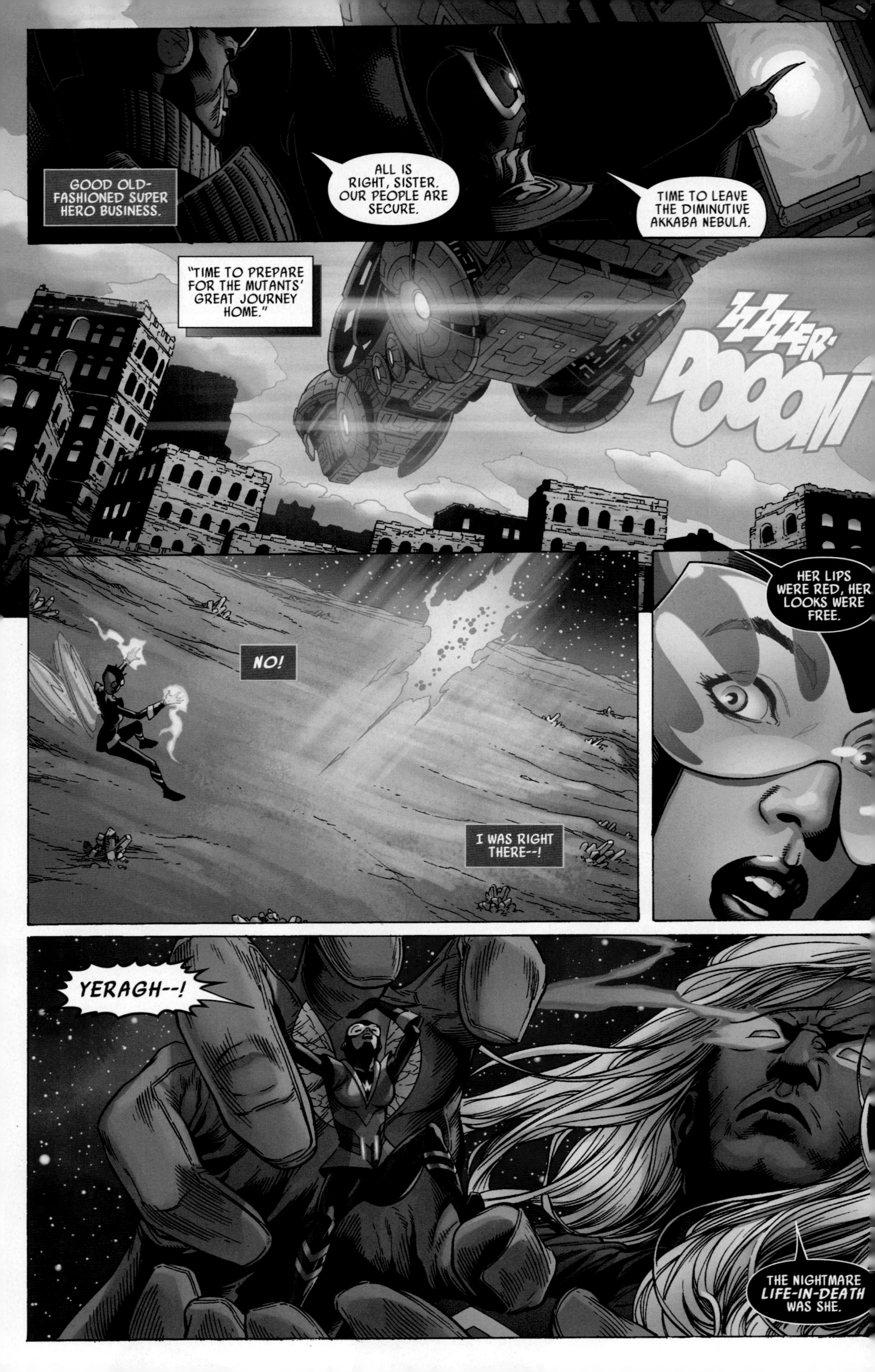
GOOD OLD-FASHIONED SUPER HERO BUSINESS.
ALL IS RIGHT, SISTER. OUR PEOPLE ARE SECURE.
TIME TO LEAVE THE DIMINUTIVE AKKABA NEBULA.
"TIME TO PREPARE FOR THE MUTANTS' GREAT JOURNEY HOME."
ZZZZER-DOOOM
NO!
I WAS RIGHT THERE--!
HER LIPS WERE RED, HER LOOKS WERE FREE.
YERAGH--!
THE NIGHTMARE LIFE-IN-DEATH WAS SHE.

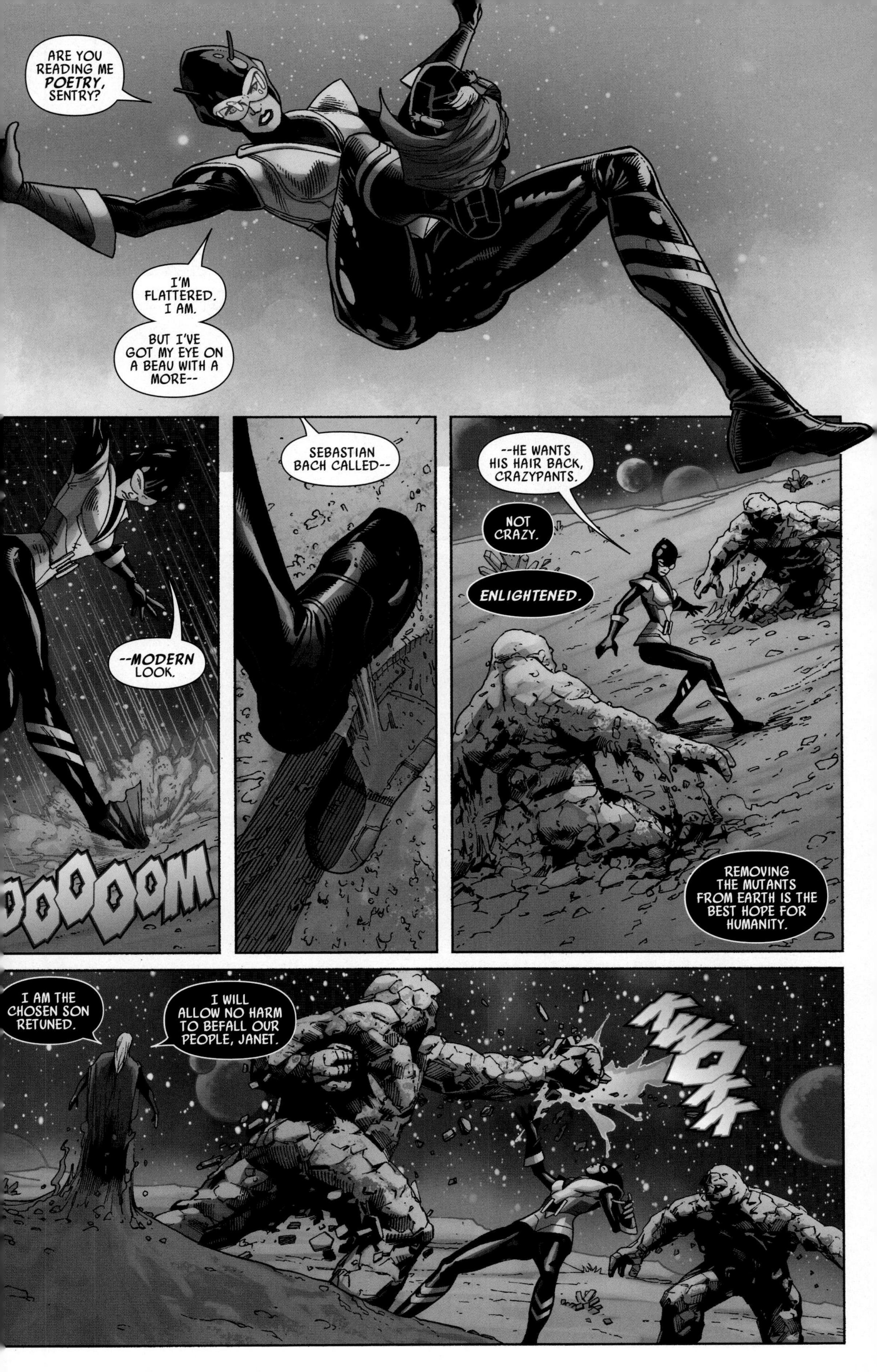
ARE YOU READING ME POETRY, SENTRY?
I'M FLATTERED. I AM.
BUT I'VE GOT MY EYE ON A BEAU WITH A MORE--
--MODERN LOOK.
DOOOOM
SEBASTIAN BACH CALLED--
--HE WANTS HIS HAIR BACK, CRAZYPANTS.
NOT CRAZY.
ENLIGHTENED.
REMOVING THE MUTANTS FROM EARTH IS THE BEST HOPE FOR HUMANITY.
I AM THE CHOSEN SON RETUNED.
I WILL ALLOW NO HARM TO BEFALL OUR PEOPLE, JANET.
KWOK

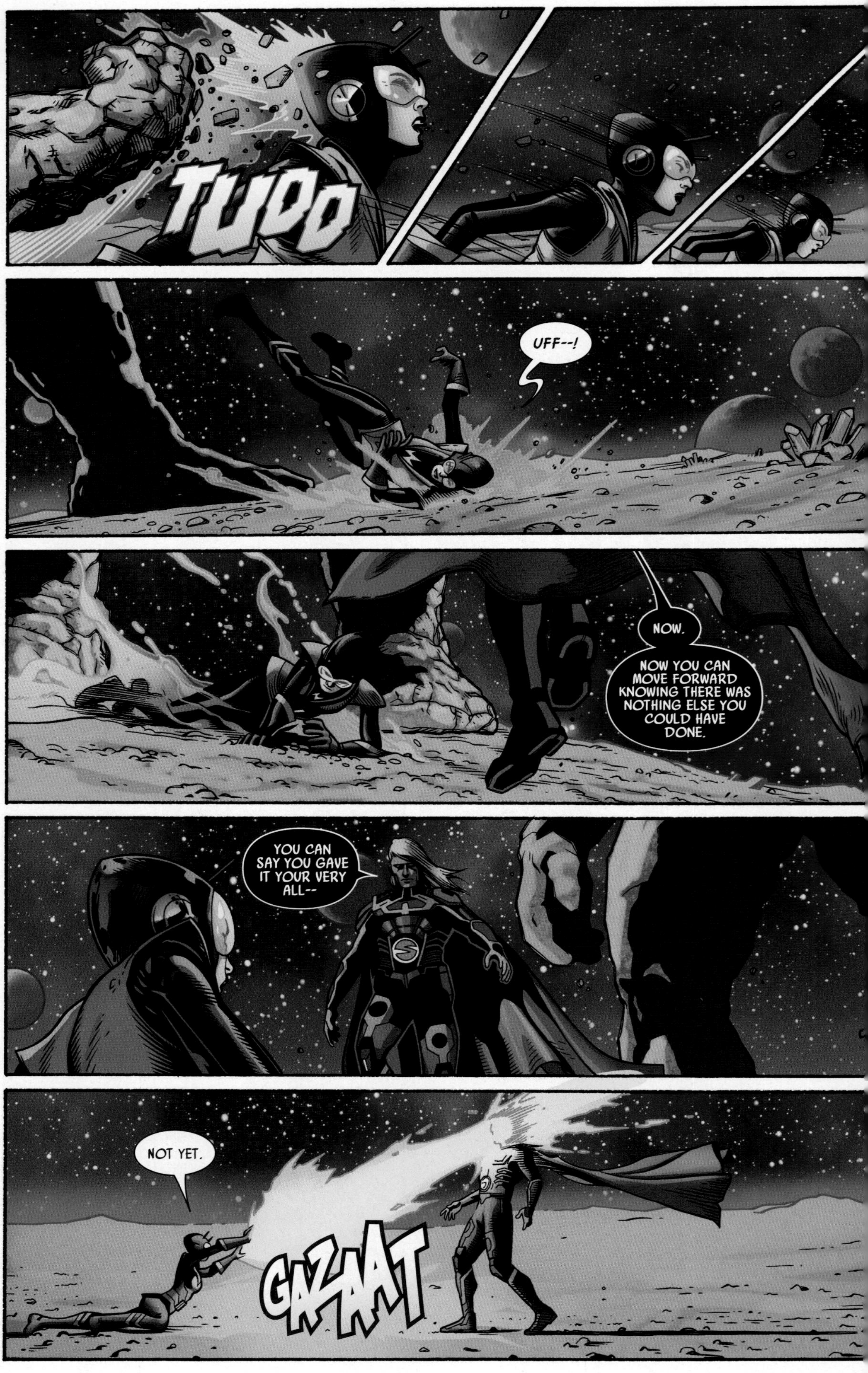
TUDD
UFF--!
NOW.
NOW YOU CAN MOVE FORWARD KNOWING THERE WAS NOTHING ELSE YOU COULD HAVE DONE.
YOU CAN SAY YOU GAVE IT YOUR VERY ALL--
NOT YET.
GAZAAT

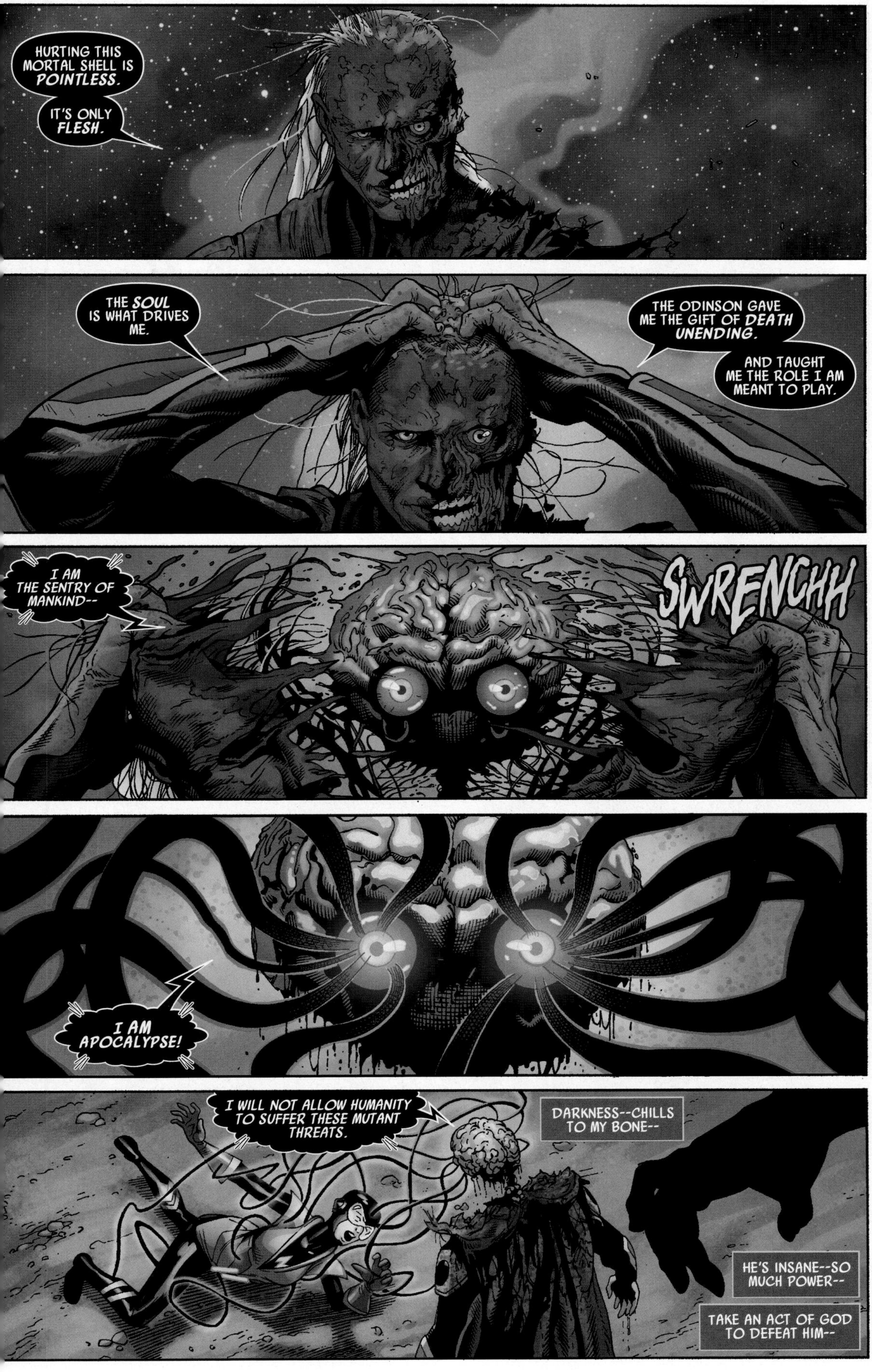
HURTING THIS MORTAL SHELL IS POINTLESS.
IT'S ONLY FLESH.
THE SOUL IS WHAT DRIVES ME.
THE ODINSON GAVE ME THE GIFT OF DEATH UNENDING.
AND TAUGHT ME THE ROLE I AM MEANT TO PLAY.
I AM THE SENTRY OF MANKIND--
SWRENCHH
I AM APOCALYPSE!
I WILL NOT ALLOW HUMANITY TO SUFFER THESE MUTANT THREATS.
DARKNESS--CHILLS TO MY BONE--
HE'S INSANE--SO MUCH POWER--
TAKE AN ACT OF GOD TO DEFEAT HIM--

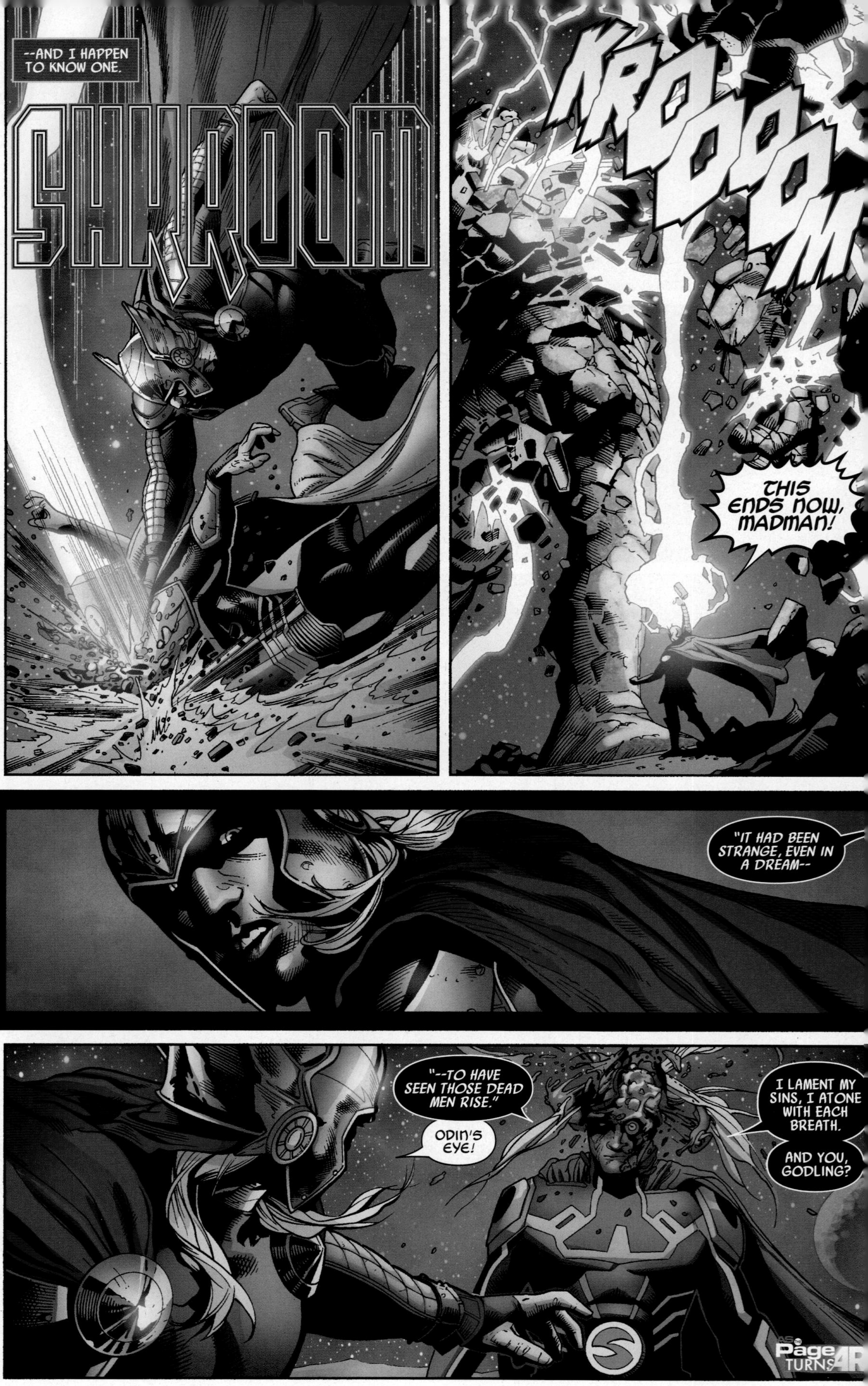
--AND I HAPPEN TO KNOW ONE.
SHROOOM
KRAKOOOM
THIS ENDS NOW, MADMAN!
"IT HAD BEEN STRANGE, EVEN IN A DREAM--
"--TO HAVE SEEN THOSE DEAD MEN RISE."
ODIN'S EYE!
I LAMENT MY SINS, I ATONE WITH EACH BREATH.
AND YOU, GODLING?
Page TURNS

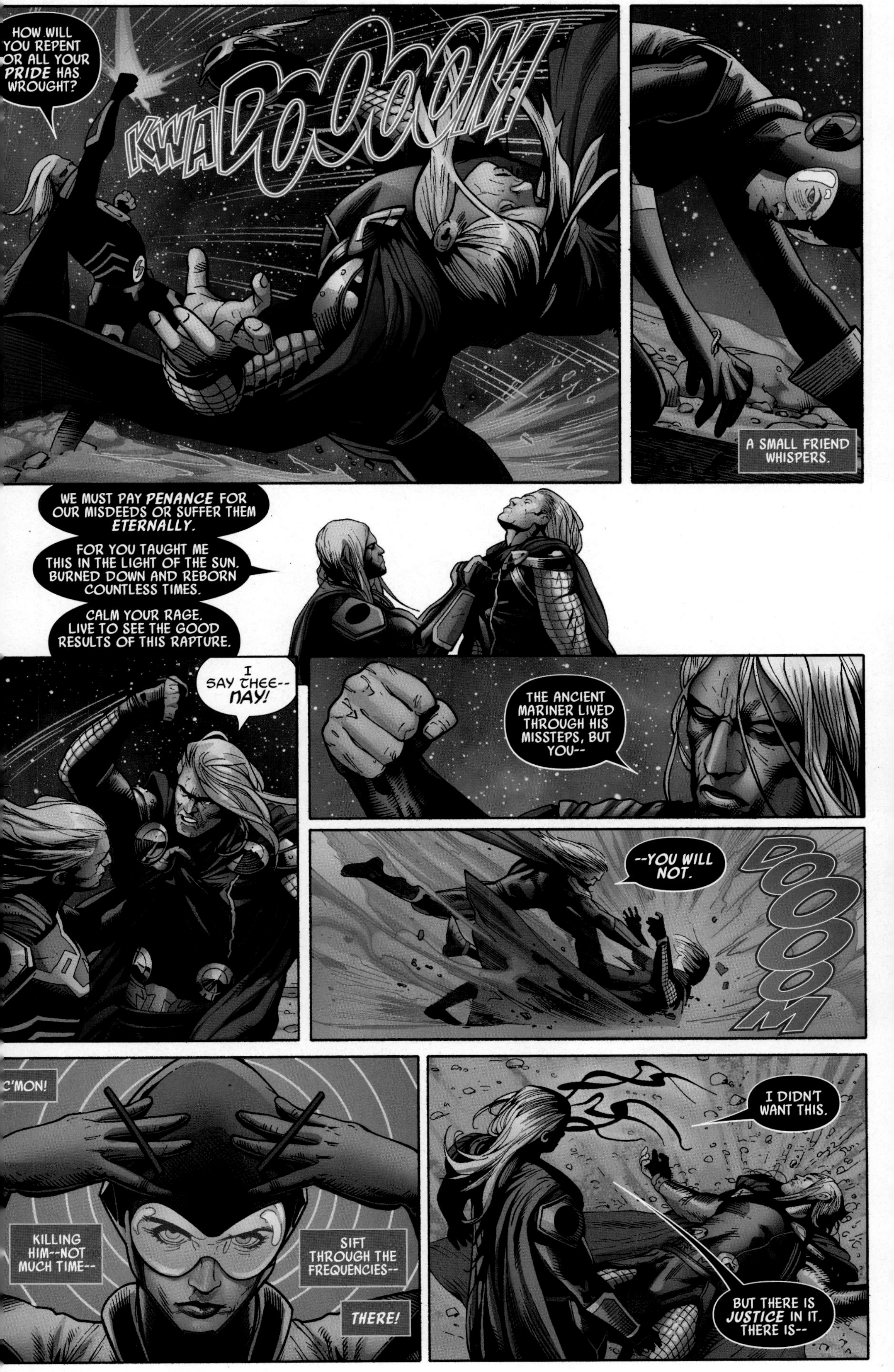

HOW WILL YOU REPENT FOR ALL YOUR PRIDE HAS WROUGHT?
KWADOOOOM
A SMALL FRIEND WHISPERS.
WE MUST PAY PENANCE FOR OUR MISDEEDS OR SUFFER THEM ETERNALLY.
FOR YOU TAUGHT ME THIS IN THE LIGHT OF THE SUN. BURNED DOWN AND REBORN COUNTLESS TIMES.
CALM YOUR RAGE. LIVE TO SEE THE GOOD RESULTS OF THIS RAPTURE.
I SAY THEE-- NAY!
THE ANCIENT MARINER LIVED THROUGH HIS MISSTEPS, BUT YOU--
--YOU WILL NOT.
DOOOOOM
C'MON!
KILLING HIM--NOT MUCH TIME--
SIFT THROUGH THE FREQUENCIES--
THERE!
I DIDN'T WANT THIS.
BUT THERE IS JUSTICE IN IT. THERE IS--

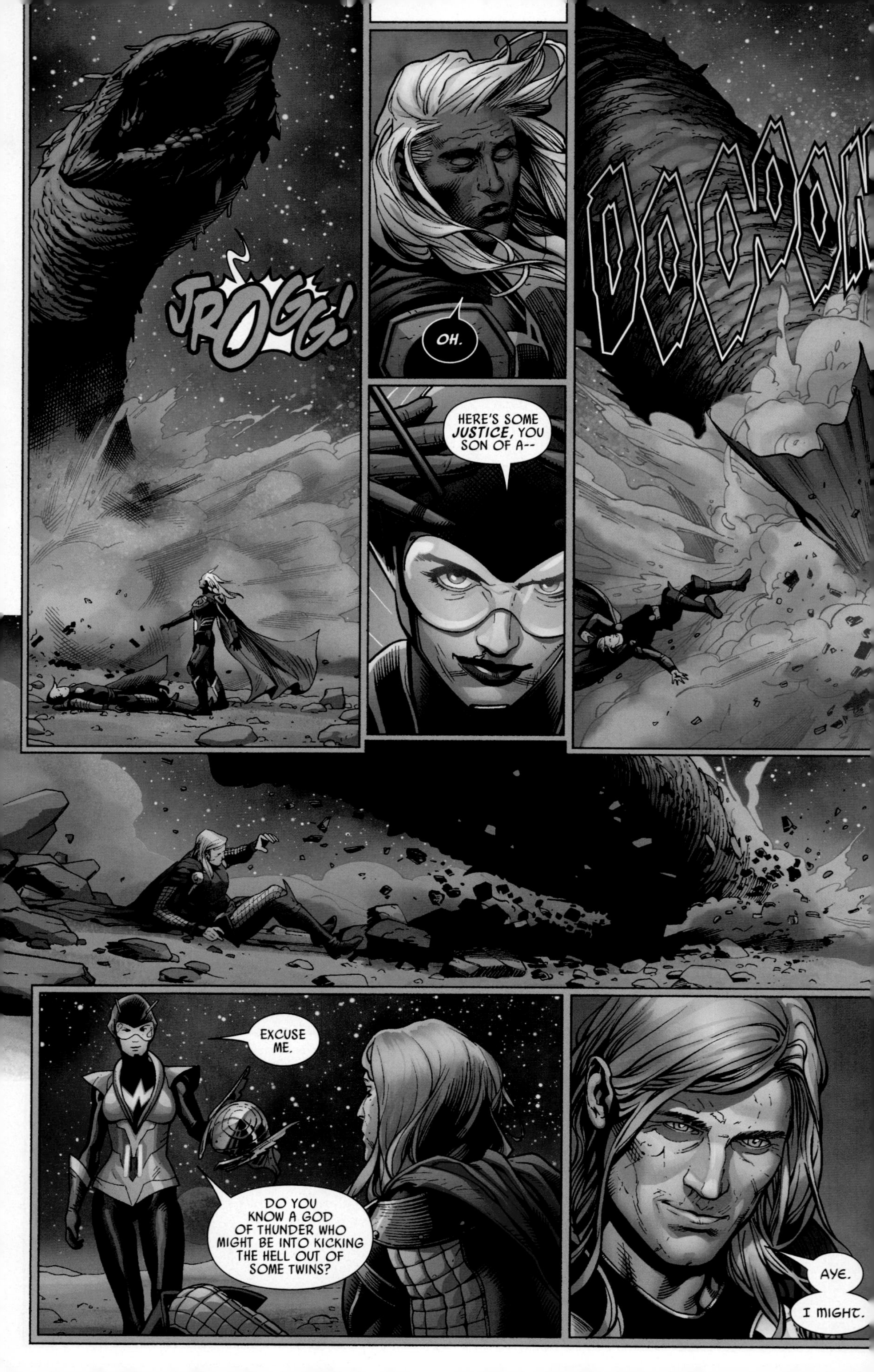
JROGG!
OH.
HERE'S SOME *JUSTICE*, YOU SON OF A--
DOOOOOM
EXCUSE ME.
DO YOU KNOW A GOD OF THUNDER WHO MIGHT BE INTO KICKING THE HELL OUT OF SOME TWINS?
AYE.
I MIGHT.

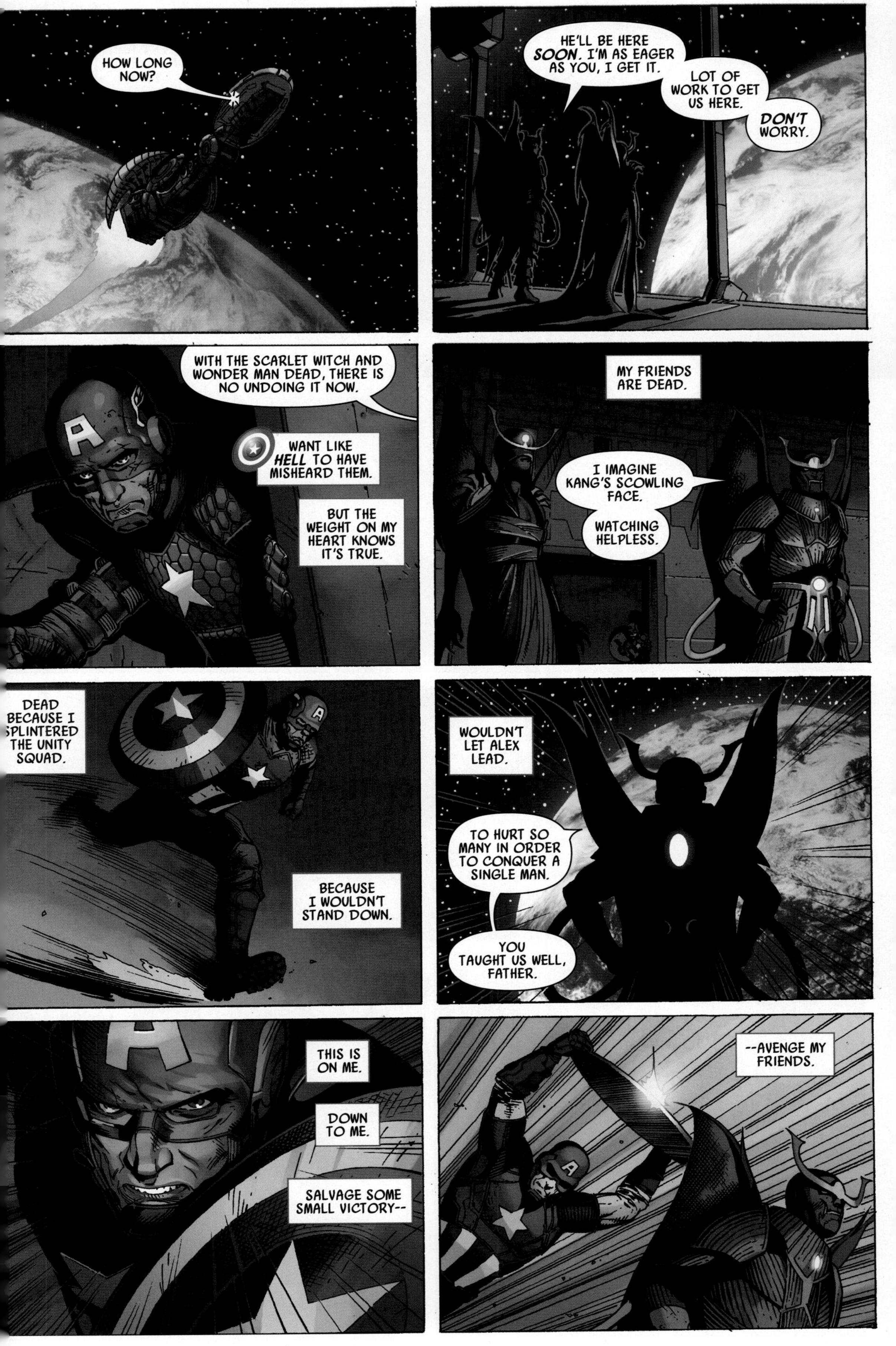

HOW LONG NOW?
HE'LL BE HERE SOON. I'M AS EAGER AS YOU, I GET IT.
LOT OF WORK TO GET US HERE.
DON'T WORRY.
WITH THE SCARLET WITCH AND WONDER MAN DEAD, THERE IS NO UNDOING IT NOW.
WANT LIKE HELL TO HAVE MISHEARD THEM.
BUT THE WEIGHT ON MY HEART KNOWS IT'S TRUE.
MY FRIENDS ARE DEAD.
I IMAGINE KANG'S SCOWLING FACE.
WATCHING HELPLESS.
DEAD BECAUSE I SPLINTERED THE UNITY SQUAD.
BECAUSE I WOULDN'T STAND DOWN.
WOULDN'T LET ALEX LEAD.
TO HURT SO MANY IN ORDER TO CONQUER A SINGLE MAN.
YOU TAUGHT US WELL, FATHER.
THIS IS ON ME.
DOWN TO ME.
SALVAGE SOME SMALL VICTORY--
--AVENGE MY FRIENDS.

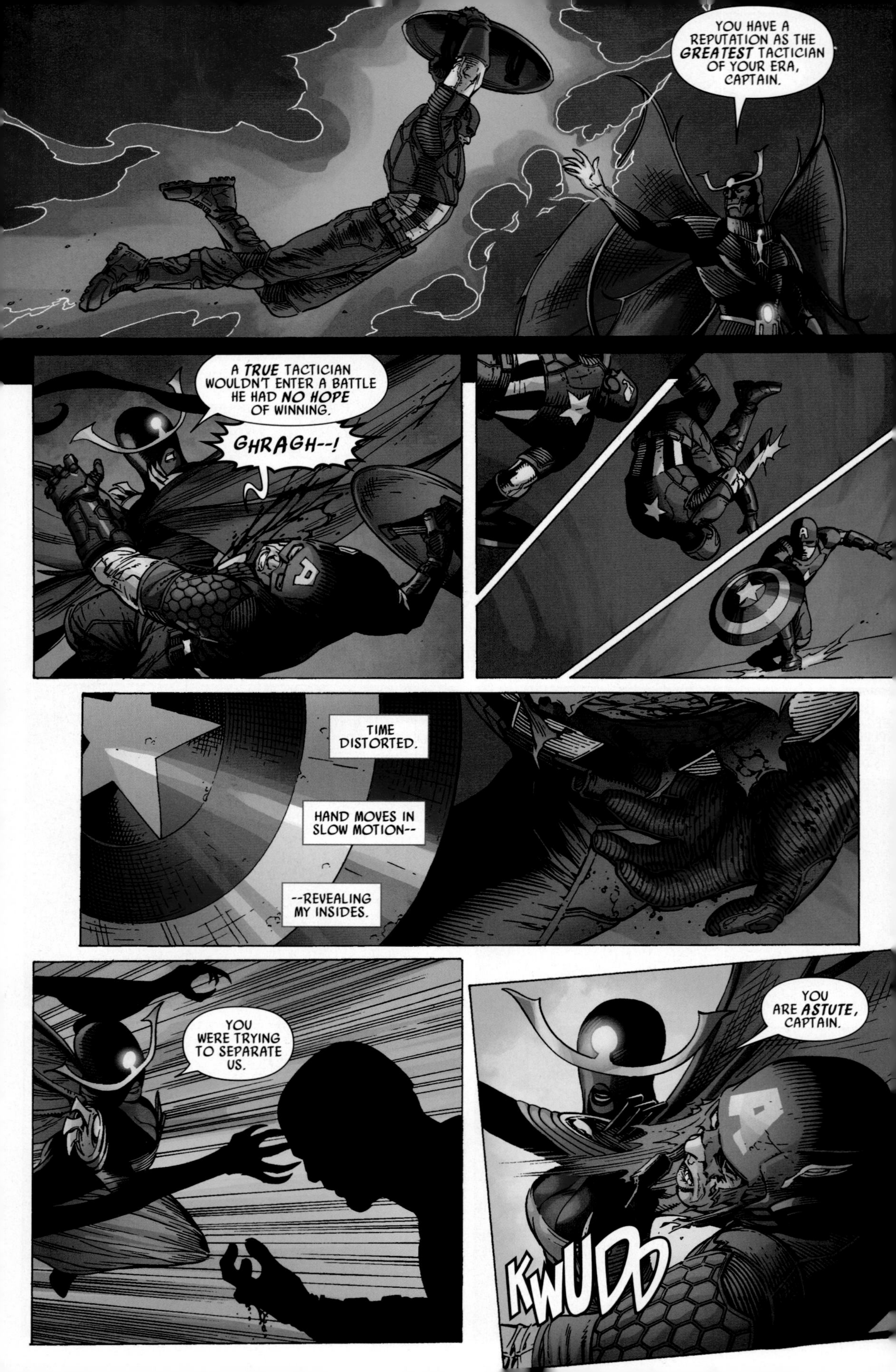

YOU HAVE A REPUTATION AS THE GREATEST TACTICIAN OF YOUR ERA, CAPTAIN.
A TRUE TACTICIAN WOULDN'T ENTER A BATTLE HE HAD NO HOPE OF WINNING.
GHRAGH--!
TIME DISTORTED.
HAND MOVES IN SLOW MOTION--
--REVEALING MY INSIDES.
YOU WERE TRYING TO SEPARATE US.
YOU ARE ASTUTE, CAPTAIN.
KWUDD

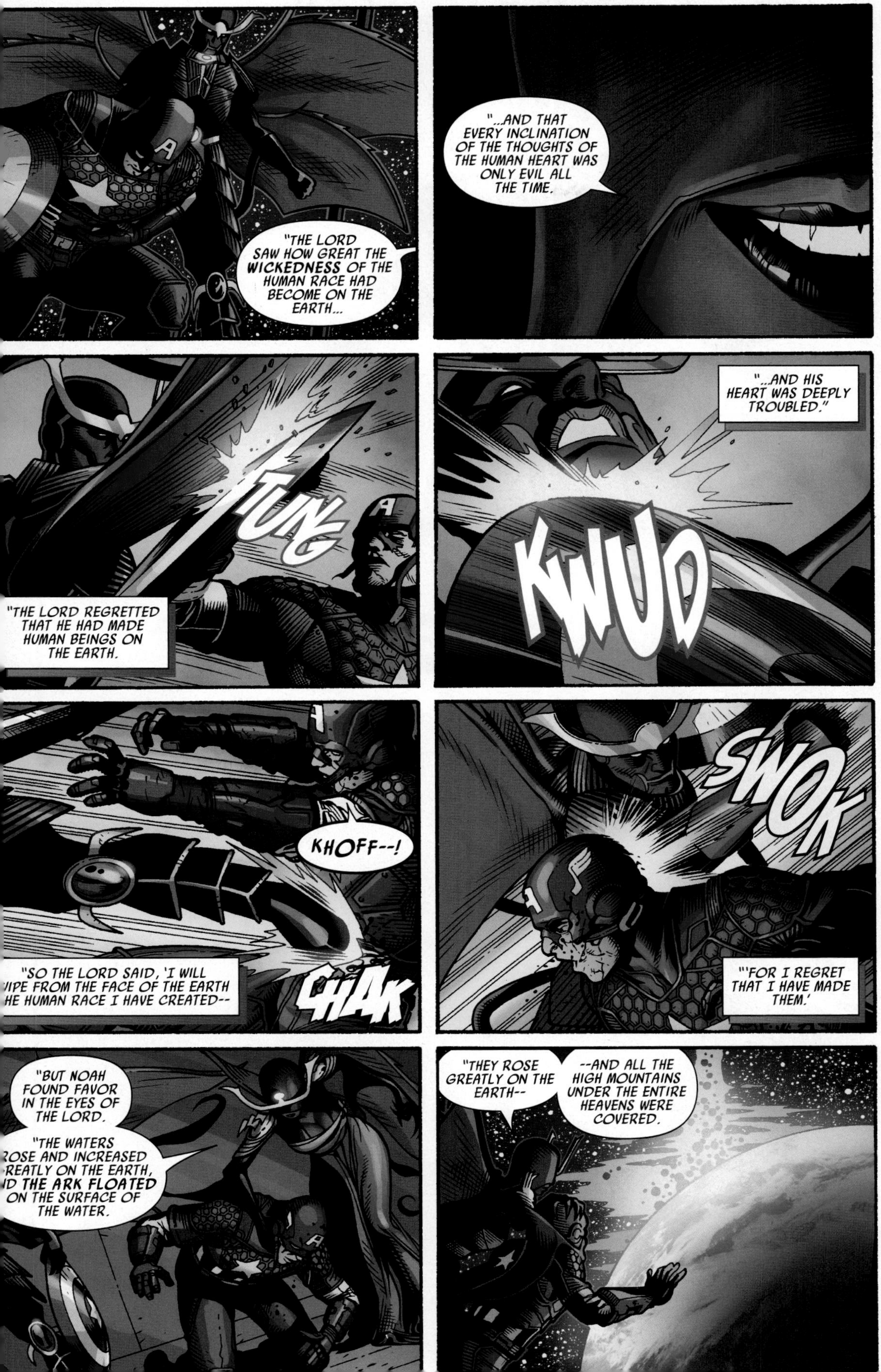
"THE LORD SAW HOW GREAT THE **WICKEDNESS** OF THE HUMAN RACE HAD BECOME ON THE EARTH...
"...AND THAT EVERY INCLINATION OF THE THOUGHTS OF THE HUMAN HEART WAS ONLY EVIL ALL THE TIME.
TUNG
"THE LORD REGRETTED THAT HE HAD MADE HUMAN BEINGS ON THE EARTH.
"...AND HIS HEART WAS DEEPLY TROUBLED."
KWUD
KHOFF--!
"SO THE LORD SAID, 'I WILL IPE FROM THE FACE OF THE EARTH HE HUMAN RACE I HAVE CREATED--
CHAK
SWOK
"'FOR I REGRET THAT I HAVE MADE THEM.'
"BUT NOAH FOUND FAVOR IN THE EYES OF THE LORD.
"THE WATERS ROSE AND INCREASED REATLY ON THE EARTH, D **THE ARK FLOATED** ON THE SURFACE OF THE WATER.
"THEY ROSE GREATLY ON THE EARTH--
--AND ALL THE HIGH MOUNTAINS UNDER THE ENTIRE HEAVENS WERE COVERED.

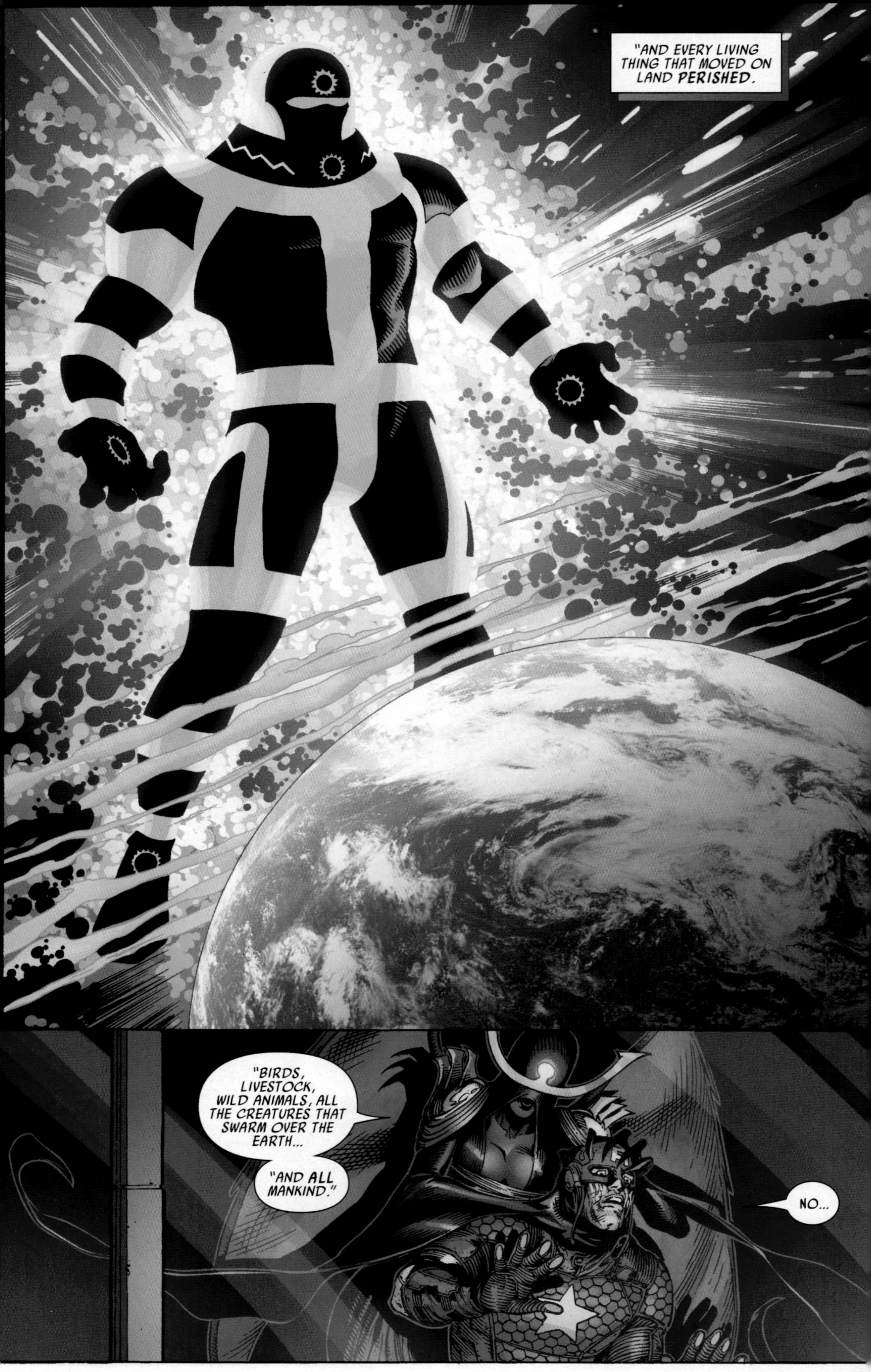
"AND EVERY LIVING THING THAT MOVED ON LAND PERISHED.
"BIRDS, LIVESTOCK, WILD ANIMALS, ALL THE CREATURES THAT SWARM OVER THE EARTH...
"AND ALL MANKIND."
NO...

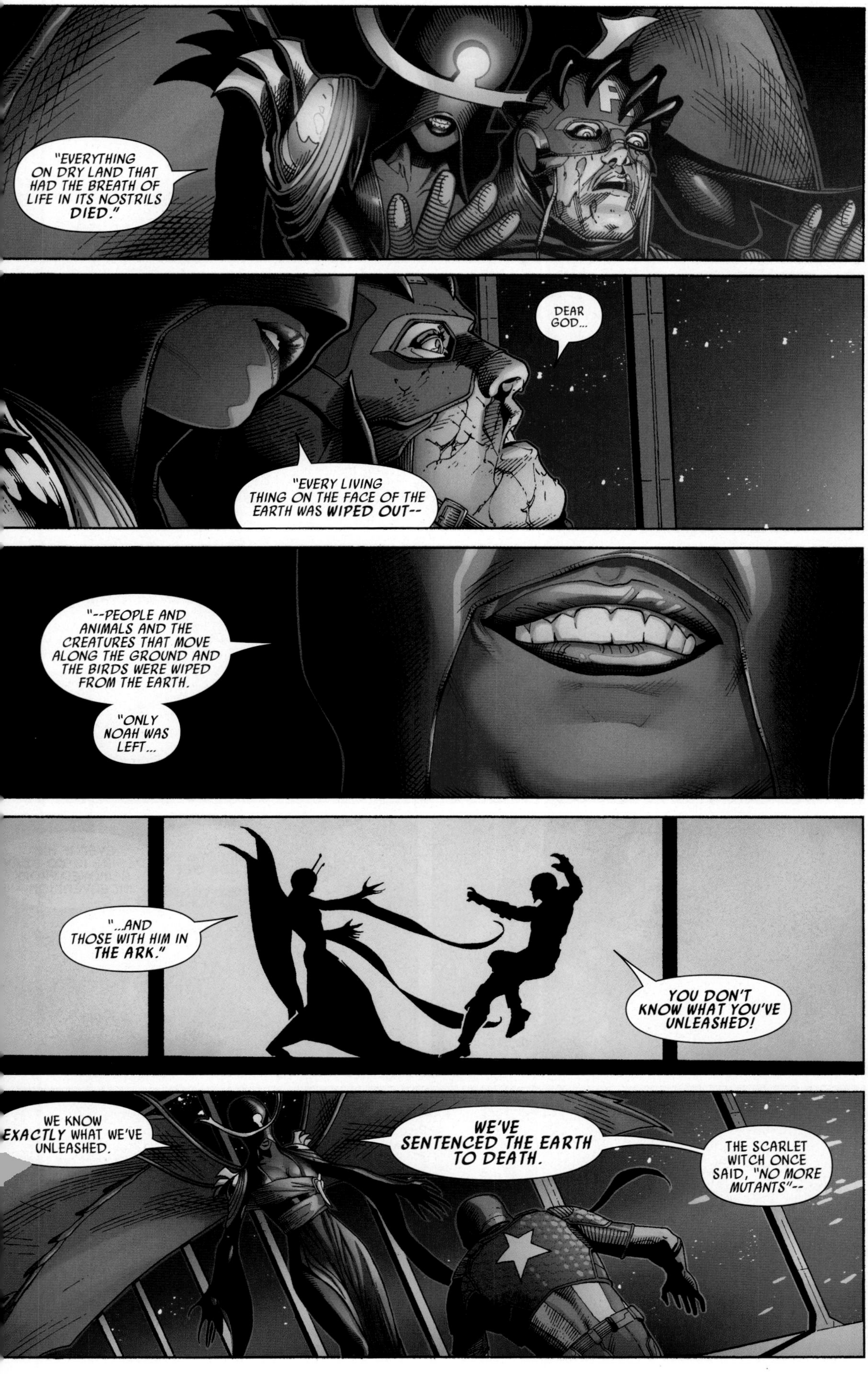
"EVERYTHING ON DRY LAND THAT HAD THE BREATH OF LIFE IN ITS NOSTRILS DIED."
DEAR GOD...
"EVERY LIVING THING ON THE FACE OF THE EARTH WAS WIPED OUT--
"--PEOPLE AND ANIMALS AND THE CREATURES THAT MOVE ALONG THE GROUND AND THE BIRDS WERE WIPED FROM THE EARTH.
"ONLY NOAH WAS LEFT...
"...AND THOSE WITH HIM IN THE ARK."
YOU DON'T KNOW WHAT YOU'VE UNLEASHED!
WE KNOW EXACTLY WHAT WE'VE UNLEASHED.
WE'VE SENTENCED THE EARTH TO DEATH.
THE SCARLET WITCH ONCE SAID, "NO MORE MUTANTS"--

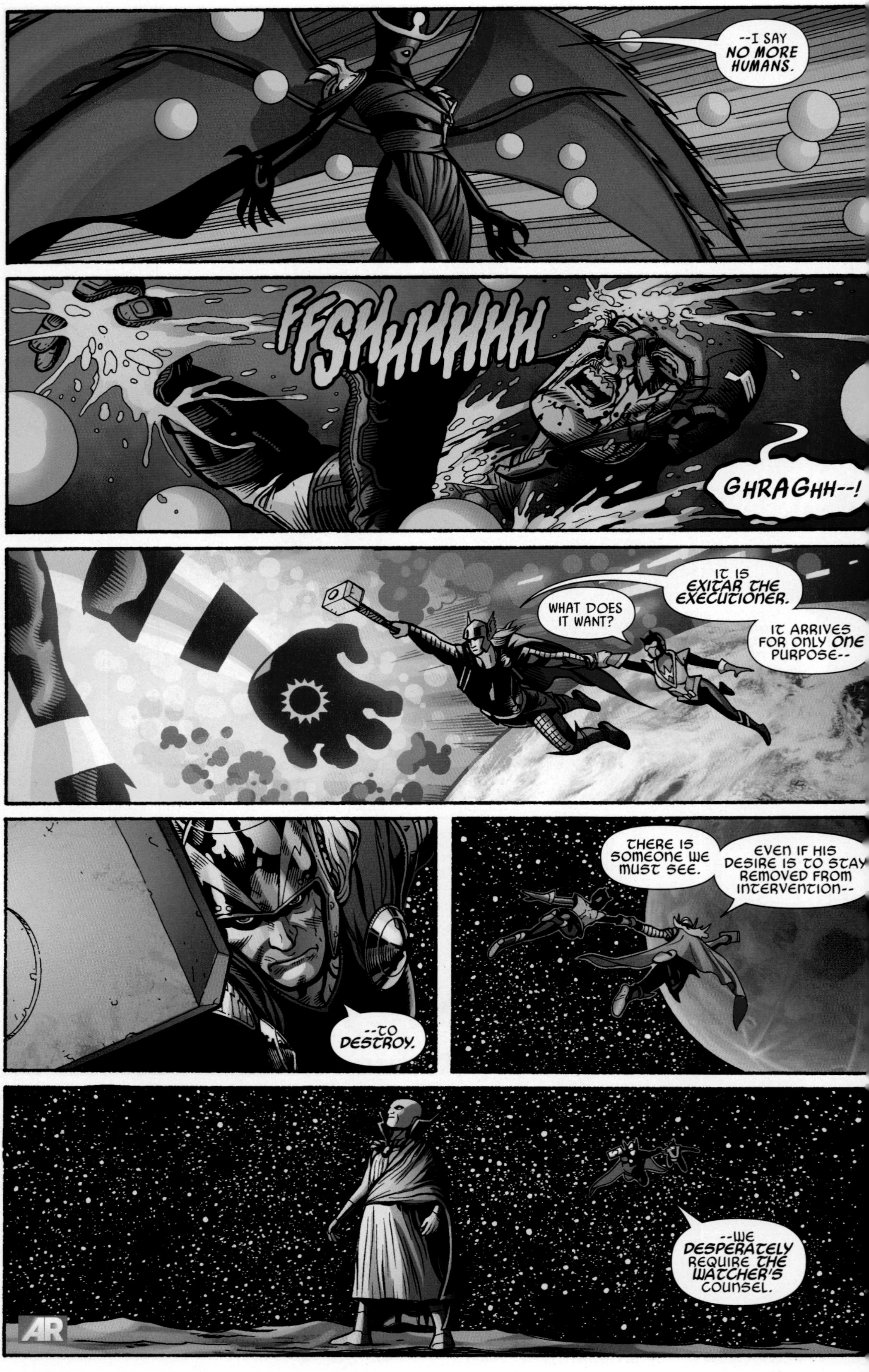
--I SAY NO MORE HUMANS.
FFSHHHHHH
GHRAGHH--!
WHAT DOES IT WANT?
IT IS EXITAR THE EXECUTIONER.
IT ARRIVES FOR ONLY ONE PURPOSE--
--TO DESTROY.
THERE IS SOMEONE WE MUST SEE.
EVEN IF HIS DESIRE IS TO STAY REMOVED FROM INTERVENTION--
--WE DESPERATELY REQUIRE THE WATCHER'S COUNSEL.
AR

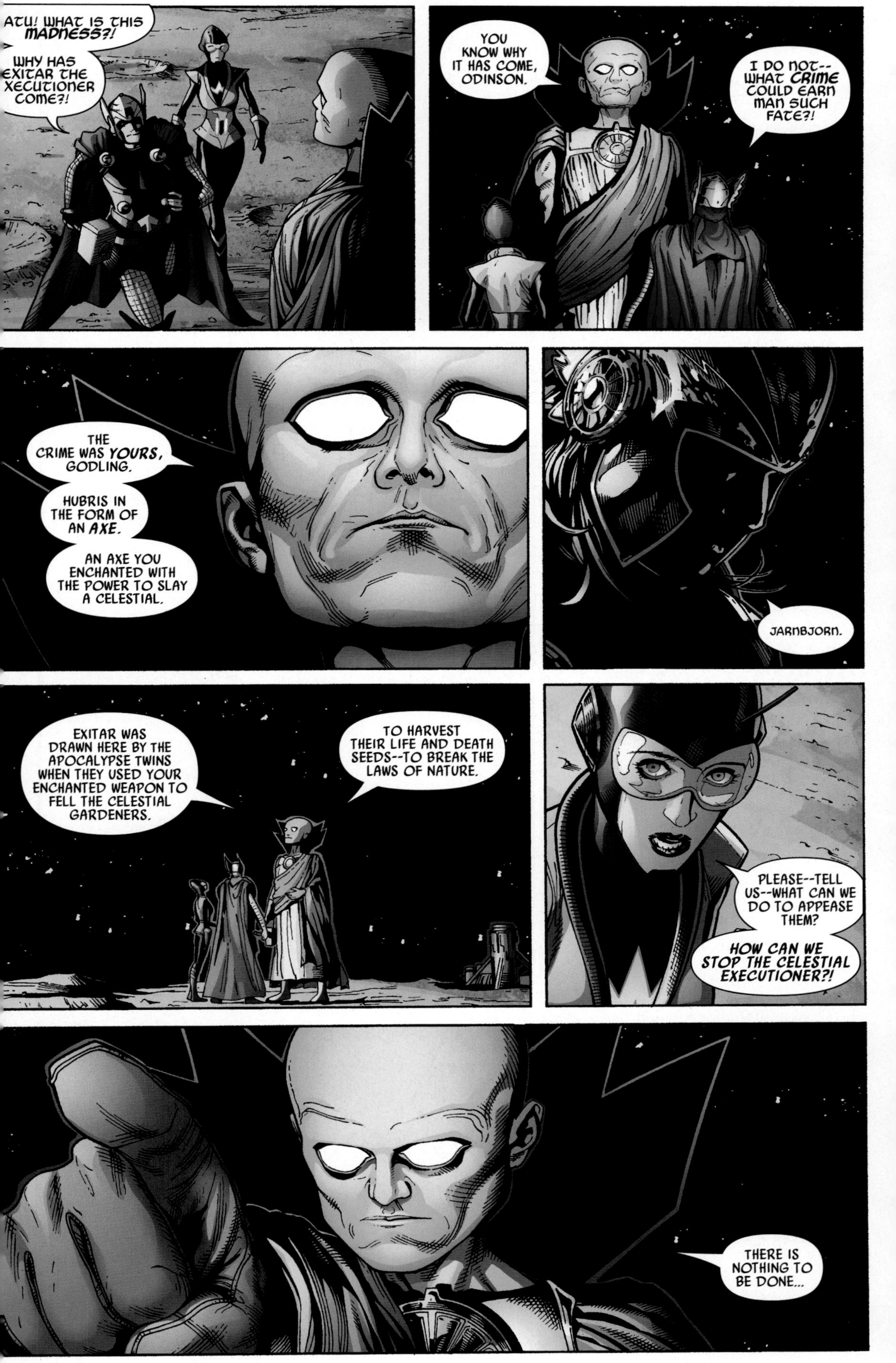

ATU! WHAT IS THIS MADNESS?!
WHY HAS EXITAR THE XECUTIONER COME?!
YOU KNOW WHY IT HAS COME, ODINSON.
I DO NOT-- WHAT CRIME COULD EARN MAN SUCH FATE?!
THE CRIME WAS YOURS, GODLING.
HUBRIS IN THE FORM OF AN AXE.
AN AXE YOU ENCHANTED WITH THE POWER TO SLAY A CELESTIAL.
JARNBJORN.
EXITAR WAS DRAWN HERE BY THE APOCALYPSE TWINS WHEN THEY USED YOUR ENCHANTED WEAPON TO FELL THE CELESTIAL GARDENERS.
TO HARVEST THEIR LIFE AND DEATH SEEDS--TO BREAK THE LAWS OF NATURE.
PLEASE--TELL US--WHAT CAN WE DO TO APPEASE THEM?
HOW CAN WE STOP THE CELESTIAL EXECUTIONER?!
THERE IS NOTHING TO BE DONE...

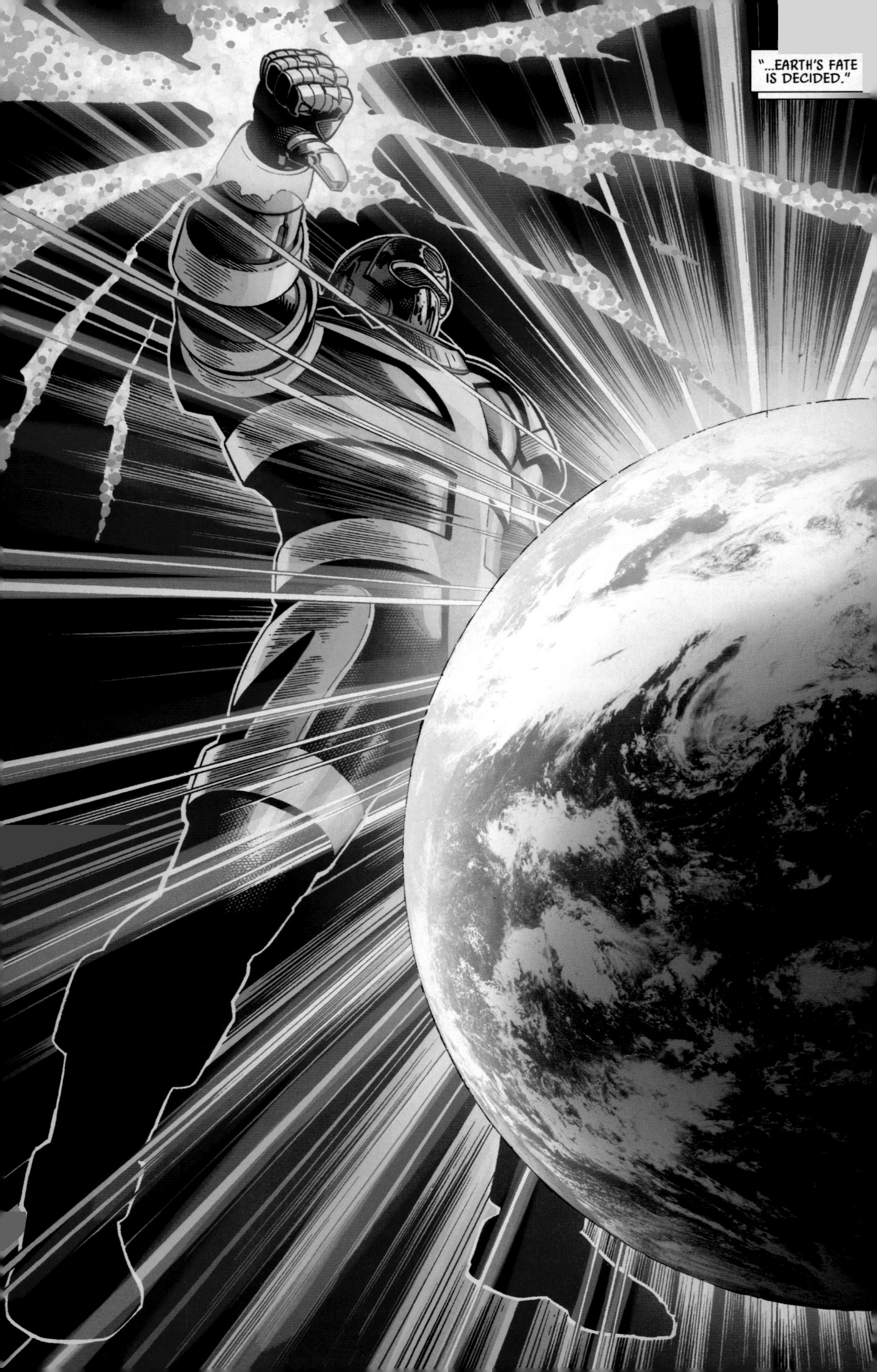
"...EARTH'S FATE IS DECIDED."

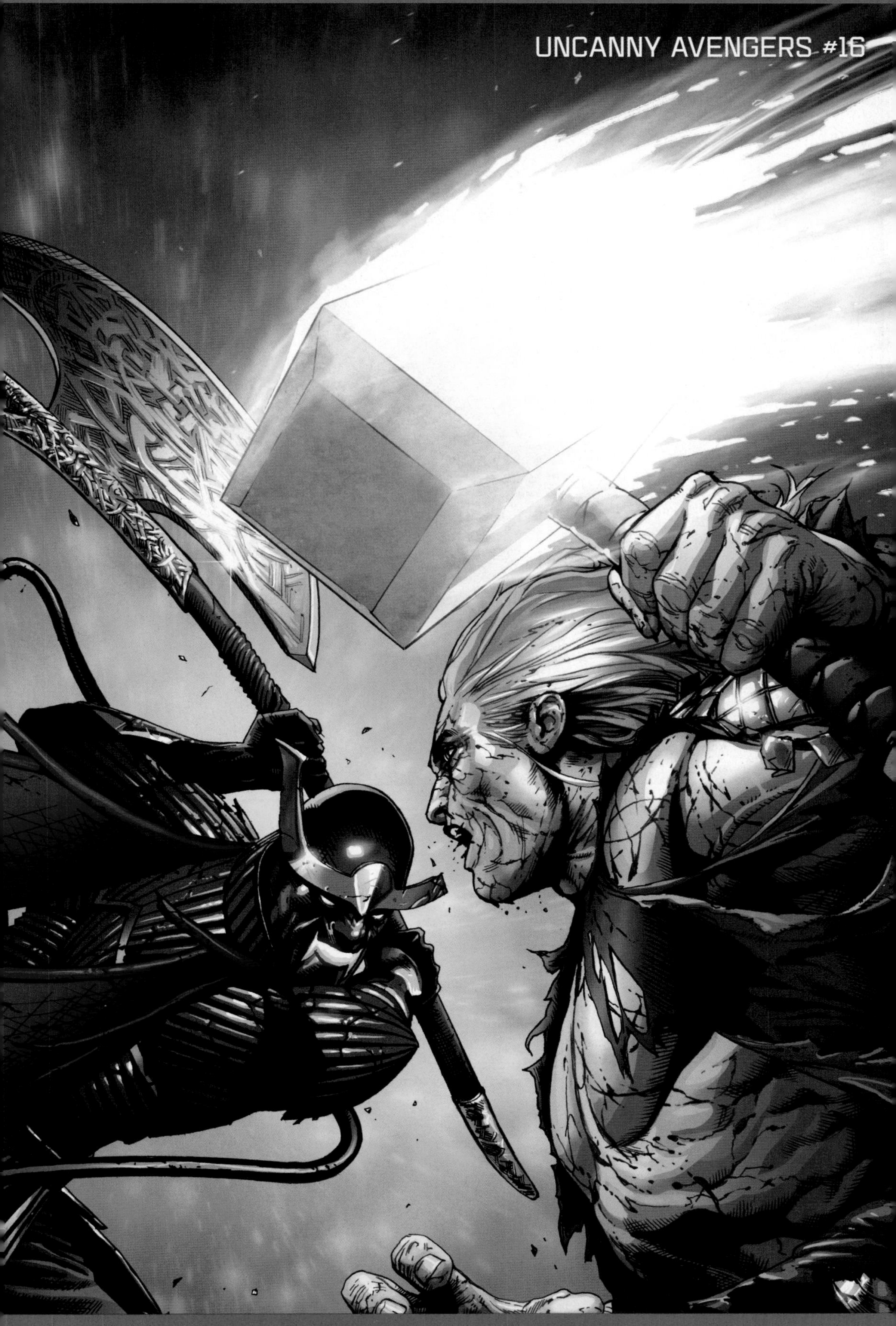
UNCANNY AVENGERS #16

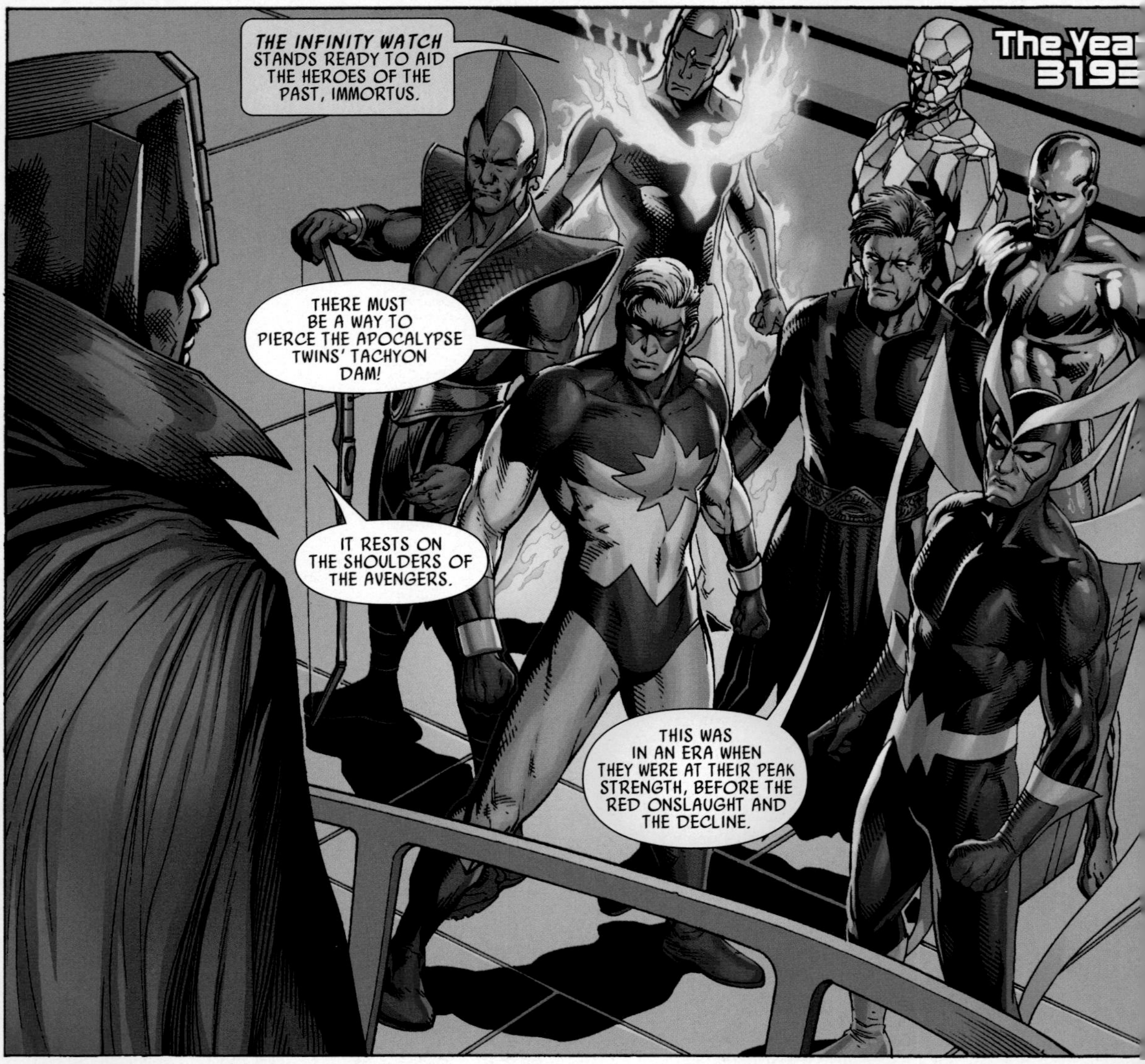
The Year 319
THE INFINITY WATCH STANDS READY TO AID THE HEROES OF THE PAST, IMMORTUS.
THERE MUST BE A WAY TO PIERCE THE APOCALYPSE TWINS' TACHYON DAM!
IT RESTS ON THE SHOULDERS OF THE AVENGERS.
THIS WAS IN AN ERA WHEN THEY WERE AT THEIR PEAK STRENGTH, BEFORE THE RED ONSLAUGHT AND THE DECLINE.

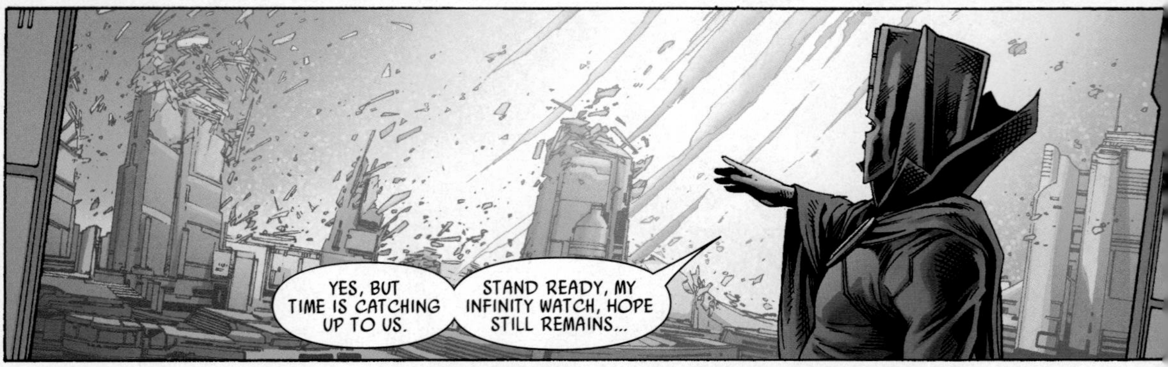
YES, BUT TIME IS CATCHING UP TO US.
STAND READY, MY INFINITY WATCH, HOPE STILL REMAINS...

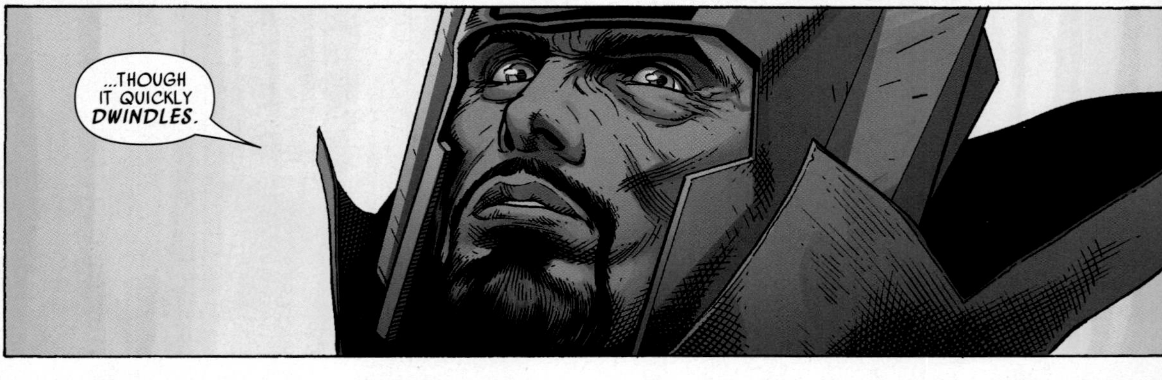
...THOUGH IT QUICKLY DWINDLES.

WITH A PORTAL LARGE ENOUGH, WE COULD HURL THE CELESTIAL INTO THE NEGATIVE ZONE.

USING A GRAVITY BELT, BENDING SPACE, TO SLINGSHOT THE CELESTIAL THROUGH.

FAR TOO *PERILOUS.*

MUTUALLY ASSURED DESTRUCTION IS THE BEST ANSWER. WE MUST LOCATE THE *ULTIMATE NULLIFIER*--

I'D SAY WE COULD JUMP BACK IN TIME AND WARN OURSELVES...

BUT SOMETHING IS BARRING TIME TRAVEL INTO OR OUT OF THIS ERA.

IF IT HAPPENED, IT HAPPENED, IT'S LOCKED IN PLACE NOW.

WE HAVEN'T EVEN BEEN ABLE TO SEND A MESSAGE--

NO-NO-NO.

STOP.

EVERYONE SHUT UP.

WE DON'T HAVE TIME TO GO HUNTING FOR THE NULLIFIER OR TO SEND ANYONE BACK IN TIME.

SIMPLIFY.

WE JUST NEED TO CONTAIN EXITAR.

JUST LONG ENOUGH TO DISCOVER WHY HE'S HERE GIVING OUR LITTLE WORLD A BIG THUMBS DOWN.

I CAN TELL YOU WHY, TONY.

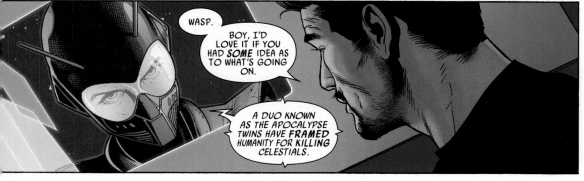

WASP.

BOY, I'D LOVE IT IF YOU HAD *SOME* IDEA AS TO WHAT'S GOING ON.

A DUO KNOWN AS THE APOCALYPSE TWINS HAVE *FRAMED* HUMANITY FOR KILLING CELESTIALS.

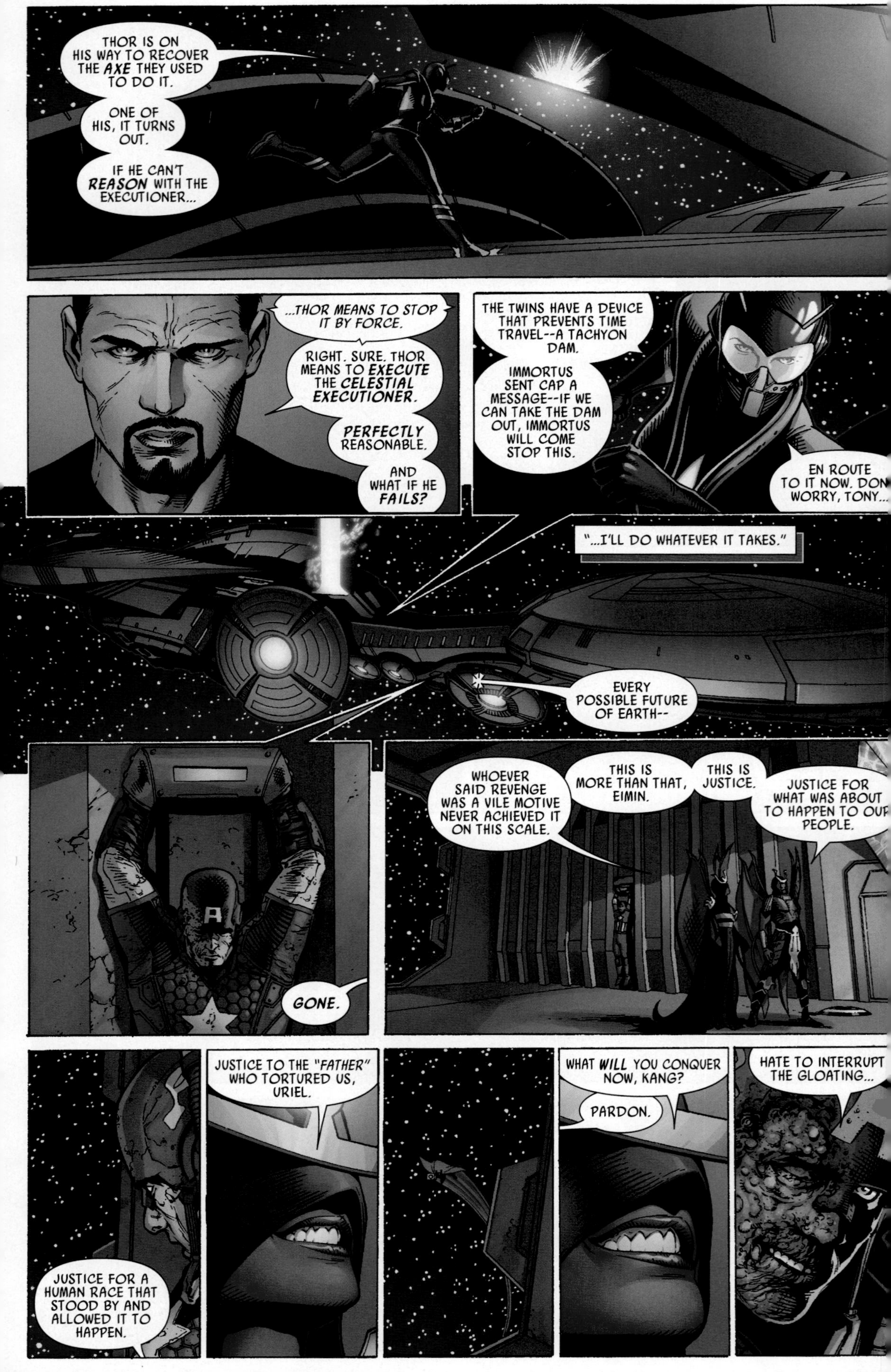
THOR IS ON HIS WAY TO RECOVER THE AXE THEY USED TO DO IT.
ONE OF HIS, IT TURNS OUT.
IF HE CAN'T REASON WITH THE EXECUTIONER...
...THOR MEANS TO STOP IT BY FORCE.
RIGHT. SURE. THOR MEANS TO EXECUTE THE CELESTIAL EXECUTIONER.
PERFECTLY REASONABLE.
AND WHAT IF HE FAILS?
THE TWINS HAVE A DEVICE THAT PREVENTS TIME TRAVEL--A TACHYON DAM.
IMMORTUS SENT CAP A MESSAGE--IF WE CAN TAKE THE DAM OUT, IMMORTUS WILL COME STOP THIS.
EN ROUTE TO IT NOW. DON WORRY, TONY...
"...I'LL DO WHATEVER IT TAKES."
EVERY POSSIBLE FUTURE OF EARTH--
GONE.
WHOEVER SAID REVENGE WAS A VILE MOTIVE NEVER ACHIEVED IT ON THIS SCALE.
THIS IS MORE THAN THAT, EIMIN.
THIS IS JUSTICE.
JUSTICE FOR WHAT WAS ABOUT TO HAPPEN TO OUR PEOPLE.
JUSTICE TO THE "FATHER" WHO TORTURED US, URIEL.
JUSTICE FOR A HUMAN RACE THAT STOOD BY AND ALLOWED IT TO HAPPEN.
WHAT WILL YOU CONQUER NOW, KANG?
PARDON.
HATE TO INTERRUPT THE GLOATING...

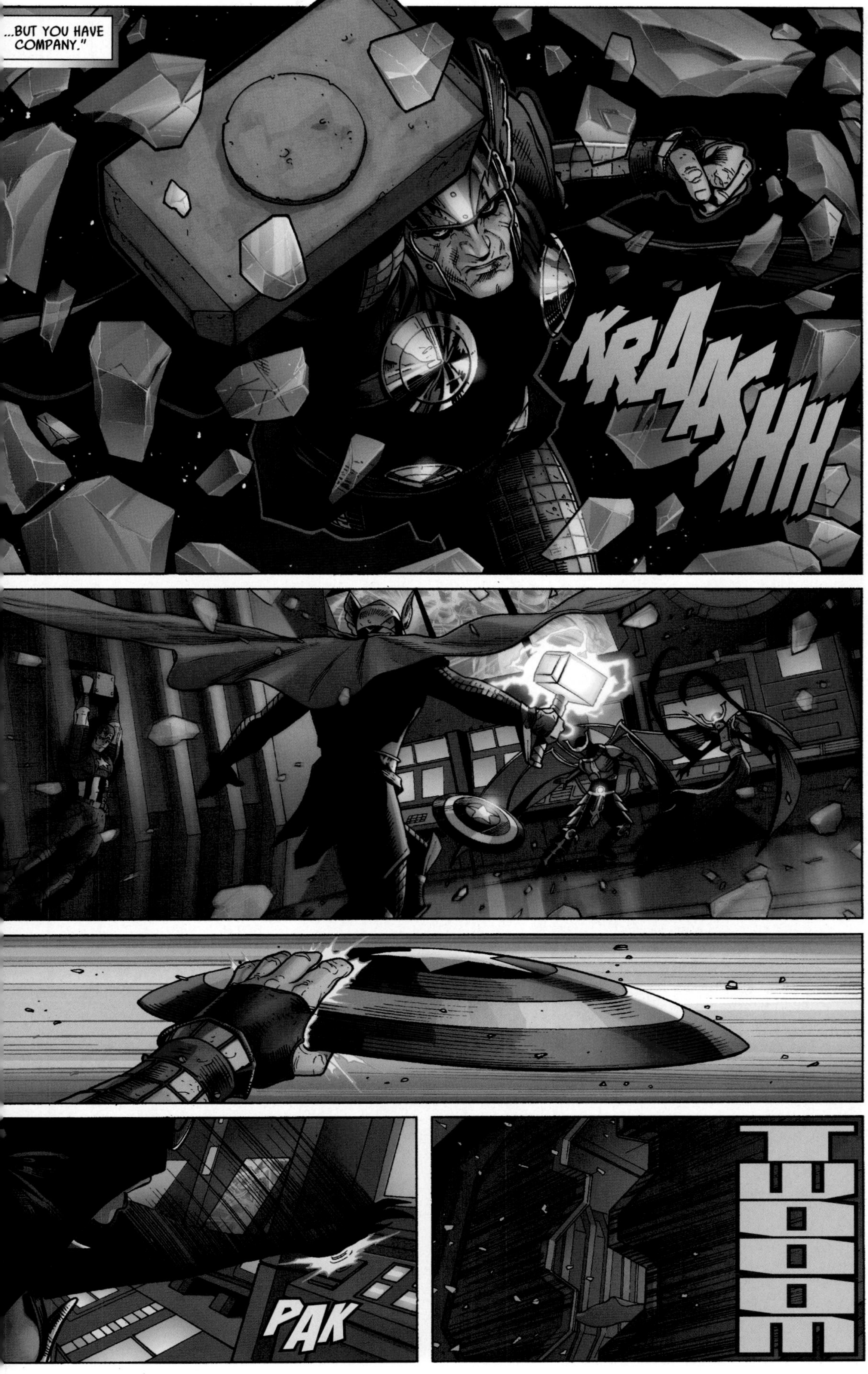
...BUT YOU HAVE COMPANY."
KRAASHH
PAK
THOOM

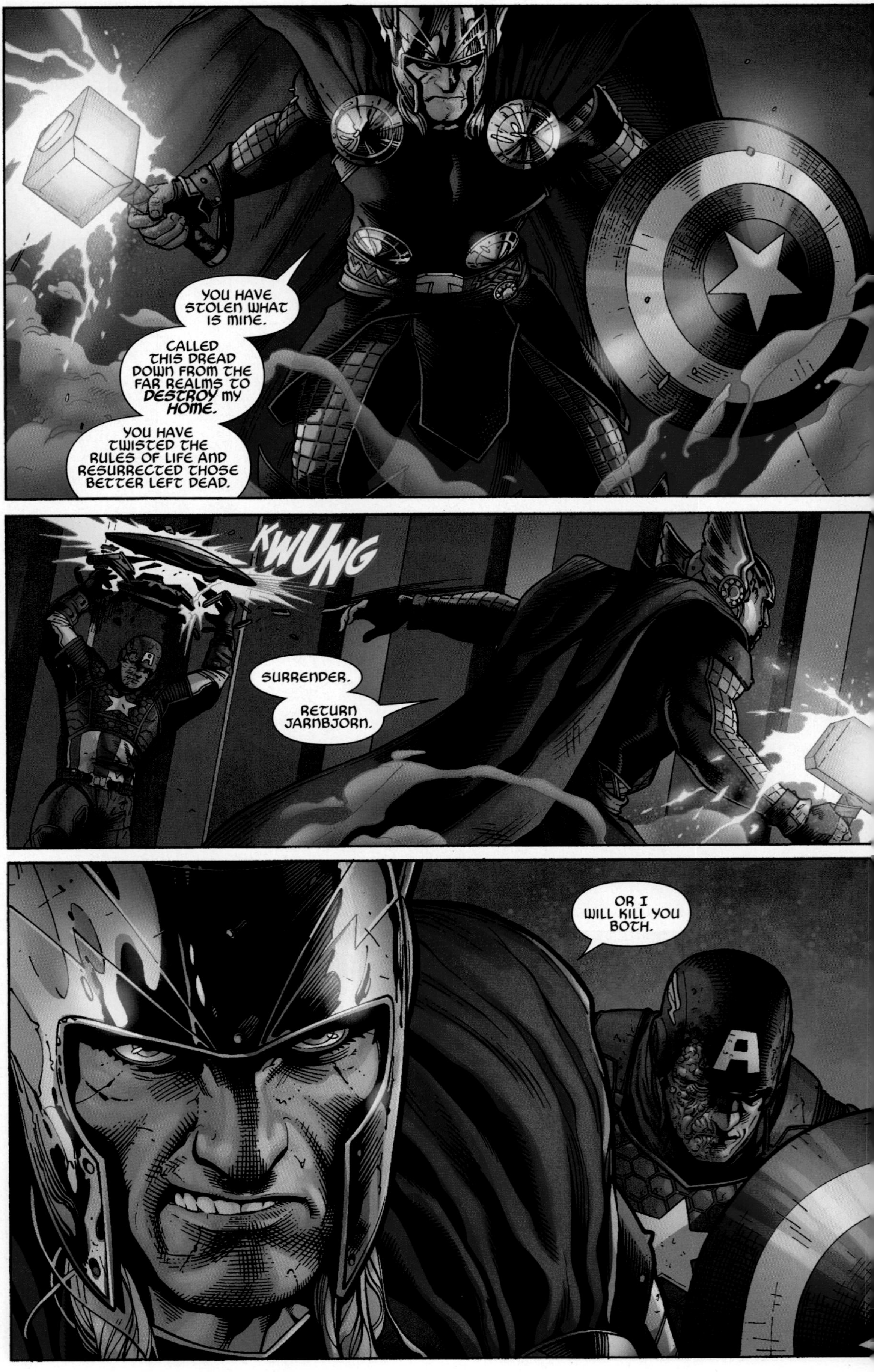
YOU HAVE STOLEN WHAT IS MINE.
CALLED THIS DREAD DOWN FROM THE FAR REALMS TO *DESTROY* MY *HOME.*
YOU HAVE TWISTED THE RULES OF LIFE AND RESURRECTED THOSE BETTER LEFT DEAD.
KWUNG
SURRENDER.
RETURN JARNBJORN.
OR I WILL KILL YOU BOTH.

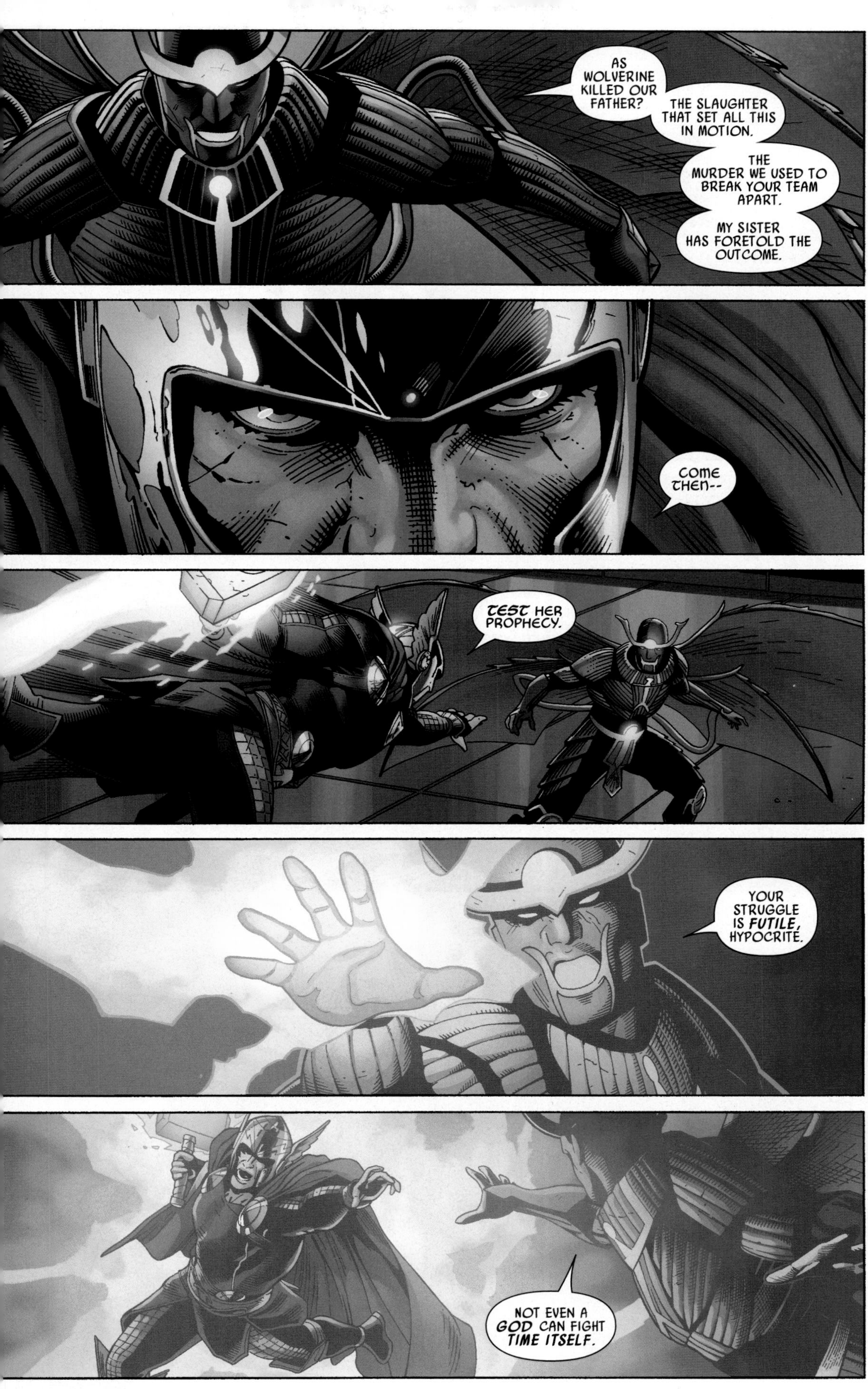
AS WOLVERINE KILLED OUR FATHER?
THE SLAUGHTER THAT SET ALL THIS IN MOTION.
THE MURDER WE USED TO BREAK YOUR TEAM APART.
MY SISTER HAS FORETOLD THE OUTCOME.
COME THEN--
TEST HER PROPHECY.
YOUR STRUGGLE IS FUTILE, HYPOCRITE.
NOT EVEN A GOD CAN FIGHT TIME ITSELF.

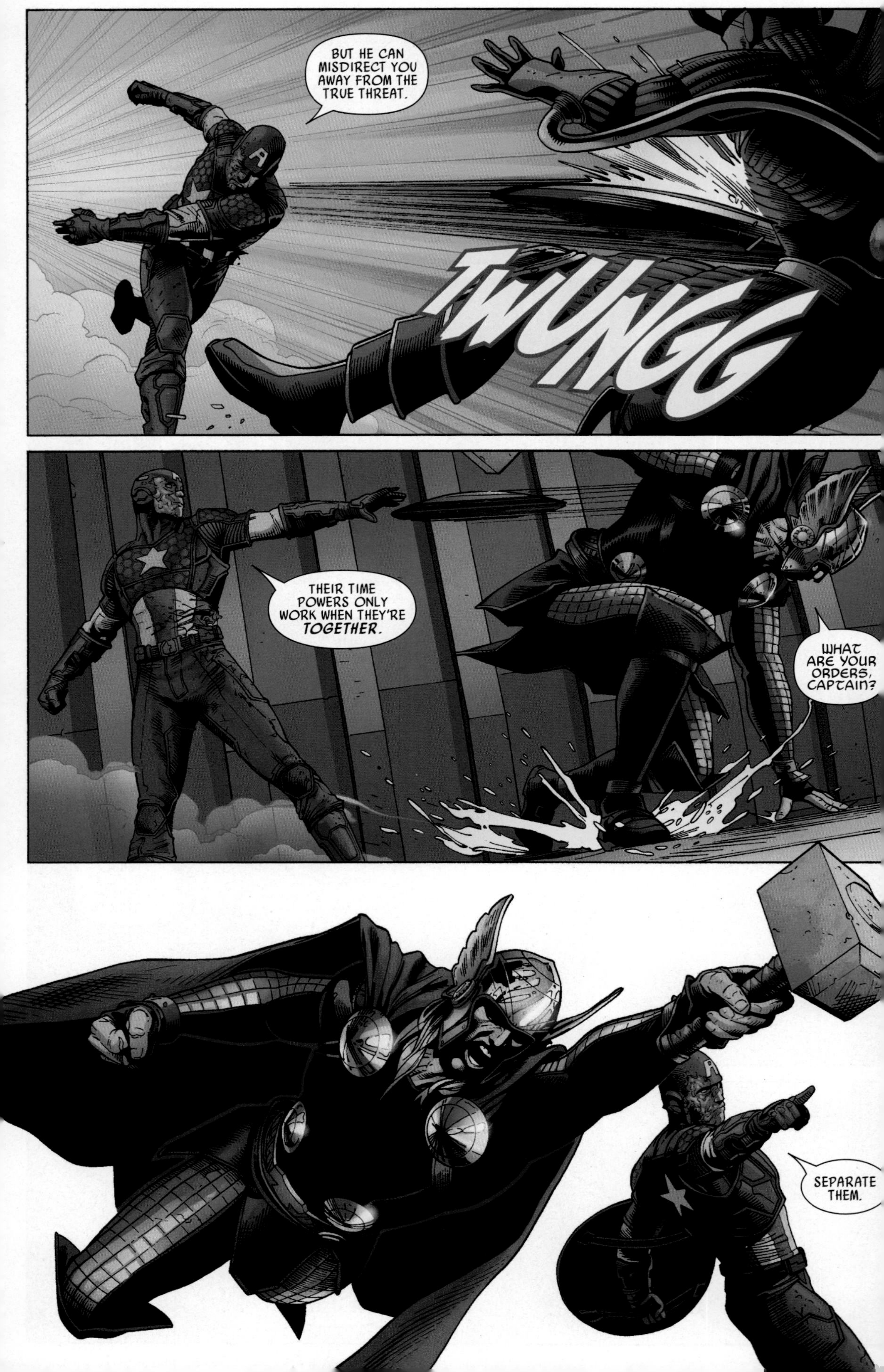
BUT HE CAN MISDIRECT YOU AWAY FROM THE TRUE THREAT.
TWUNGG
THEIR TIME POWERS ONLY WORK WHEN THEY'RE *TOGETHER*.
WHAT ARE YOUR ORDERS, CAPTAIN?
SEPARATE THEM.

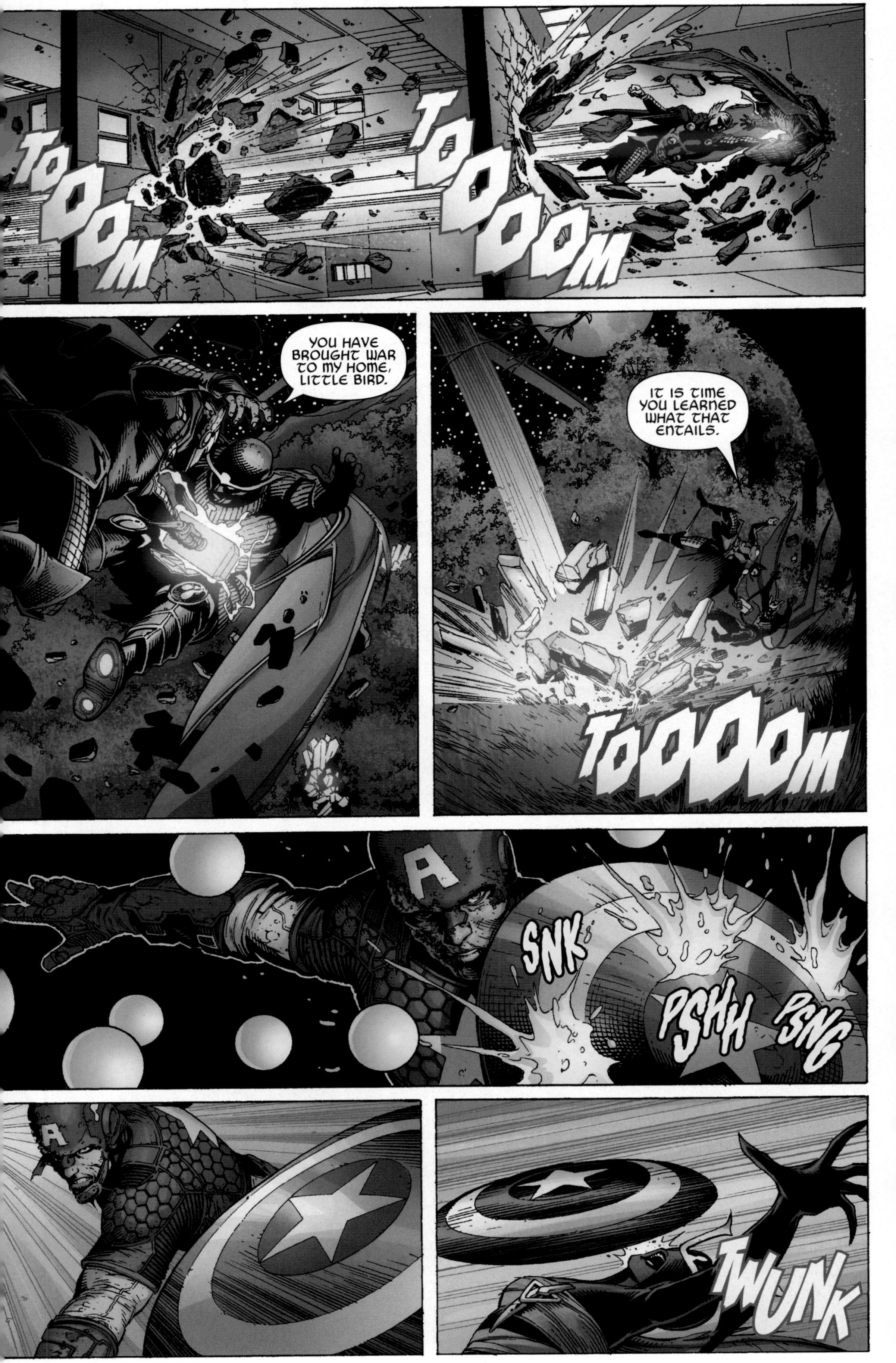
TOOOM
TOOOOM
YOU HAVE BROUGHT WAR TO MY HOME, LITTLE BIRD.
IT IS TIME YOU LEARNED WHAT THAT ENTAILS.
TOOOOM
SNK
PSHH
PSNG
TWUNK

I'VE ALREADY WON THIS WAR! DEFEATED THE TERRIBLE FOES YOU COULDN'T!

FOREDOOMED THE RED SKULL!

OUTMANEUVERED KANG!

I CARE--

NOT!

TWOOOM

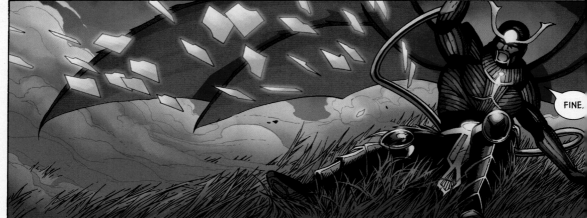

FINE.

WE'LL PLAY THIS OUT TO THE END.

GHRAGHH--!

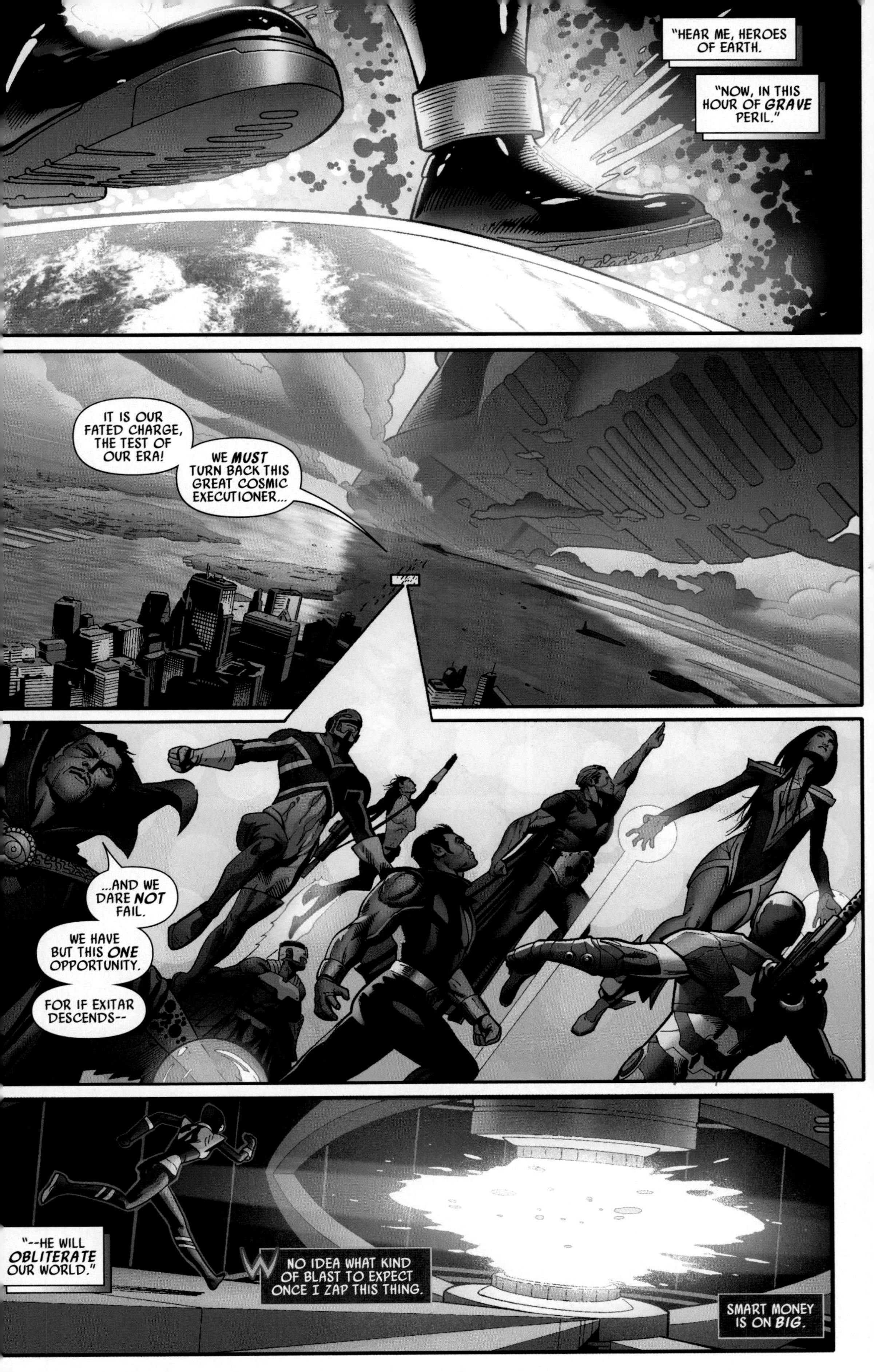
"HEAR ME, HEROES OF EARTH.
"NOW, IN THIS HOUR OF GRAVE PERIL."
IT IS OUR FATED CHARGE, THE TEST OF OUR ERA!
WE MUST TURN BACK THIS GREAT COSMIC EXECUTIONER...
...AND WE DARE NOT FAIL.
WE HAVE BUT THIS ONE OPPORTUNITY.
FOR IF EXITAR DESCENDS--
"--HE WILL OBLITERATE OUR WORLD."
NO IDEA WHAT KIND OF BLAST TO EXPECT ONCE I ZAP THIS THING.
SMART MONEY IS ON BIG.

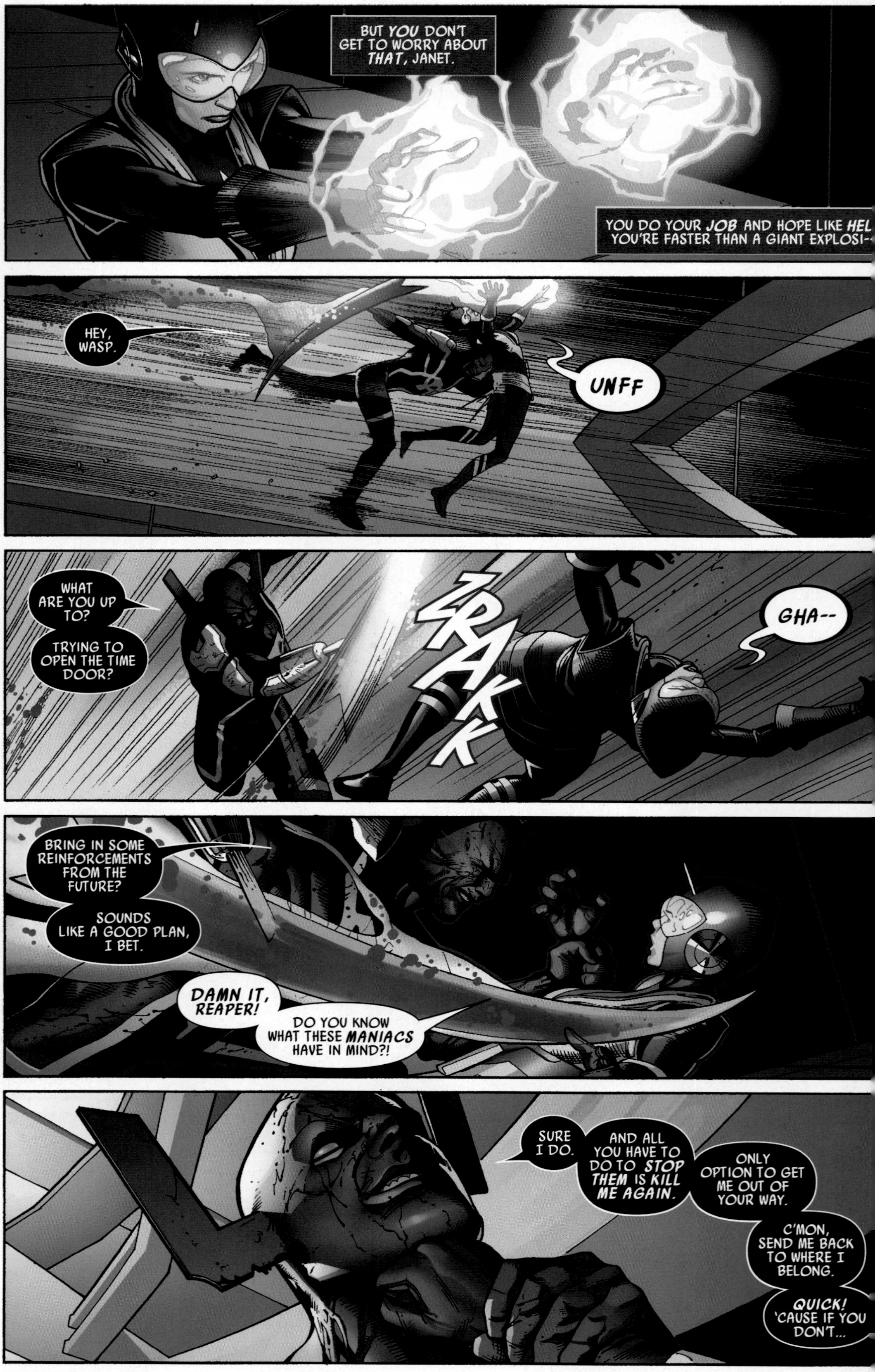
BUT *YOU* DON'T GET TO WORRY ABOUT *THAT*, JANET.
YOU DO YOUR *JOB* AND HOPE LIKE *HEL*
YOU'RE FASTER THAN A GIANT EXPLOSI--
HEY, WASP.
UNFF
WHAT ARE YOU UP TO?
TRYING TO OPEN THE TIME DOOR?
ZRAKK
GHA--
BRING IN SOME REINFORCEMENTS FROM THE FUTURE?
SOUNDS LIKE A GOOD PLAN, I BET.
DAMN IT, REAPER!
DO YOU KNOW WHAT THESE *MANIACS* HAVE IN MIND?!
SURE I DO.
AND ALL YOU HAVE TO DO TO *STOP THEM* IS *KILL ME AGAIN*.
ONLY OPTION TO GET ME OUT OF YOUR WAY.
C'MON, SEND ME BACK TO WHERE I BELONG.
QUICK! 'CAUSE IF YOU DON'T...

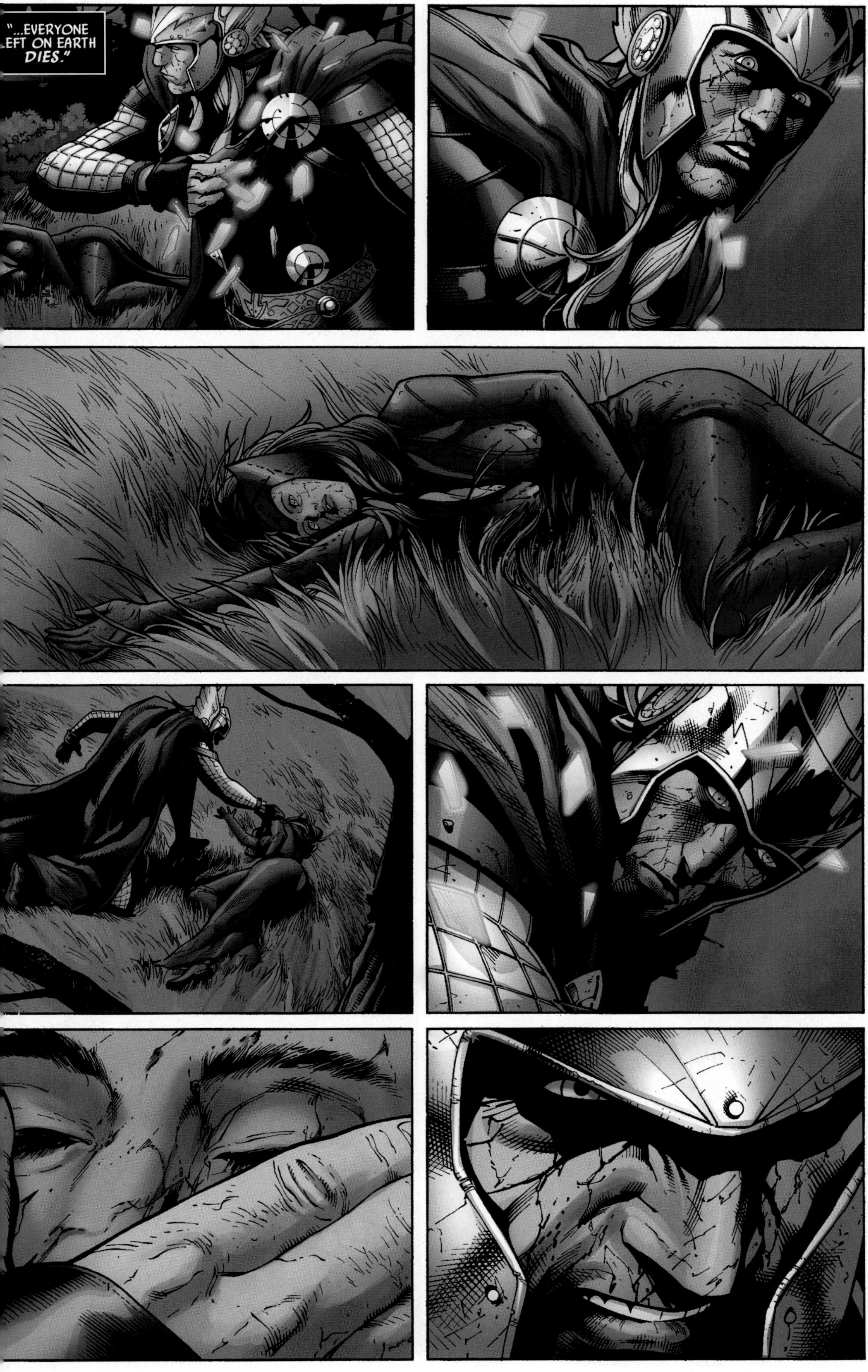
"...EVERYONE
LEFT ON EARTH
DIES."

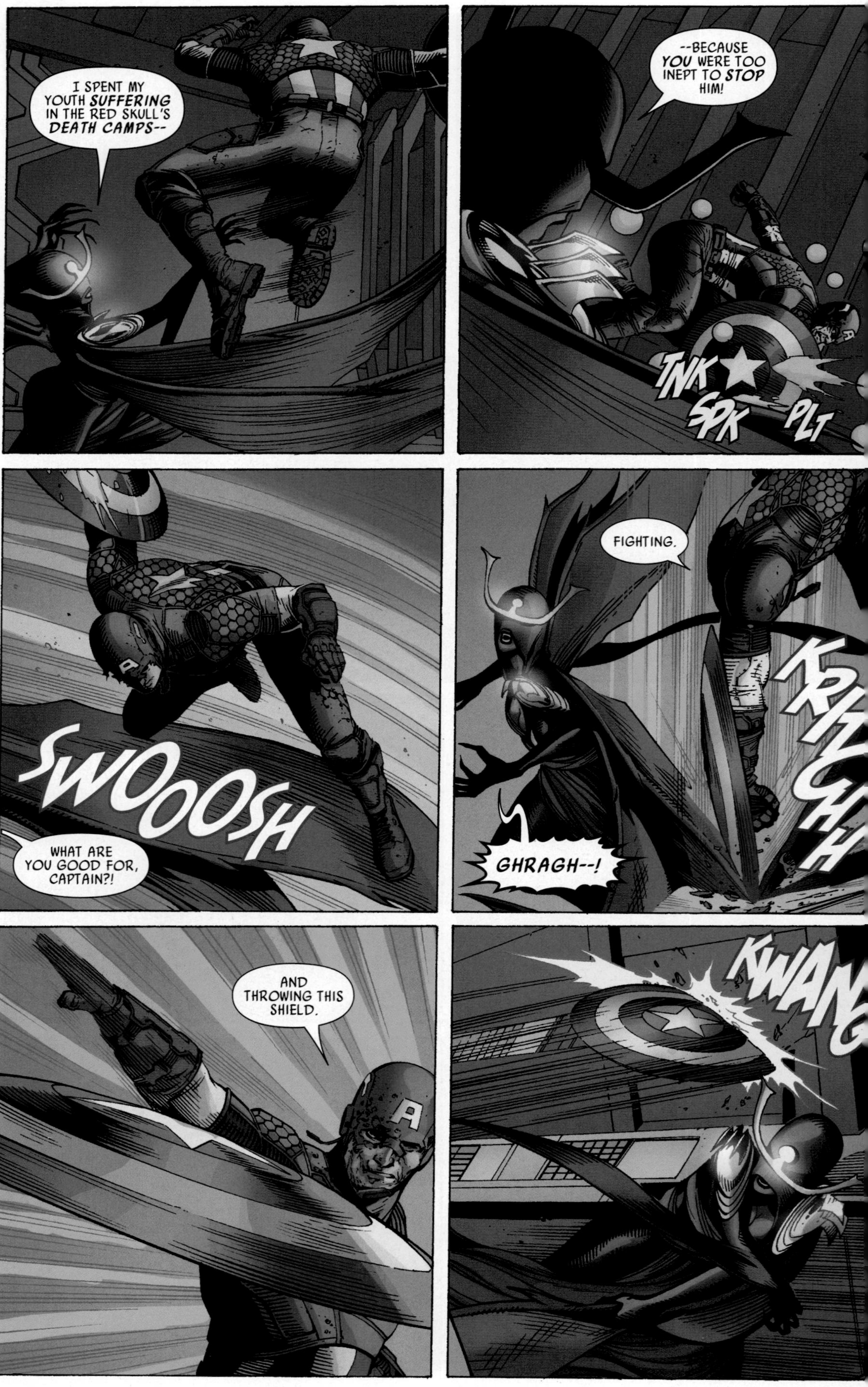
I SPENT MY YOUTH SUFFERING IN THE RED SKULL'S DEATH CAMPS--
--BECAUSE YOU WERE TOO INEPT TO STOP HIM!
TNK
SPK
PLT
SWOOOSH
WHAT ARE YOU GOOD FOR, CAPTAIN?!
FIGHTING.
GHRAGH--!
AND THROWING THIS SHIELD.
KWANG

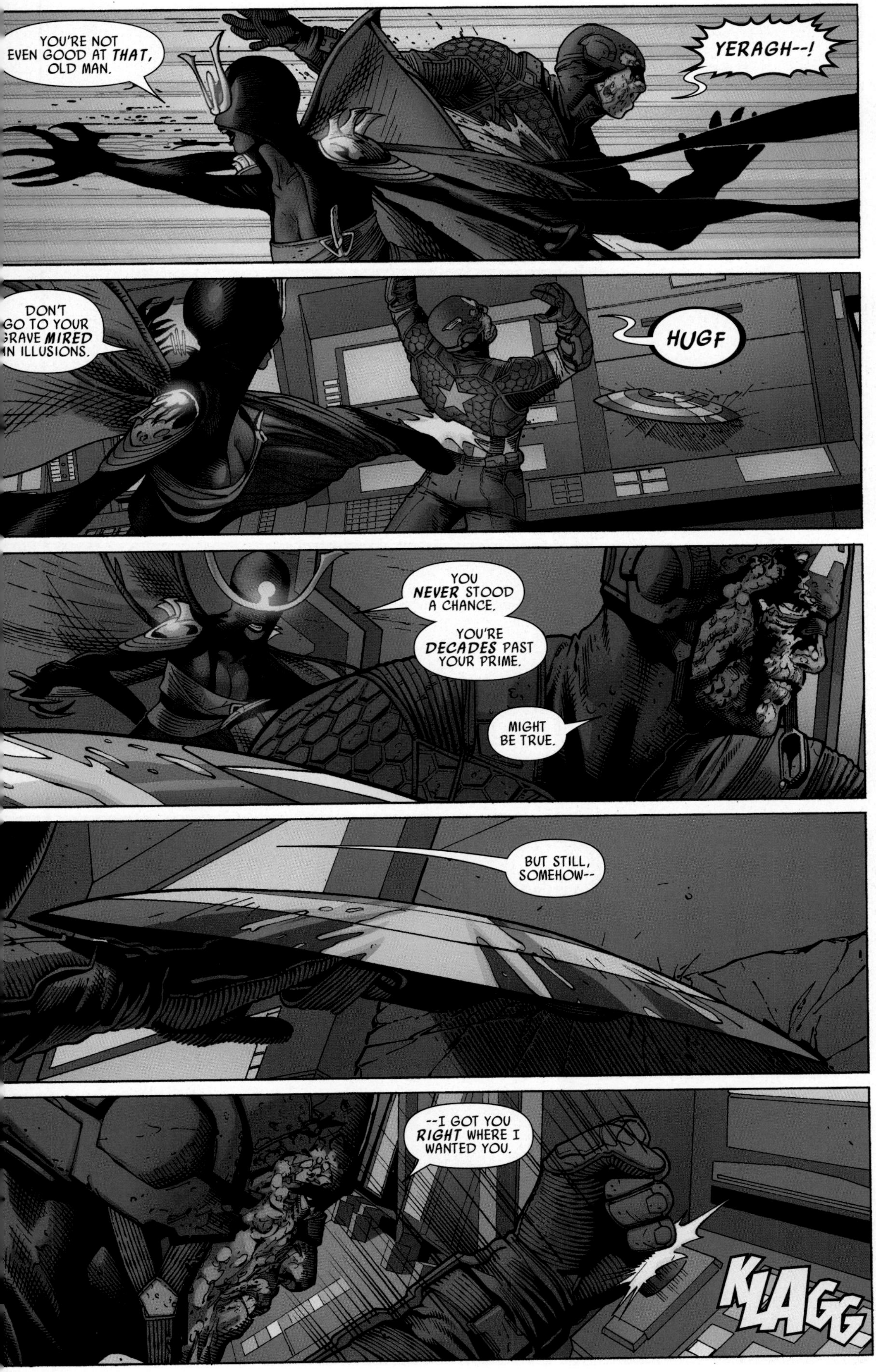
YOU'RE NOT EVEN GOOD AT THAT, OLD MAN.
YERAGH--!
DON'T GO TO YOUR GRAVE MIRED IN ILLUSIONS.
HUGF
YOU NEVER STOOD A CHANCE.
YOU'RE DECADES PAST YOUR PRIME.
MIGHT BE TRUE.
BUT STILL, SOMEHOW--
--I GOT YOU RIGHT WHERE I WANTED YOU.
KLAGG.

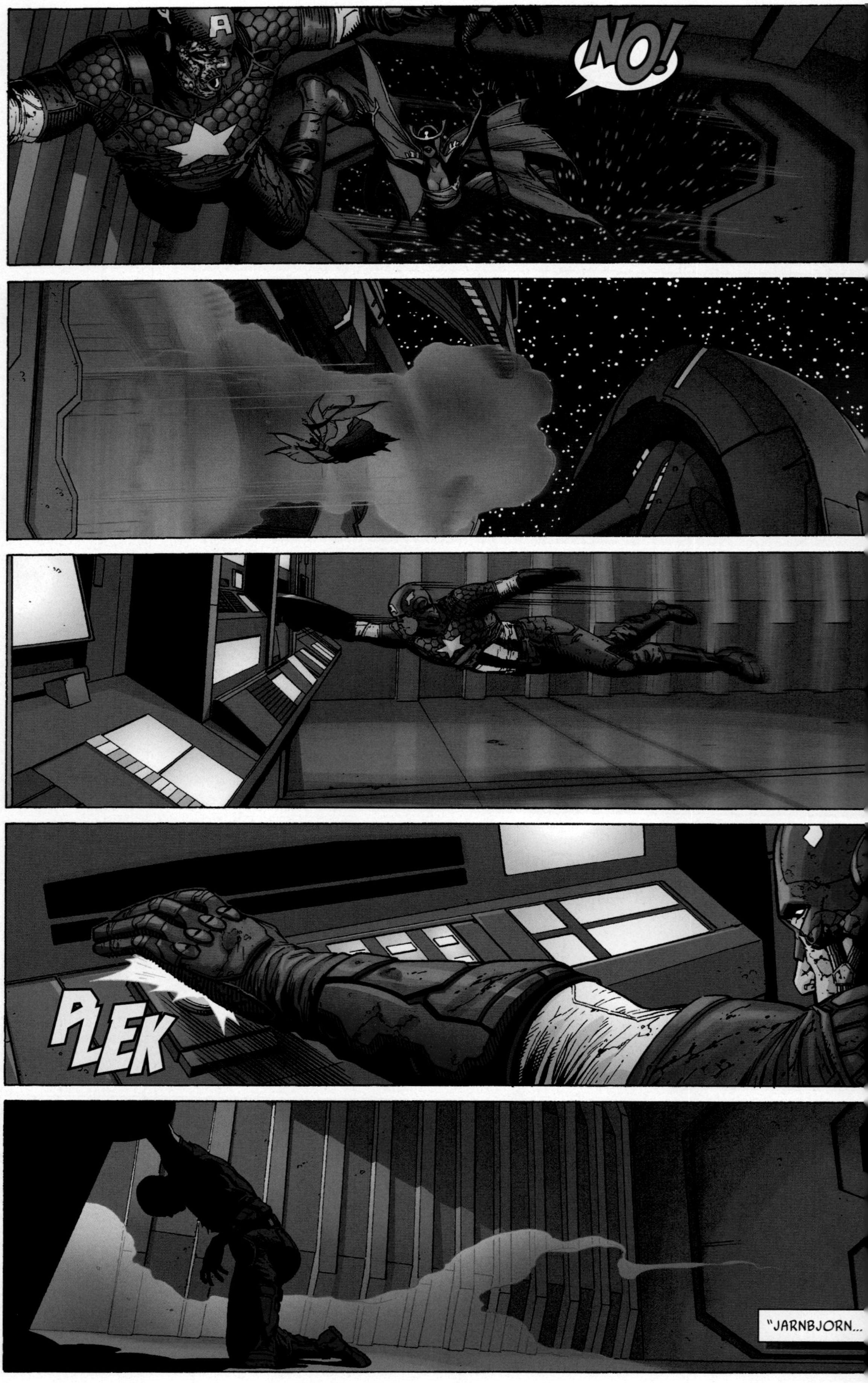
NO!
PLEK
"JARNBJORN...

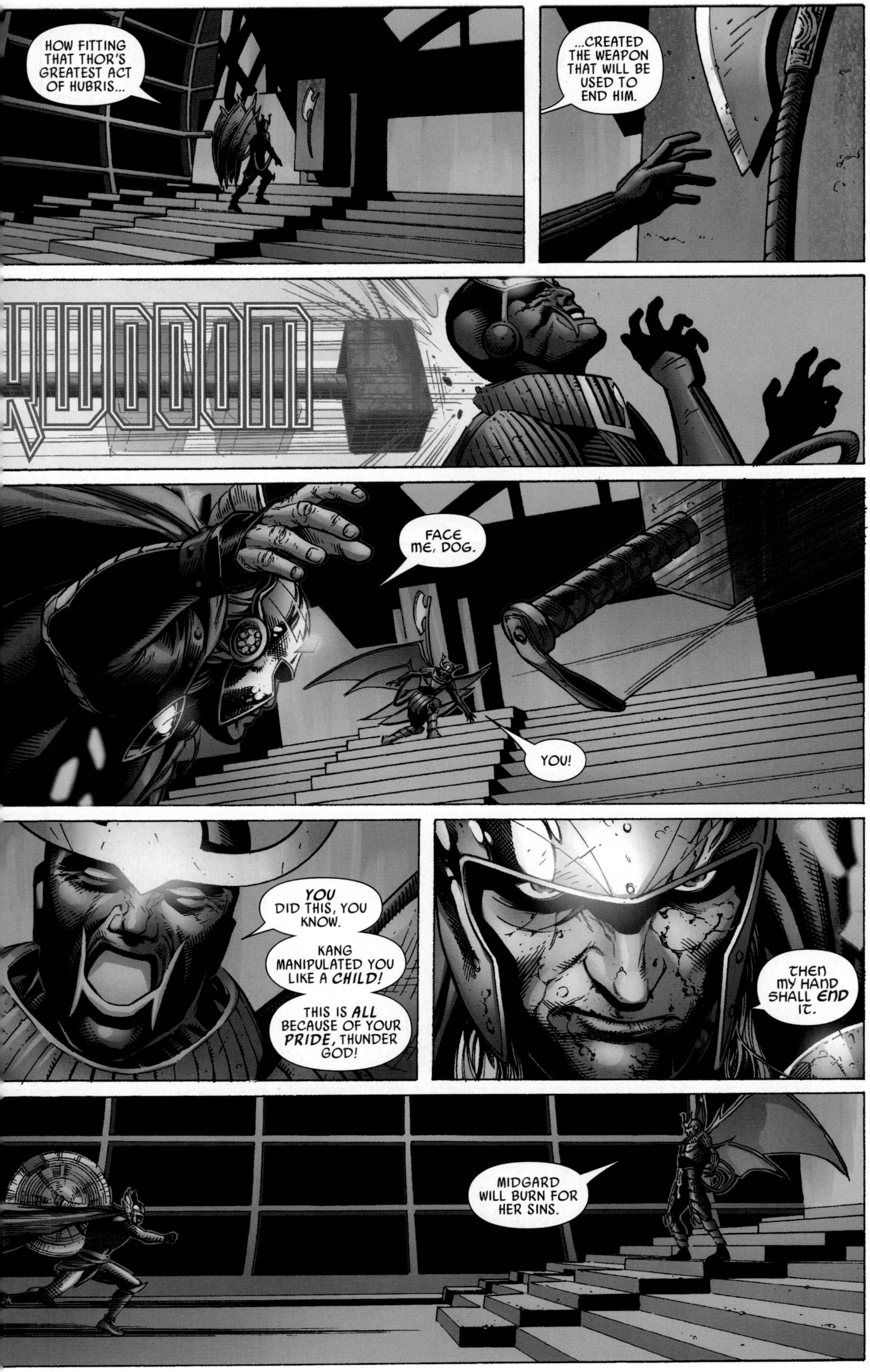
HOW FITTING THAT THOR'S GREATEST ACT OF HUBRIS...
...CREATED THE WEAPON THAT WILL BE USED TO END HIM.
KRWOOOM
FACE ME, DOG.
YOU!
YOU DID THIS, YOU KNOW.
KANG MANIPULATED YOU LIKE A CHILD!
THIS IS ALL BECAUSE OF YOUR PRIDE, THUNDER GOD!
THEN MY HAND SHALL END IT.
MIDGARD WILL BURN FOR HER SINS.

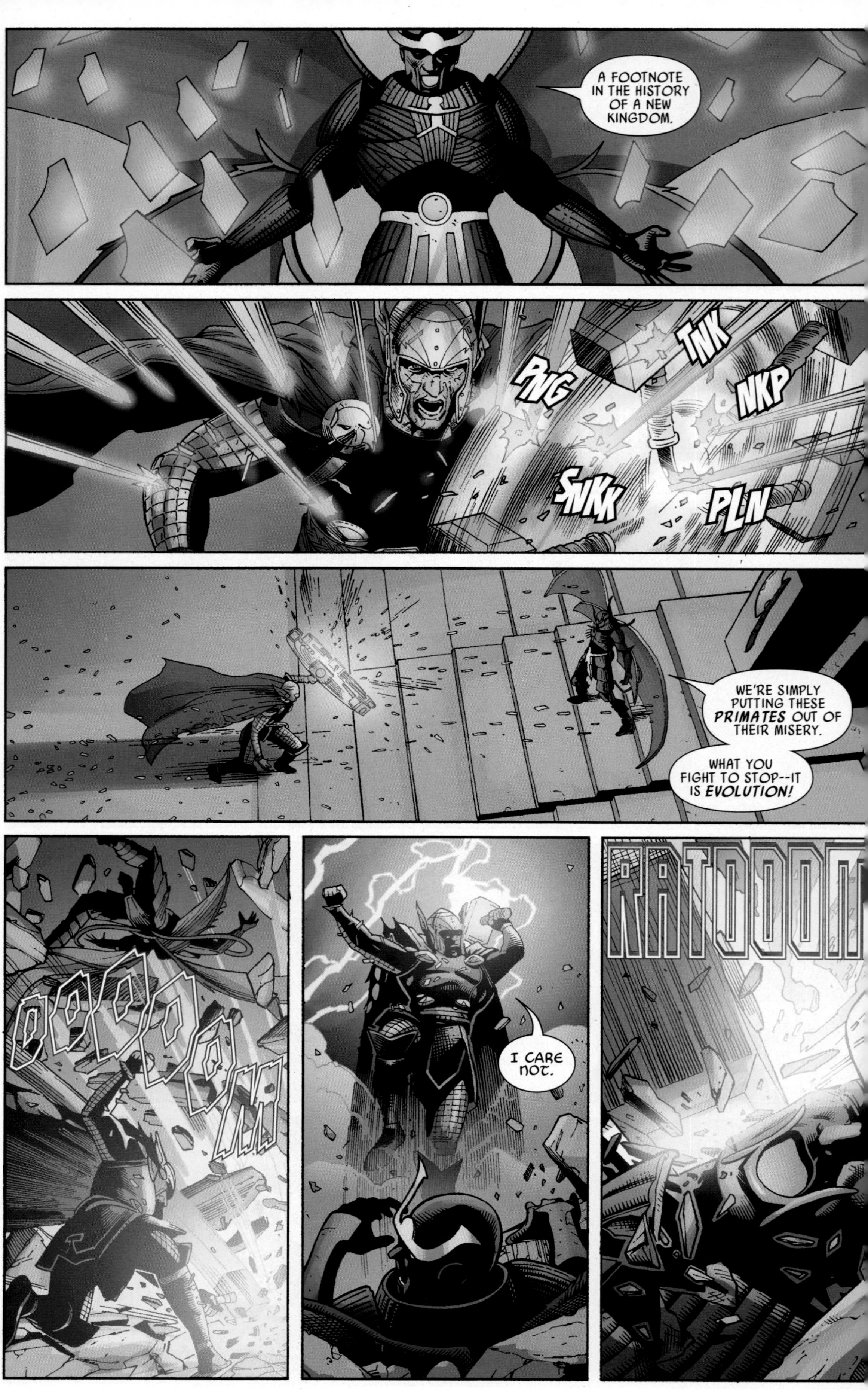
A FOOTNOTE IN THE HISTORY OF A NEW KINGDOM.
PNG
TNK
NKP
SNKK
PLN
WE'RE SIMPLY PUTTING THESE *PRIMATES* OUT OF THEIR MISERY.
WHAT YOU FIGHT TO STOP--IT IS *EVOLUTION!*
OOOOOOM
I CARE NOT.
RATOOOM

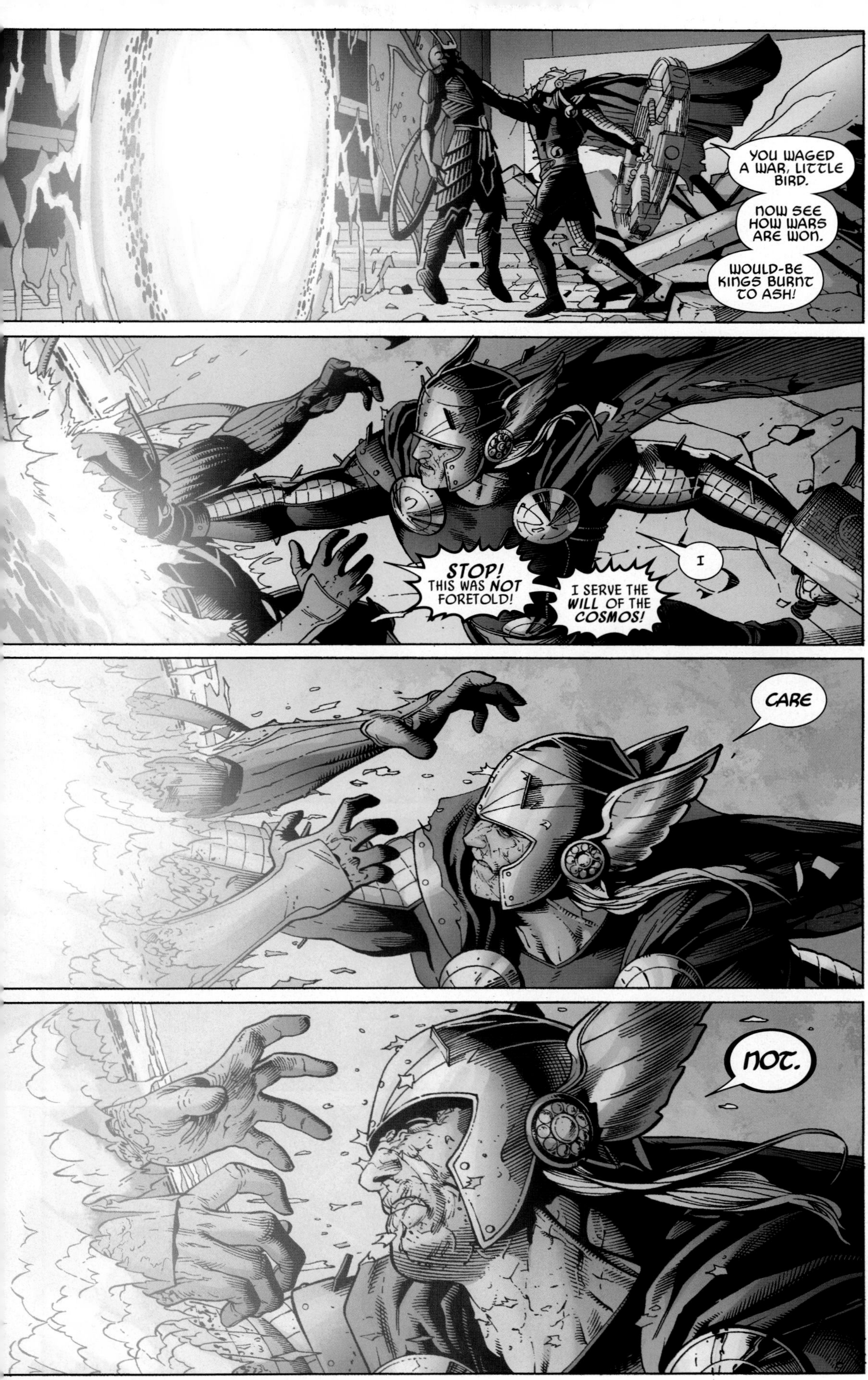
YOU WAGED A WAR, LITTLE BIRD.
NOW SEE HOW WARS ARE WON.
WOULD-BE KINGS BURNT TO ASH!
STOP! THIS WAS NOT FORETOLD!
I SERVE THE WILL OF THE COSMOS!
I
CARE
NOT.

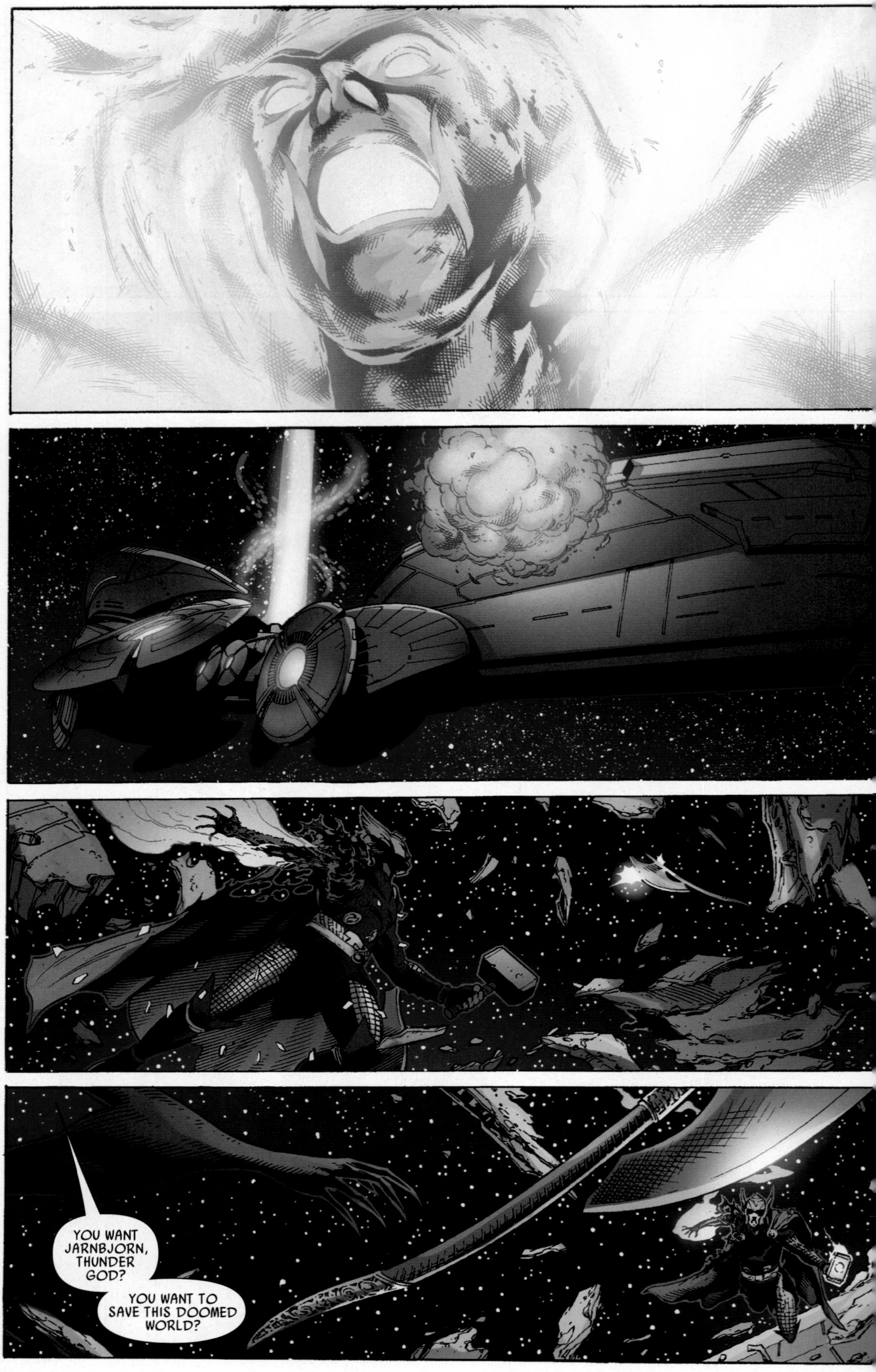
YOU WANT JARNBJORN, THUNDER GOD?
YOU WANT TO SAVE THIS DOOMED WORLD?

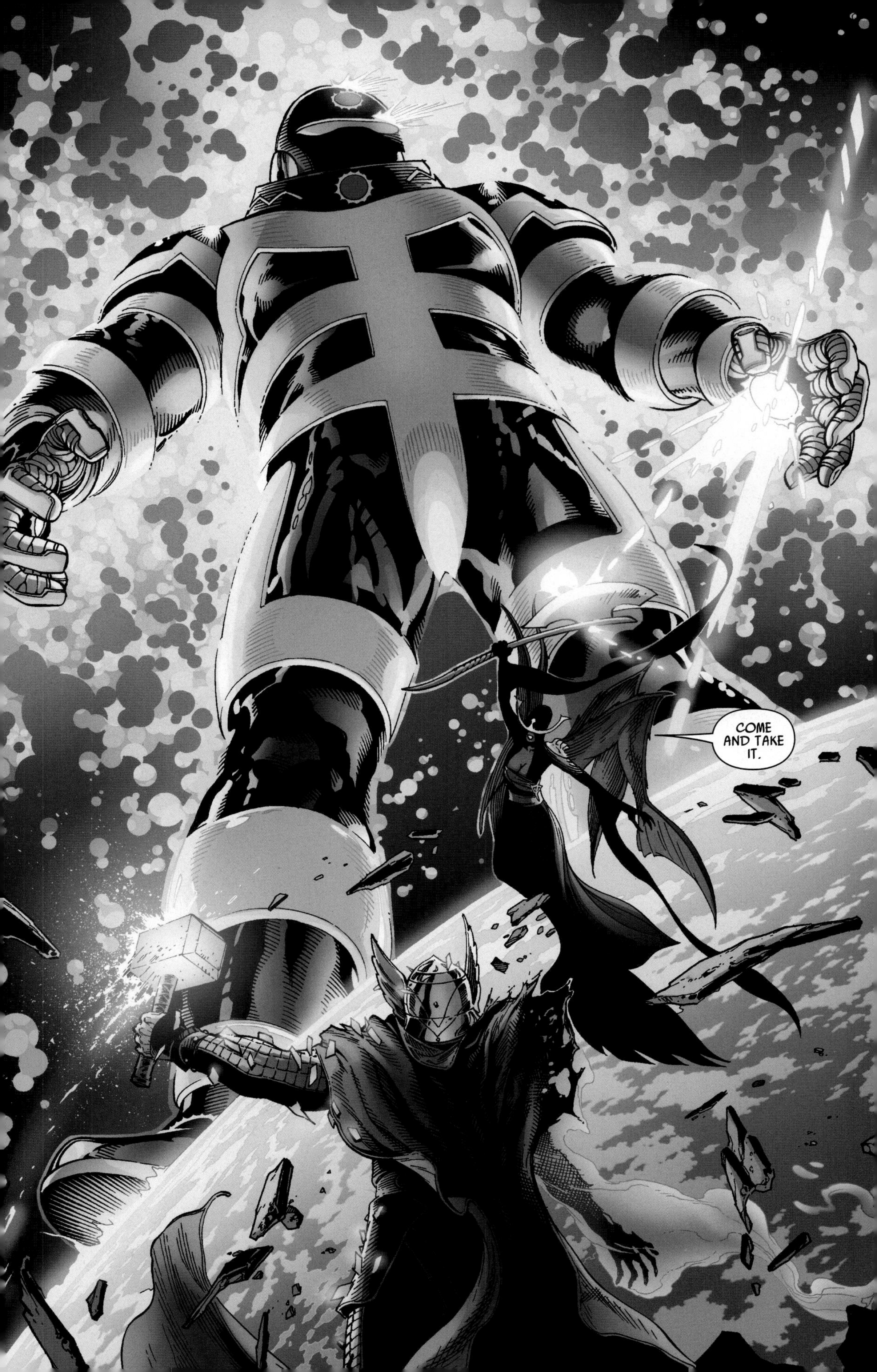
COME AND TAKE IT.

UNCANNY AVENGERS #17

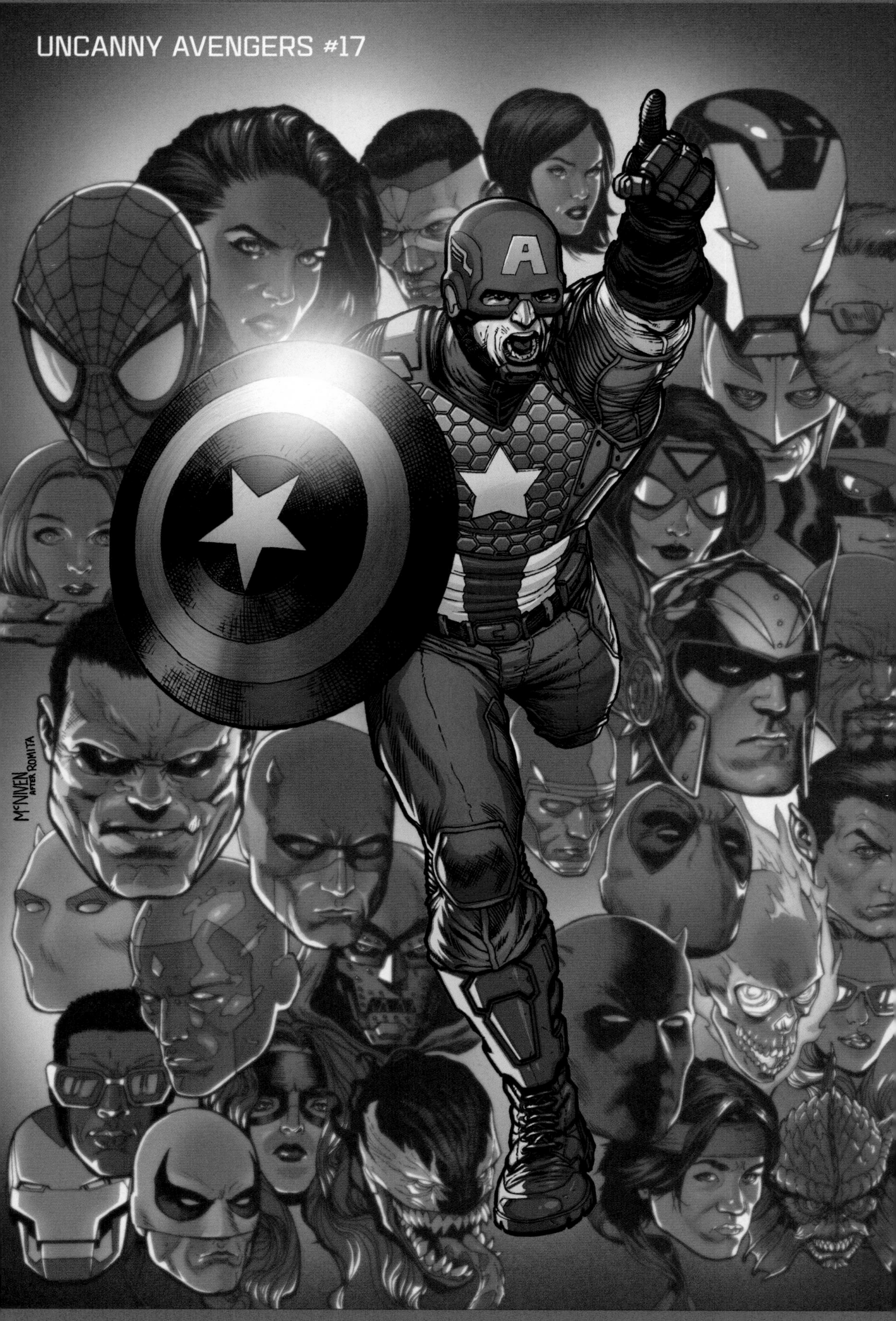

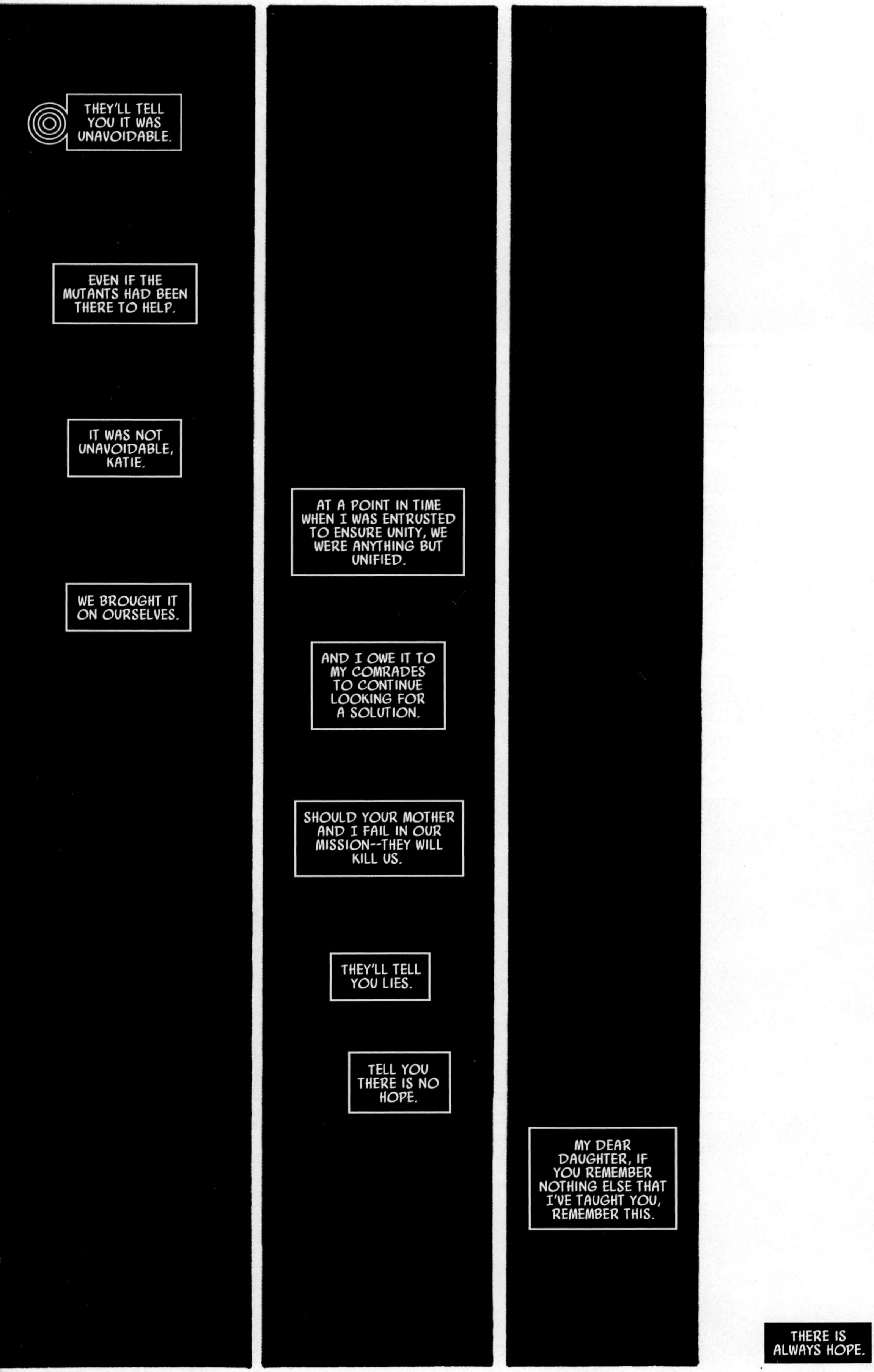
THEY'LL TELL YOU IT WAS UNAVOIDABLE.
EVEN IF THE MUTANTS HAD BEEN THERE TO HELP.
IT WAS NOT UNAVOIDABLE, KATIE.
WE BROUGHT IT ON OURSELVES.
AT A POINT IN TIME WHEN I WAS ENTRUSTED TO ENSURE UNITY, WE WERE ANYTHING BUT UNIFIED.
AND I OWE IT TO MY COMRADES TO CONTINUE LOOKING FOR A SOLUTION.
SHOULD YOUR MOTHER AND I FAIL IN OUR MISSION--THEY WILL KILL US.
THEY'LL TELL YOU LIES.
TELL YOU THERE IS NO HOPE.
MY DEAR DAUGHTER, IF YOU REMEMBER NOTHING ELSE THAT I'VE TAUGHT YOU, REMEMBER THIS.
THERE IS ALWAYS HOPE.

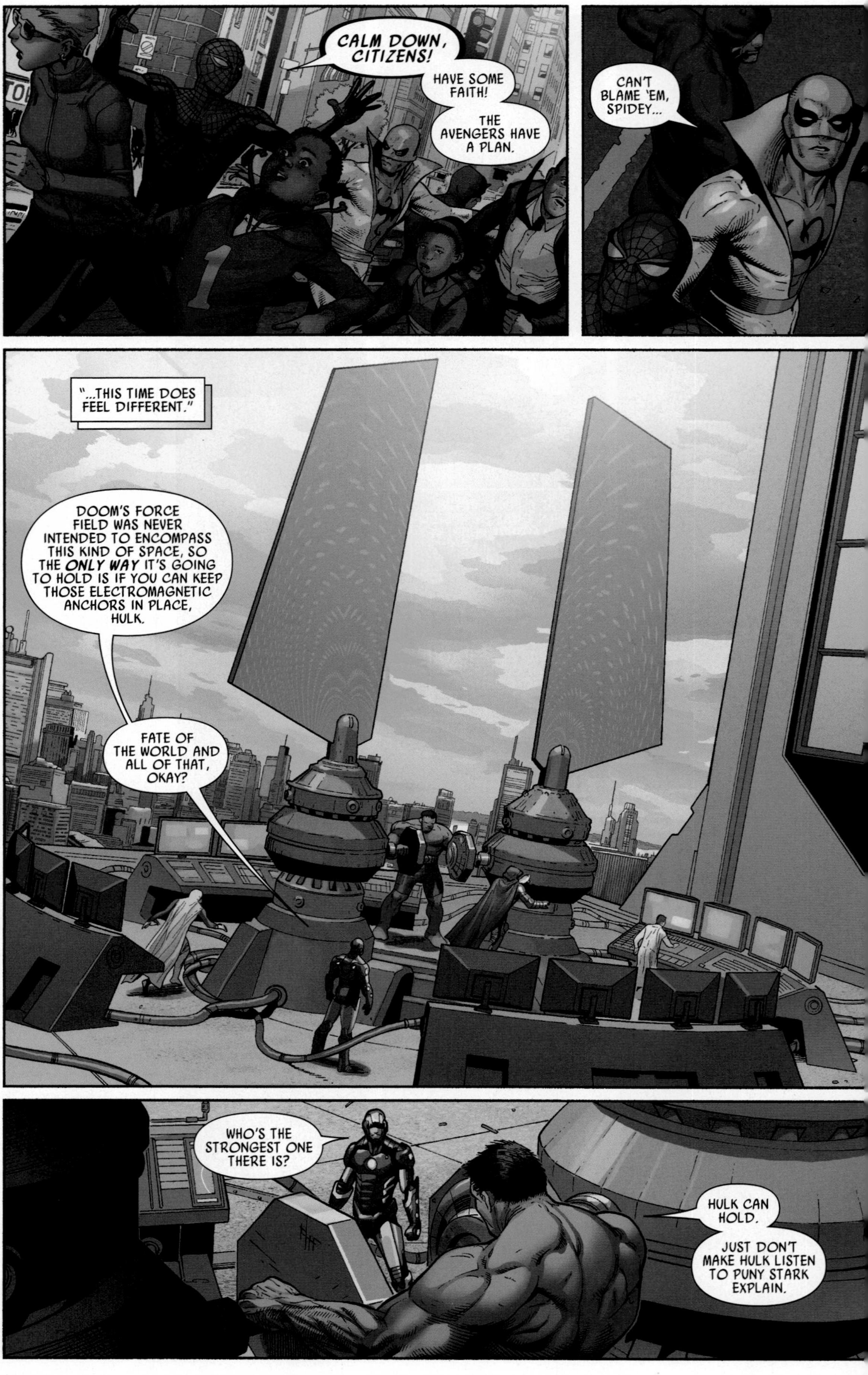
CALM DOWN, CITIZENS!
HAVE SOME FAITH!
THE AVENGERS HAVE A PLAN.
CAN'T BLAME 'EM, SPIDEY...
"...THIS TIME DOES FEEL DIFFERENT."
DOOM'S FORCE FIELD WAS NEVER INTENDED TO ENCOMPASS THIS KIND OF SPACE, SO THE ONLY WAY IT'S GOING TO HOLD IS IF YOU CAN KEEP THOSE ELECTROMAGNETIC ANCHORS IN PLACE, HULK.
FATE OF THE WORLD AND ALL OF THAT, OKAY?
WHO'S THE STRONGEST ONE THERE IS?
HULK CAN HOLD.
JUST DON'T MAKE HULK LISTEN TO PUNY STARK EXPLAIN.

FIGURED THAT MIGHT ANGRY UP THE BLOOD A BIT AND--

MY GOD...

HE'S COMING.

DR. STRANGE, WE NEED A FEW MORE MINUTES TO COMPLETE THIS THING!

CAN YOUR TEAM BUY US SOME TIME?

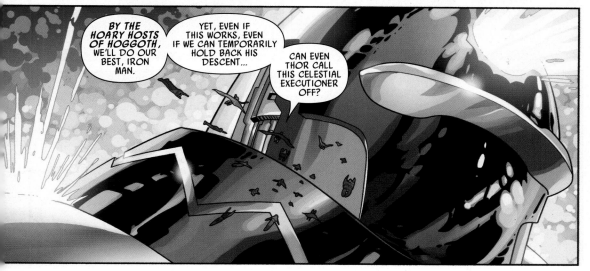

BY THE HOARY HOSTS OF HOGGOTH, WE'LL DO OUR BEST, IRON MAN.

YET, EVEN IF THIS WORKS, EVEN IF WE CAN TEMPORARILY HOLD BACK HIS DESCENT...

CAN EVEN THOR CALL THIS CELESTIAL EXECUTIONER OFF?

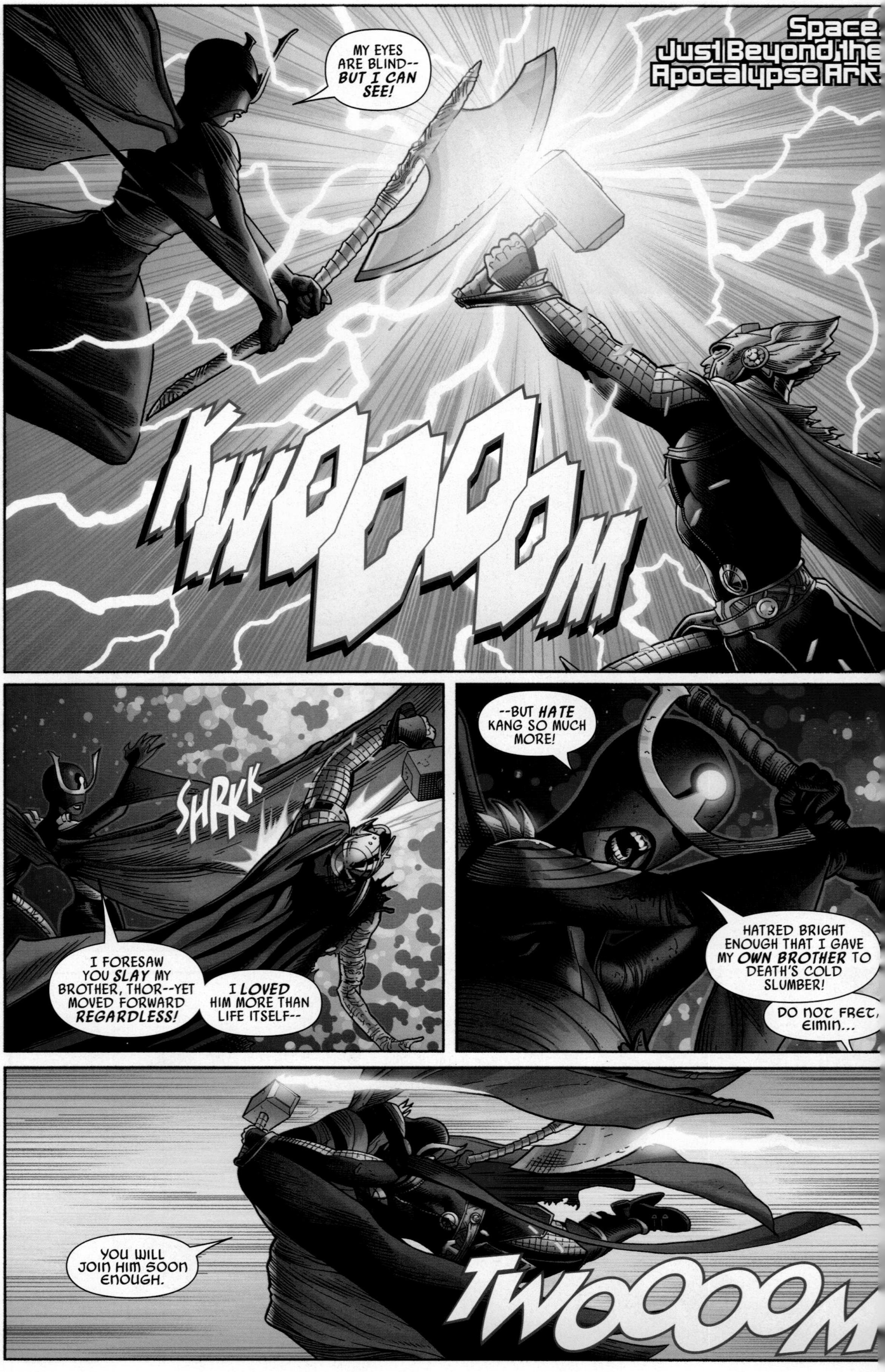

Space. Just Beyond the Apocalypse Ark.
MY EYES ARE BLIND-- BUT I CAN SEE!
KWOOOOOM
SHRKK
I FORESAW YOU SLAY MY BROTHER, THOR--YET MOVED FORWARD REGARDLESS!
I LOVED HIM MORE THAN LIFE ITSELF--
--BUT HATE KANG SO MUCH MORE!
HATRED BRIGHT ENOUGH THAT I GAVE MY OWN BROTHER TO DEATH'S COLD SLUMBER!
DO NOT FRET, EIMIN...
YOU WILL JOIN HIM SOON ENOUGH.
TWOOOOM

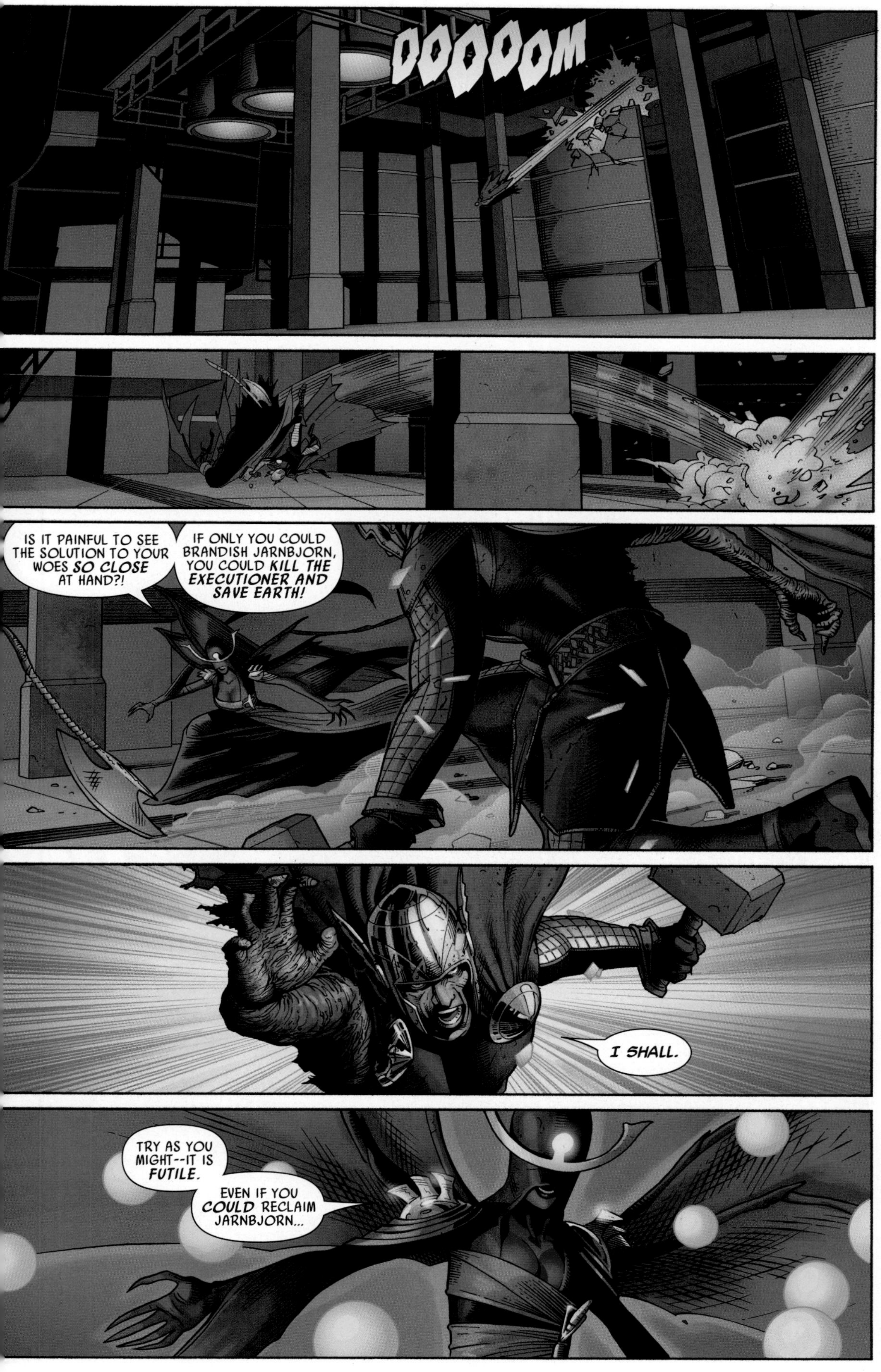

DOOOOM
IS IT PAINFUL TO SEE THE SOLUTION TO YOUR WOES SO CLOSE AT HAND?!
IF ONLY YOU COULD BRANDISH JARNBJORN, YOU COULD KILL THE EXECUTIONER AND SAVE EARTH!
I SHALL.
TRY AS YOU MIGHT--IT IS FUTILE.
EVEN IF YOU COULD RECLAIM JARNBJORN...

"...EARTH'S FATE LIES IN THE HANDS OF ANOTHER."

G'MON--

HURRY, WASP!

TIME'S SHORT! GET TO IT!

RELEASE ME FROM THIS *NIGHTMARE* AND *SAVE THE WORLD!*

HERE IT IS-- THE HARD LINE YOU JUDGED WOLVERINE *SO HARSHLY* FOR!

MAKE THE CHOICE!

COMPROMISE YOUR ETHICS OR LOSE *EVERYTHING!*

I-I'LL FIND ANOTHER WAY--

I WON'T KILL YOU, REAPER!

THEN YOU'VE ALREADY *LOST*, INSECT!

TWUDD

GAA--

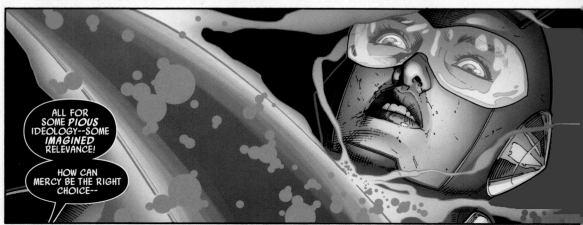

ALL FOR SOME *PIOUS* IDEOLOGY--SOME *IMAGINED* RELEVANCE!

HOW CAN MERCY BE THE RIGHT CHOICE--

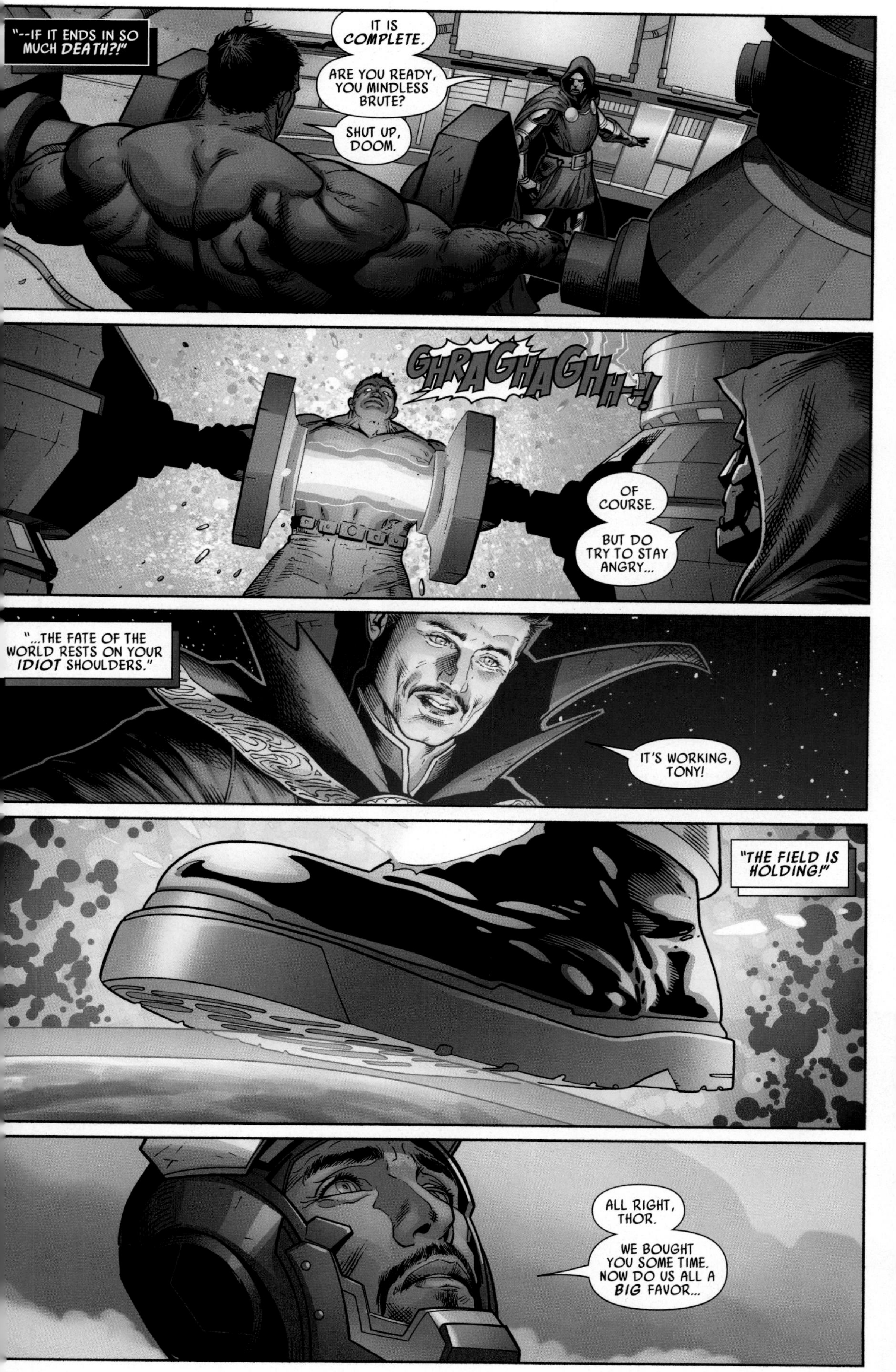
"--IF IT ENDS IN SO MUCH DEATH?!"
IT IS COMPLETE.
ARE YOU READY, YOU MINDLESS BRUTE?
SHUT UP, DOOM.
GHRAGHAGHH--!
OF COURSE.
BUT DO TRY TO STAY ANGRY...
"...THE FATE OF THE WORLD RESTS ON YOUR IDIOT SHOULDERS."
IT'S WORKING, TONY!
"THE FIELD IS HOLDING!"
ALL RIGHT, THOR.
WE BOUGHT YOU SOME TIME. NOW DO US ALL A BIG FAVOR...

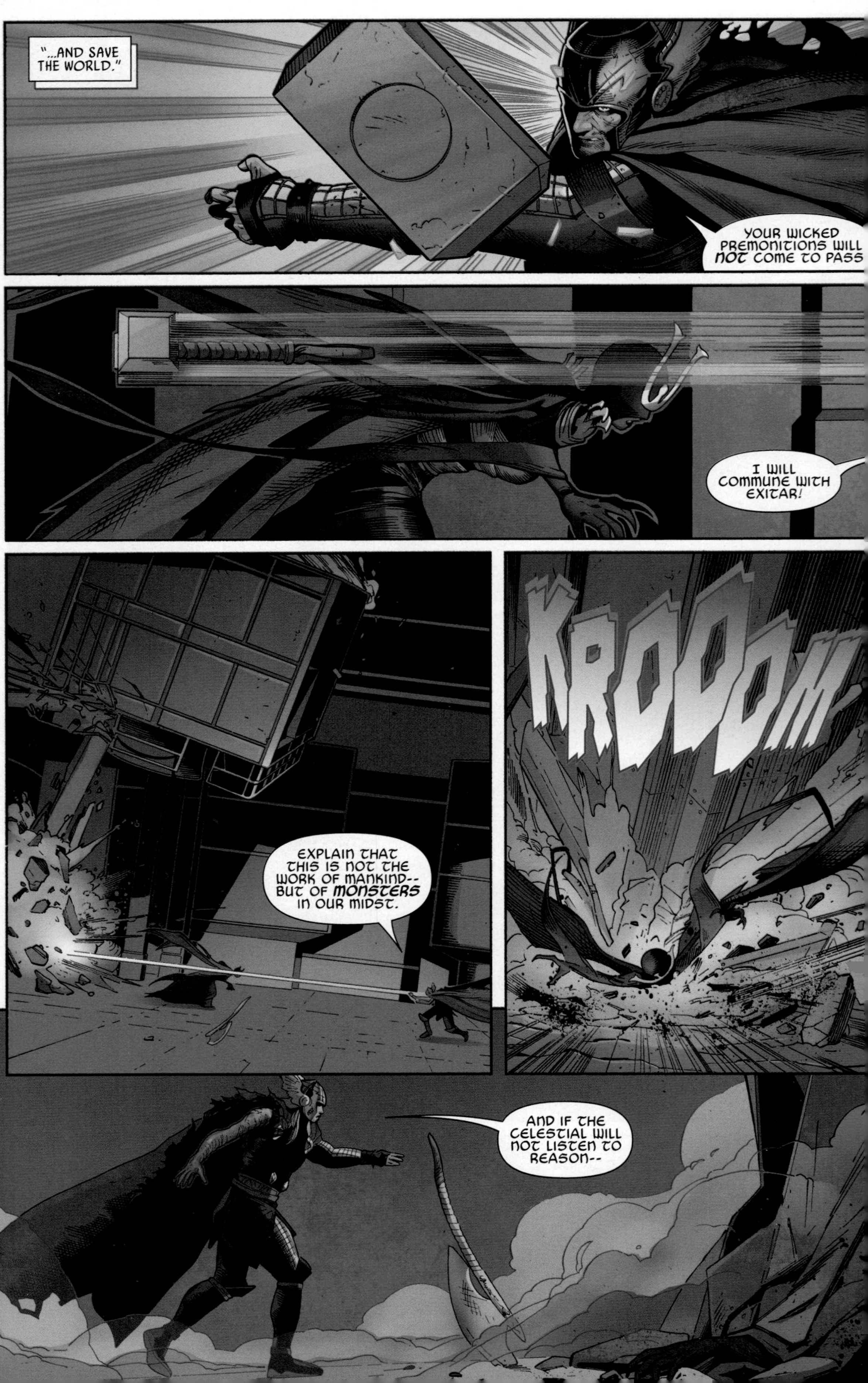
"...AND SAVE THE WORLD."
YOUR WICKED PREMONITIONS WILL NOT COME TO PASS
I WILL COMMUNE WITH EXITAR!
EXPLAIN THAT THIS IS NOT THE WORK OF MANKIND-- BUT OF MONSTERS IN OUR MIDST.
KROOOM
AND IF THE CELESTIAL WILL NOT LISTEN TO REASON--

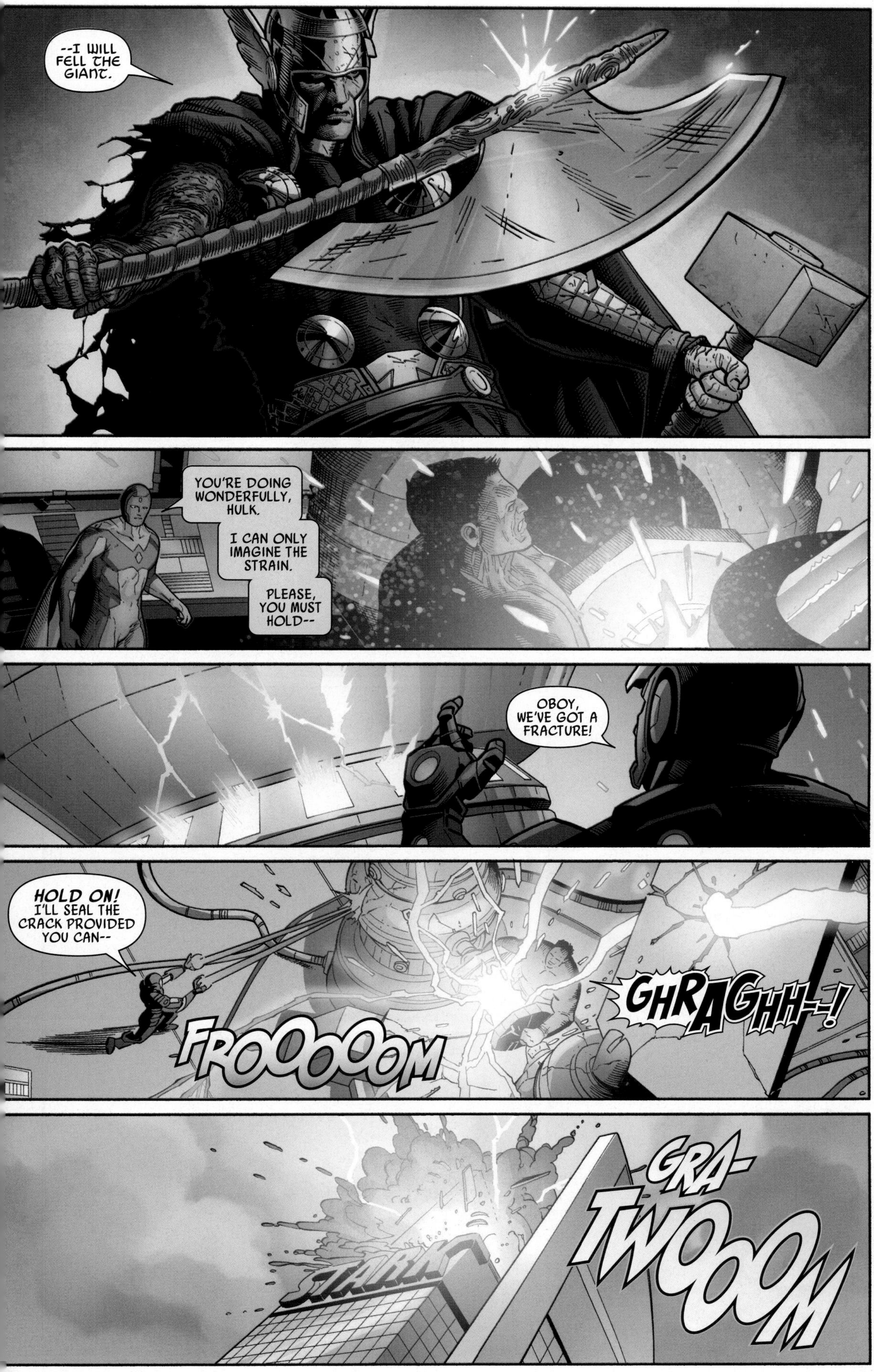
--I WILL FELL THE GIANT.
YOU'RE DOING WONDERFULLY, HULK.
I CAN ONLY IMAGINE THE STRAIN.
PLEASE, YOU MUST HOLD--
OBOY, WE'VE GOT A FRACTURE!
HOLD ON! I'LL SEAL THE CRACK PROVIDED YOU CAN--
FROOOOOOM
GHRAGHH--!
STARK
GRA-TWOOOM

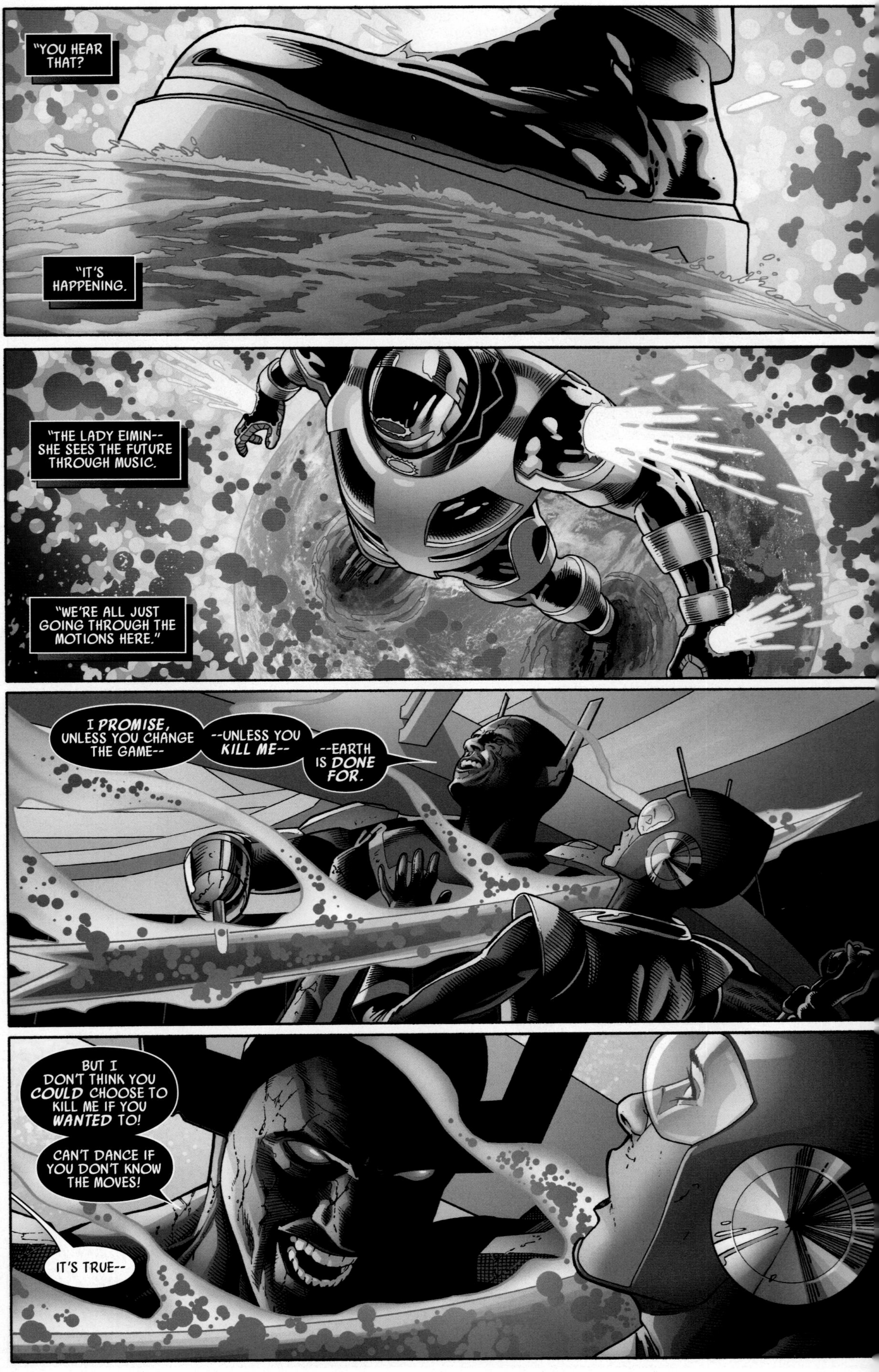
"YOU HEAR THAT?
"IT'S HAPPENING.
"THE LADY EIMIN-- SHE SEES THE FUTURE THROUGH MUSIC.
"WE'RE ALL JUST GOING THROUGH THE MOTIONS HERE."
I PROMISE, UNLESS YOU CHANGE THE GAME--
--UNLESS YOU KILL ME--
--EARTH IS DONE FOR.
BUT I DON'T THINK YOU COULD CHOOSE TO KILL ME IF YOU WANTED TO!
CAN'T DANCE IF YOU DON'T KNOW THE MOVES!
IT'S TRUE--

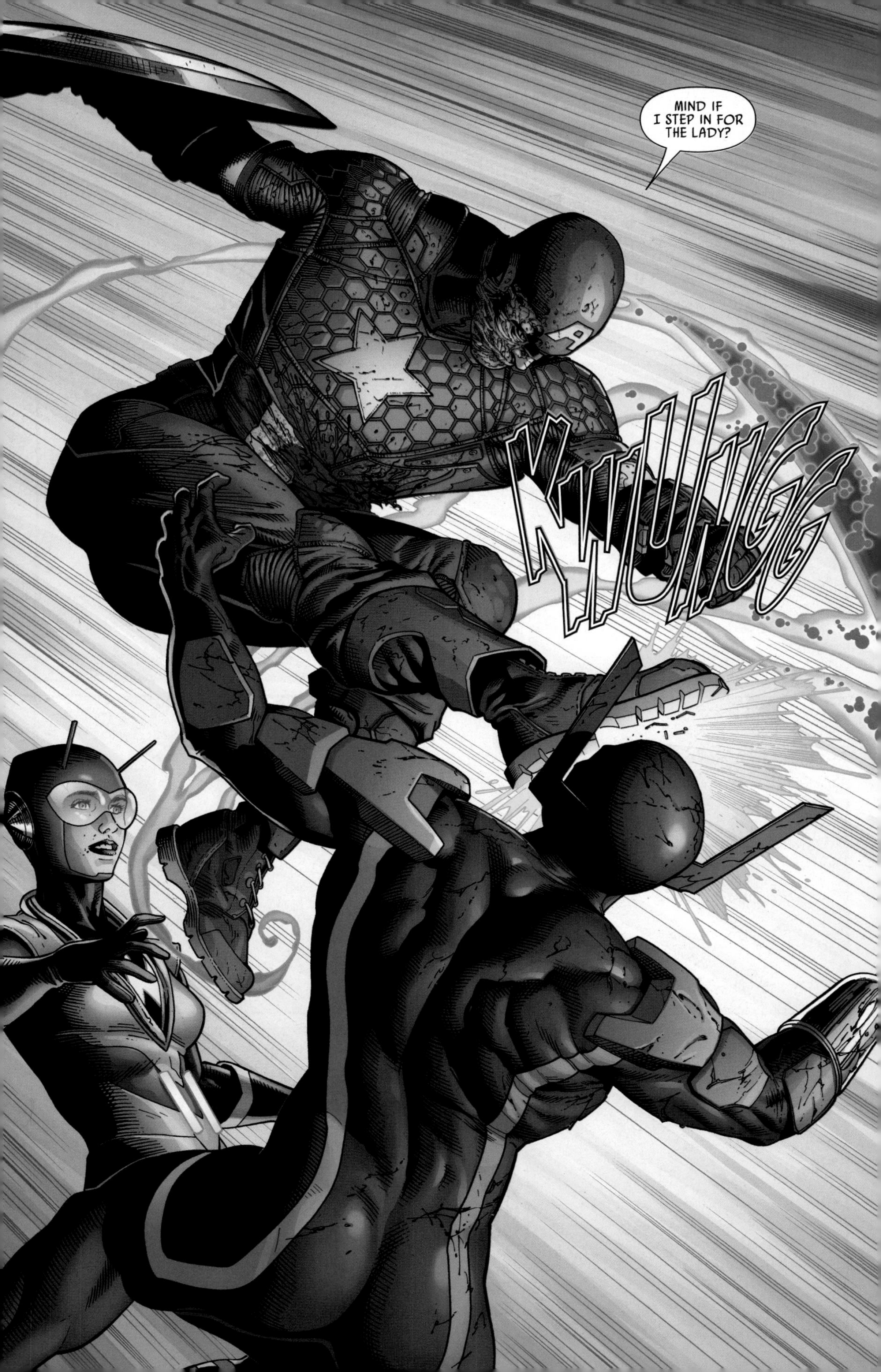
MIND IF I STEP IN FOR THE LADY?
KWUUNGG

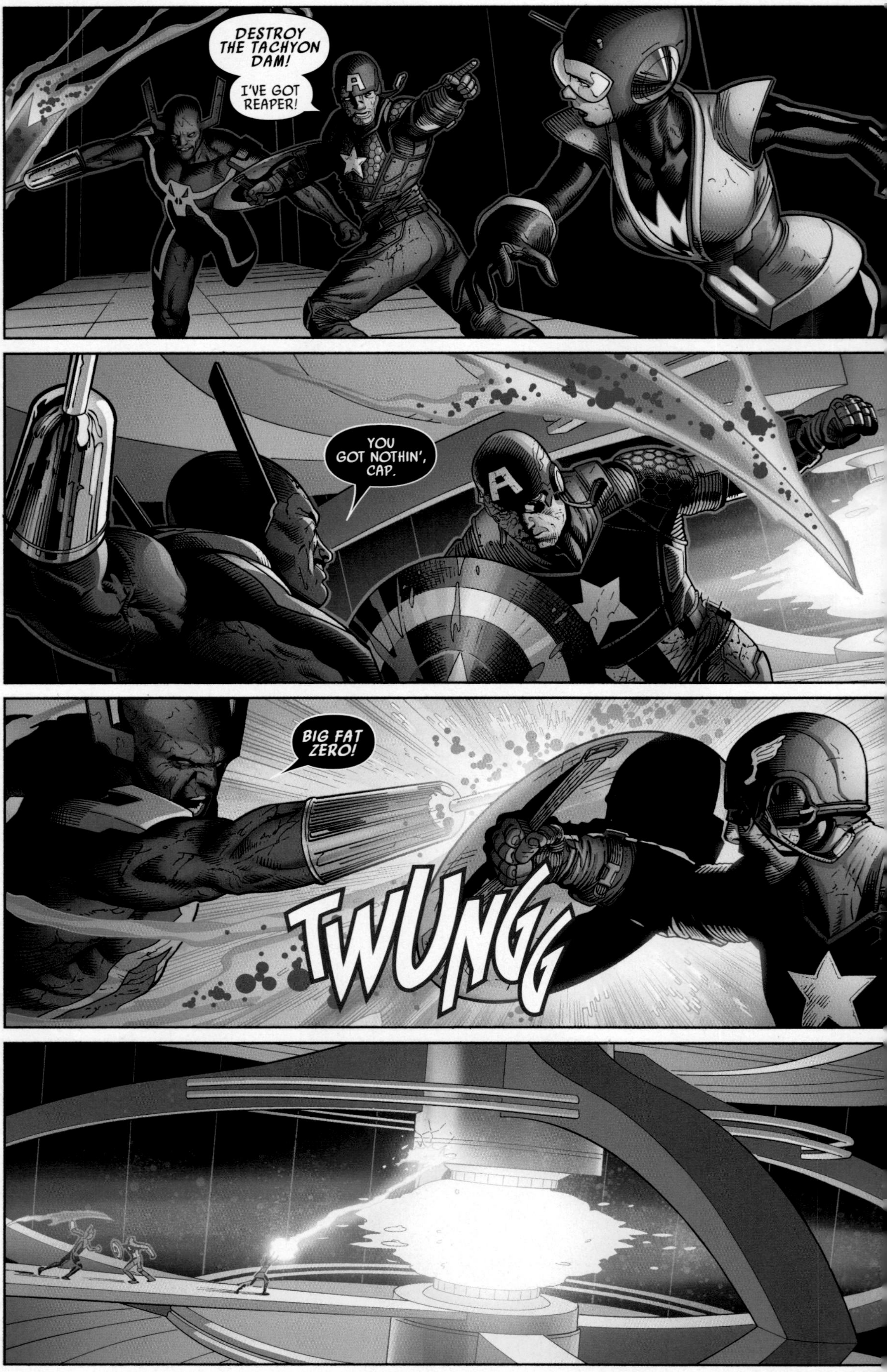
DESTROY THE TACHYON DAM!
I'VE GOT REAPER!
YOU GOT NOTHIN', CAP.
BIG FAT ZERO!
TWUNGG

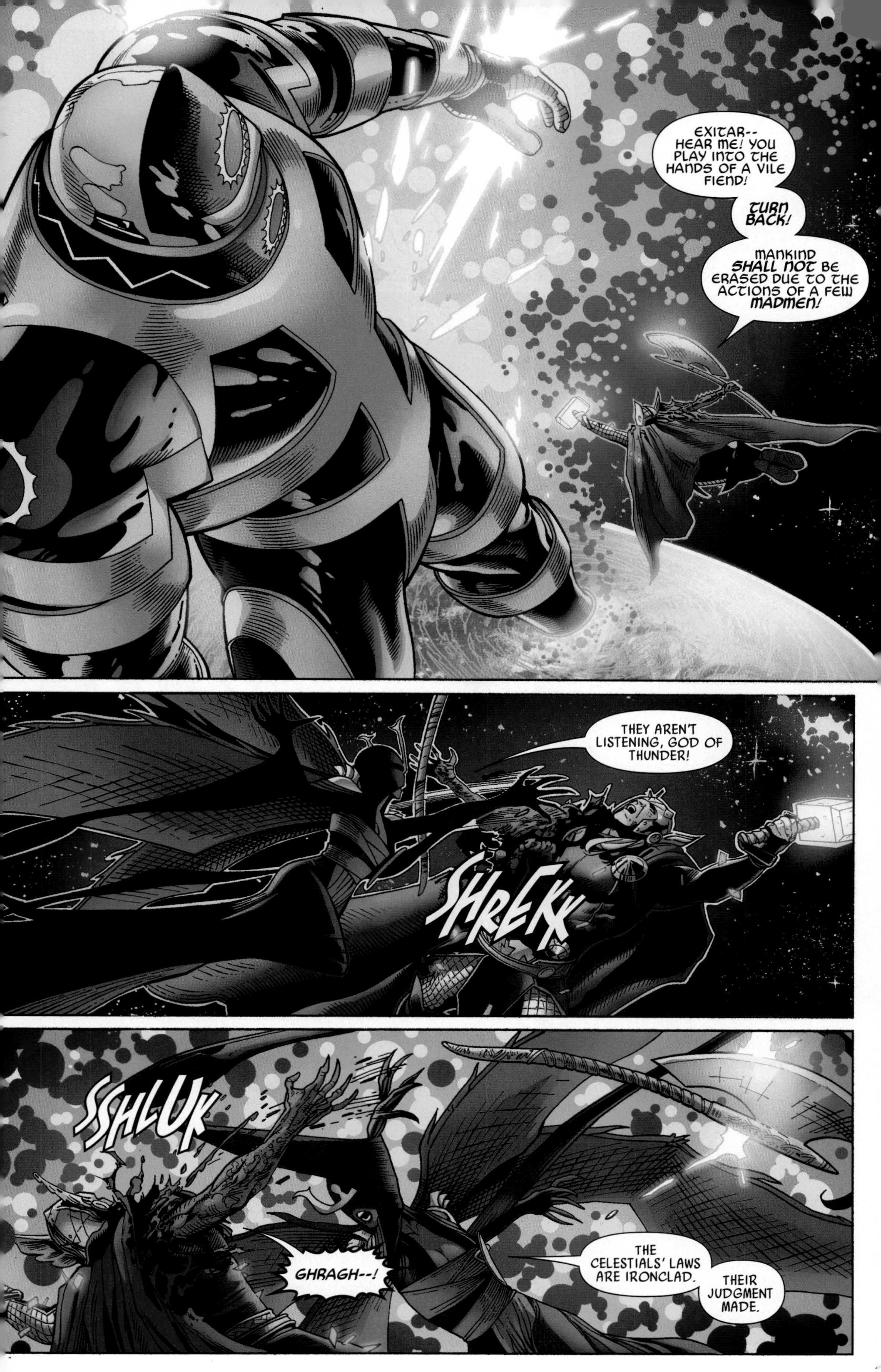
EXITAR-- HEAR ME! YOU PLAY INTO THE HANDS OF A VILE FIEND!
TURN BACK!
MANKIND SHALL NOT BE ERASED DUE TO THE ACTIONS OF A FEW MADMEN!
THEY AREN'T LISTENING, GOD OF THUNDER!
SHREKK
SSHLUK
GHRAGH--!
THE CELESTIALS' LAWS ARE IRONCLAD.
THEIR JUDGMENT MADE.

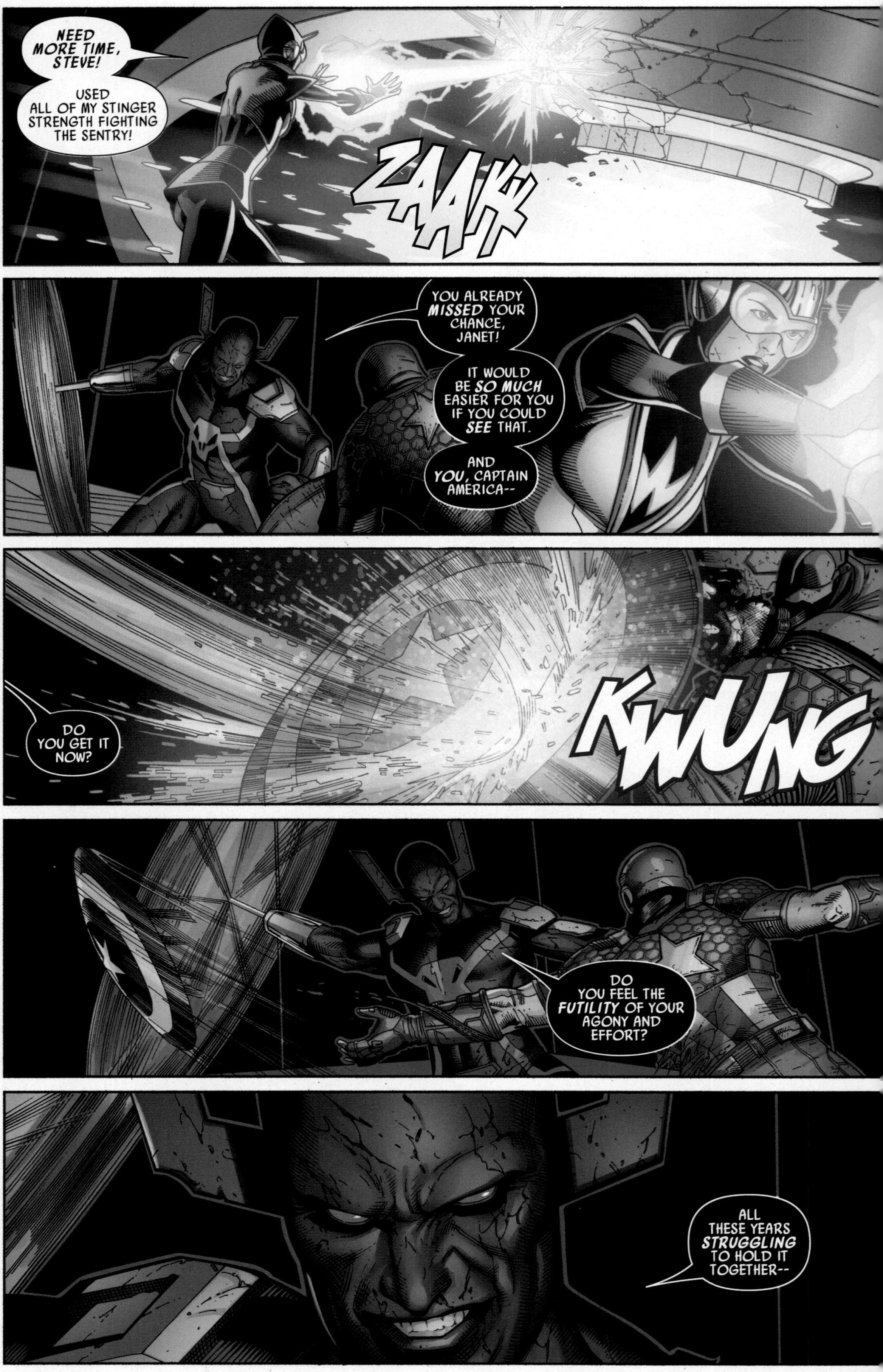
NEED MORE TIME, STEVE!
USED ALL OF MY STINGER STRENGTH FIGHTING THE SENTRY!
ZAAKK
YOU ALREADY MISSED YOUR CHANCE, JANET!
IT WOULD BE SO MUCH EASIER FOR YOU IF YOU COULD SEE THAT.
AND YOU, CAPTAIN AMERICA--
KWUNG
DO YOU GET IT NOW?
DO YOU FEEL THE FUTILITY OF YOUR AGONY AND EFFORT?
ALL THESE YEARS STRUGGLING TO HOLD IT TOGETHER--

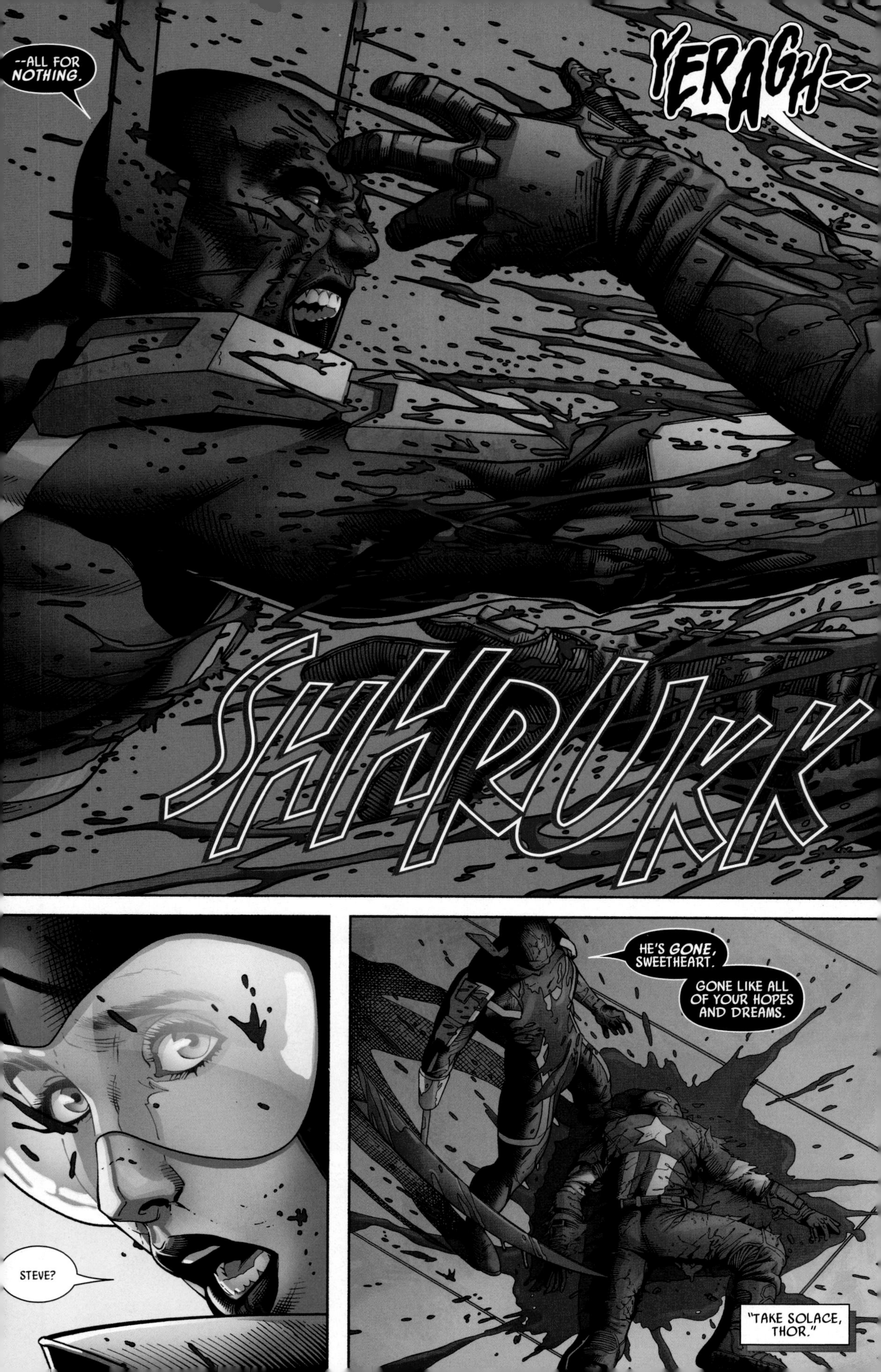
--ALL FOR NOTHING.
YERAGH--
SHHRUKK
STEVE?
HE'S GONE, SWEETHEART.
GONE LIKE ALL OF YOUR HOPES AND DREAMS.
"TAKE SOLACE, THOR."

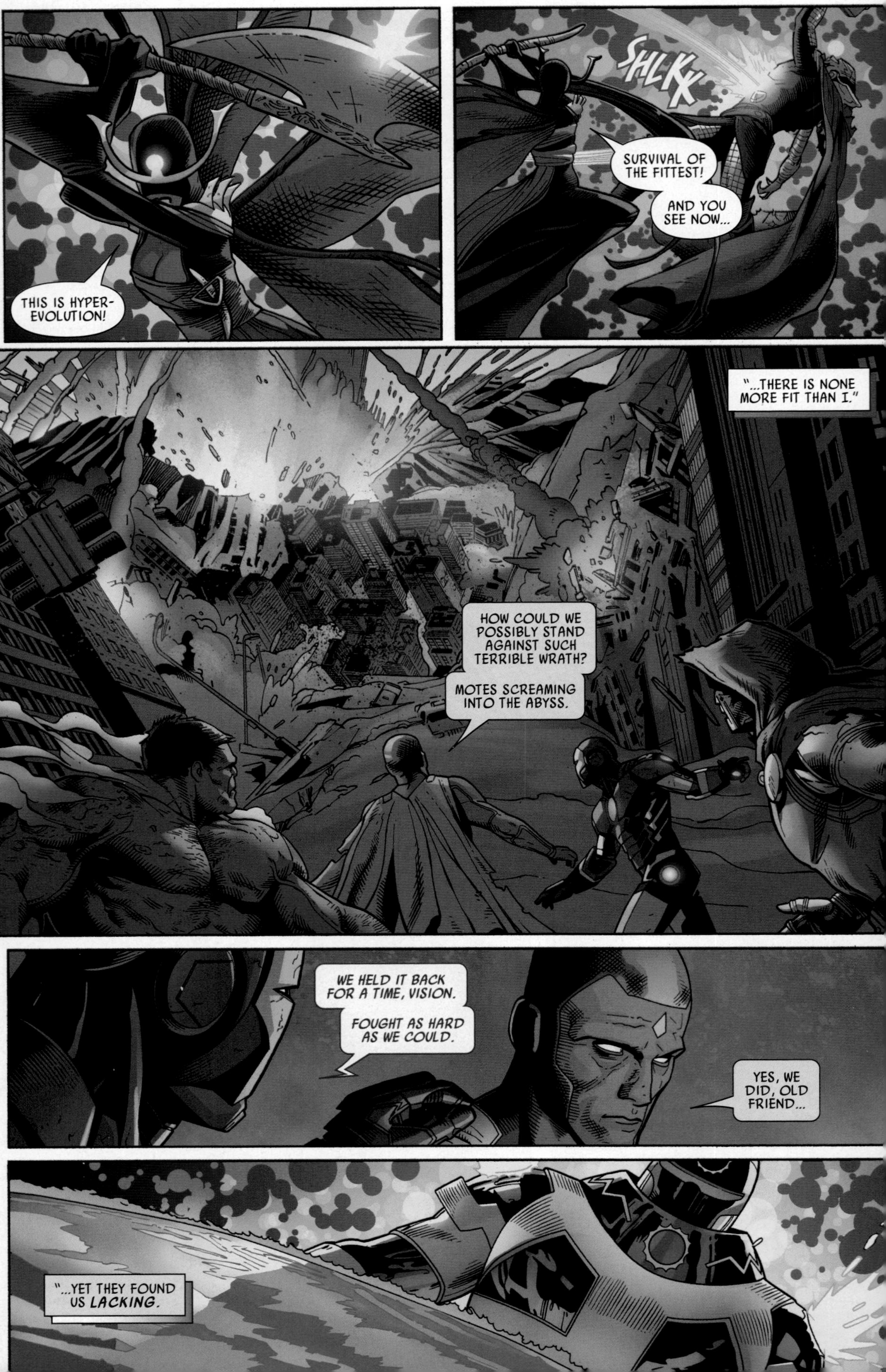
THIS IS HYPER-EVOLUTION!
SHLKK
SURVIVAL OF THE FITTEST!
AND YOU SEE NOW...
"...THERE IS NONE MORE FIT THAN I."
HOW COULD WE POSSIBLY STAND AGAINST SUCH TERRIBLE WRATH?
MOTES SCREAMING INTO THE ABYSS.
WE HELD IT BACK FOR A TIME, VISION.
FOUGHT AS HARD AS WE COULD.
YES, WE DID, OLD FRIEND...
"...YET THEY FOUND US LACKING.

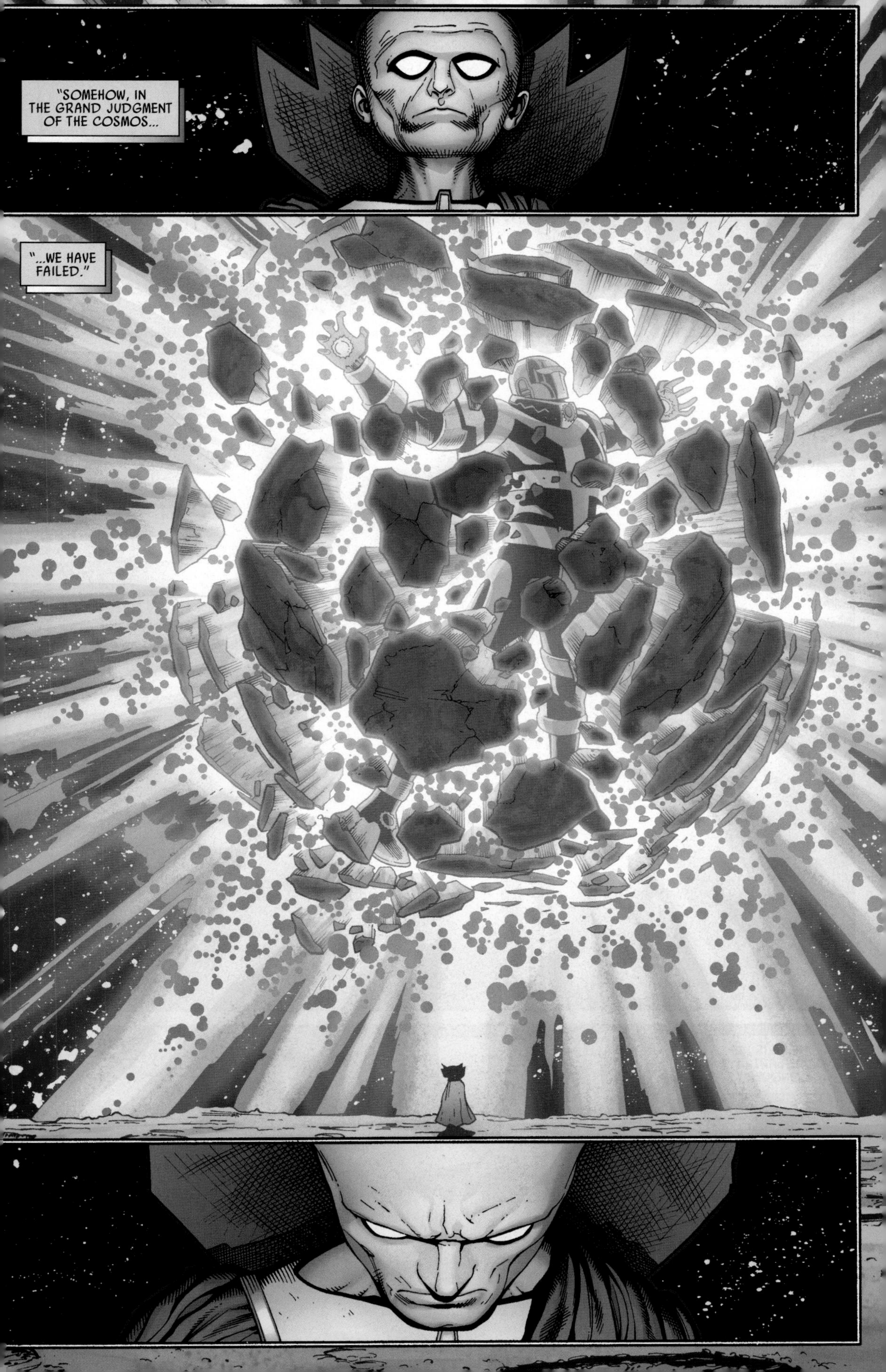
"SOMEHOW, IN THE GRAND JUDGMENT OF THE COSMOS...
"...WE HAVE FAILED."

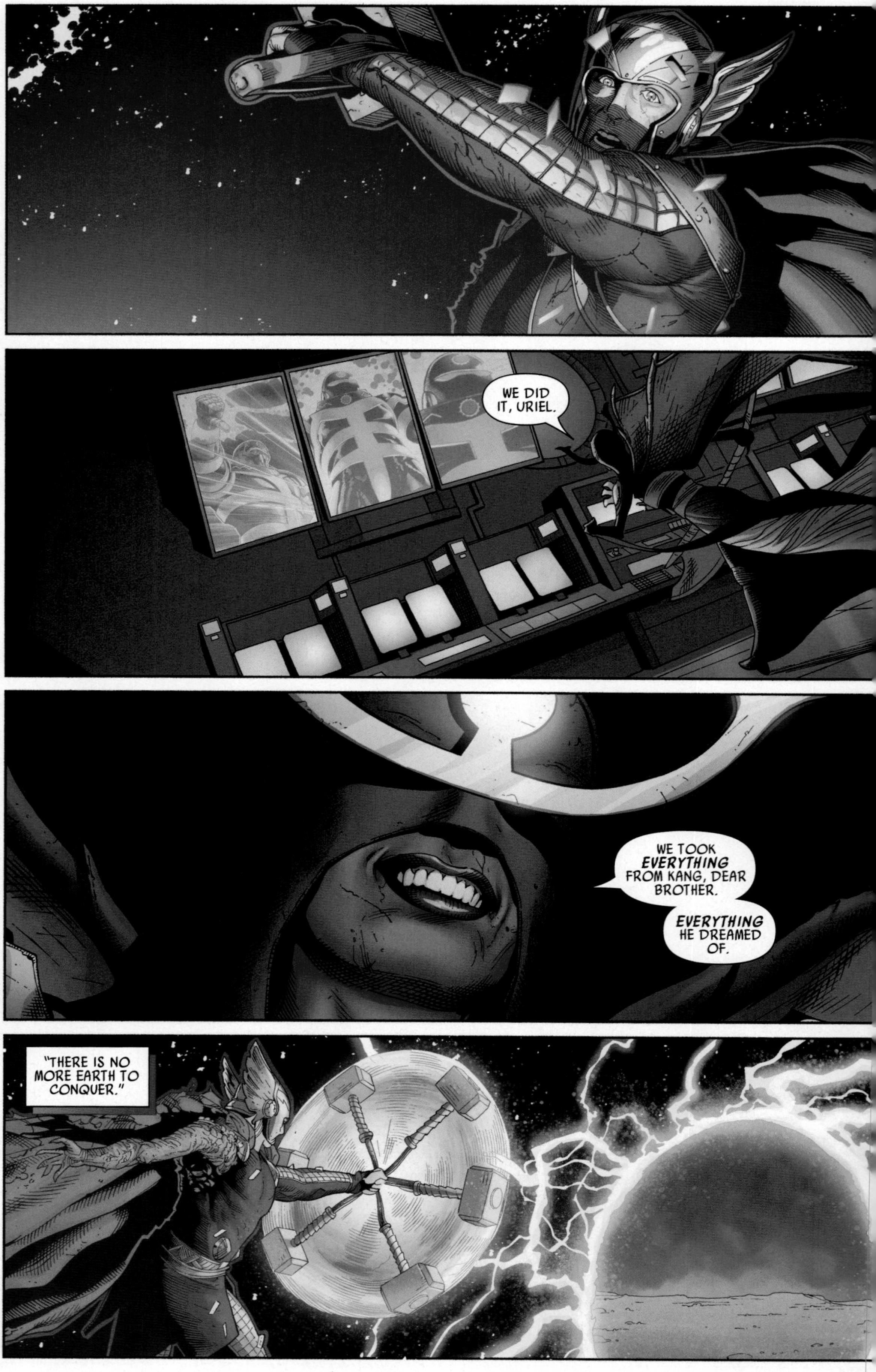
WE DID IT, URIEL.
WE TOOK *EVERYTHING* FROM KANG, DEAR BROTHER.
EVERYTHING HE DREAMED OF.
"THERE IS NO MORE EARTH TO CONQUER."

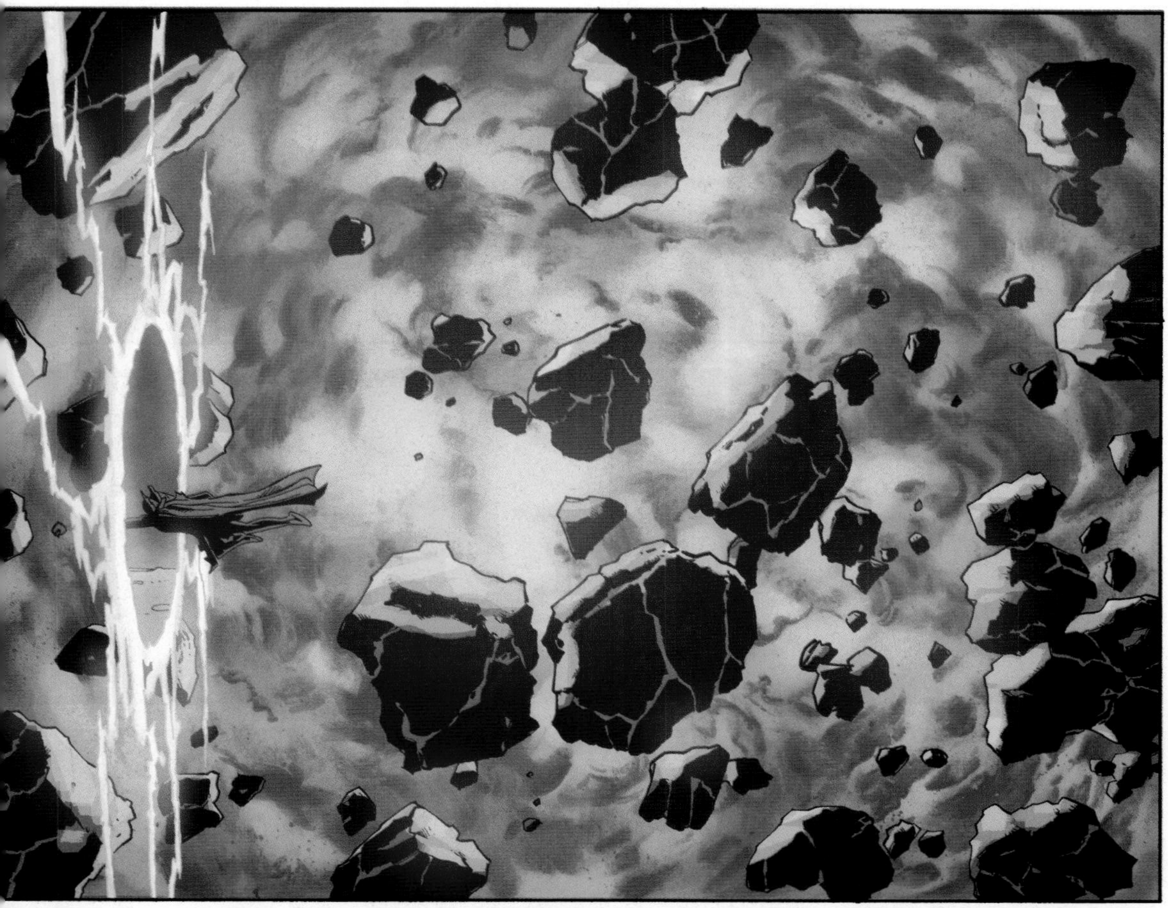
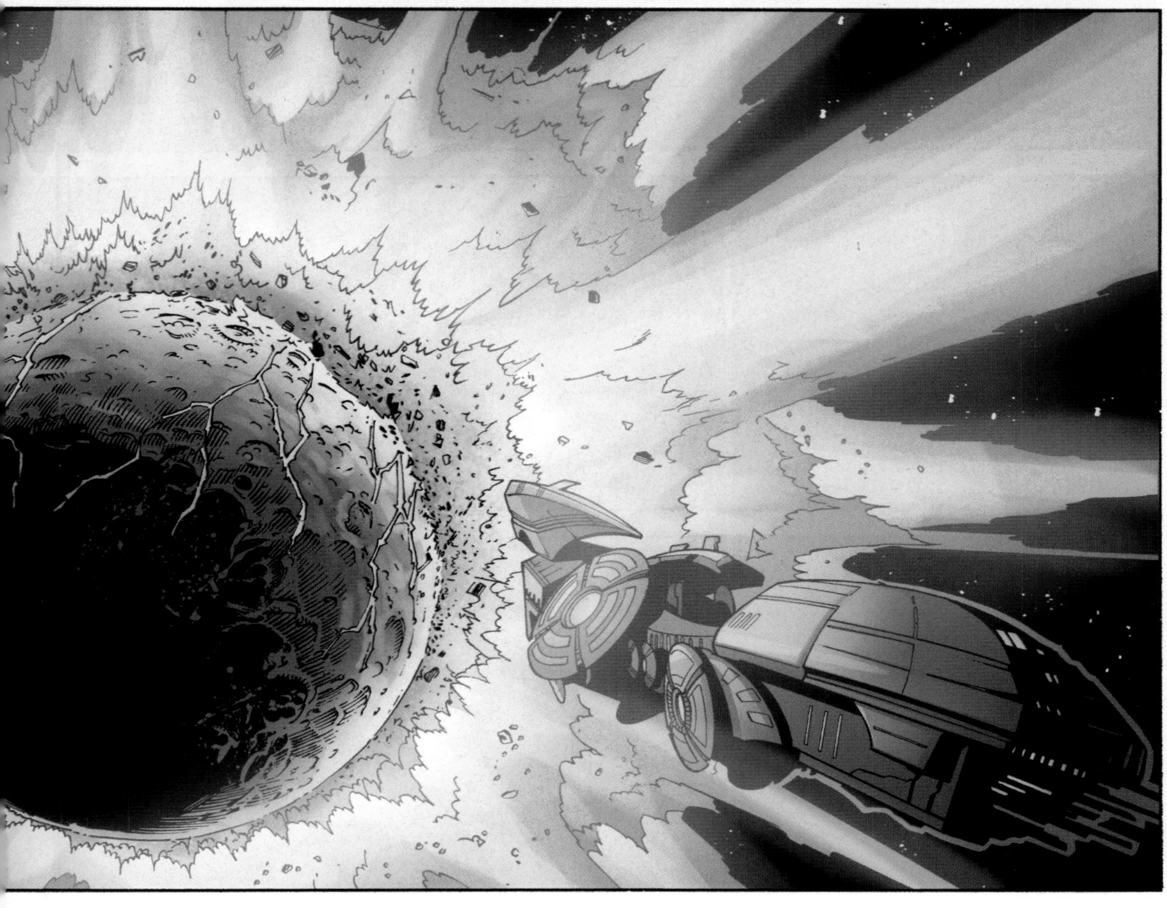

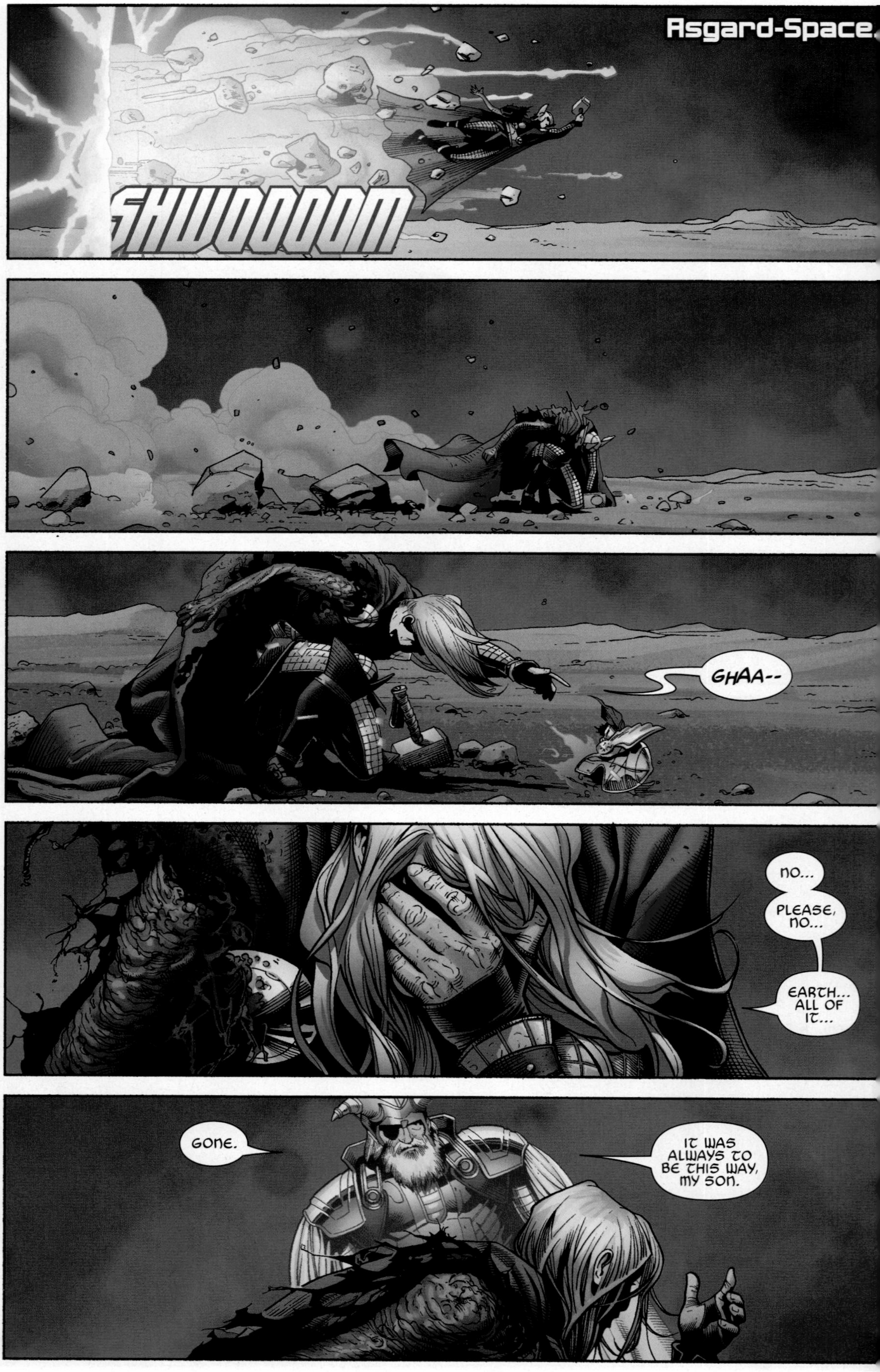
Asgard-Space.
SHWOOOOM
GHAA--
NO...
PLEASE, NO...
EARTH... ALL OF IT...
GONE.
IT WAS ALWAYS TO BE THIS WAY, MY SON.

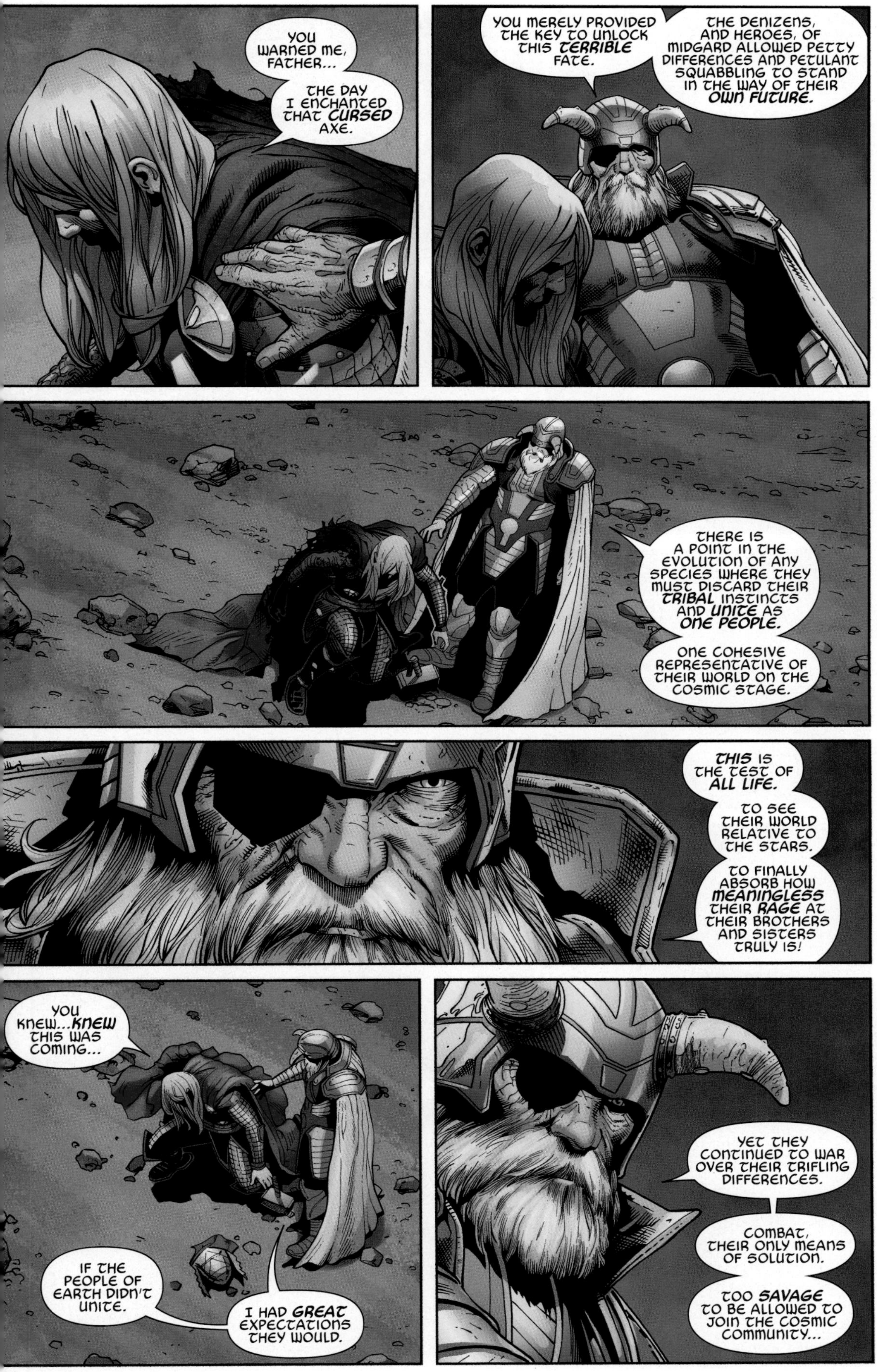

YOU WARNED ME, FATHER...
THE DAY I ENCHANTED THAT CURSED AXE.
YOU MERELY PROVIDED THE KEY TO UNLOCK THIS TERRIBLE FATE.
THE DENIZENS, AND HEROES, OF MIDGARD ALLOWED PETTY DIFFERENCES AND PETULANT SQUABBLING TO STAND IN THE WAY OF THEIR OWN FUTURE.
THERE IS A POINT IN THE EVOLUTION OF ANY SPECIES WHERE THEY MUST DISCARD THEIR TRIBAL INSTINCTS AND UNITE AS ONE PEOPLE.
ONE COHESIVE REPRESENTATIVE OF THEIR WORLD ON THE COSMIC STAGE.
THIS IS THE TEST OF ALL LIFE.
TO SEE THEIR WORLD RELATIVE TO THE STARS.
TO FINALLY ABSORB HOW MEANINGLESS THEIR RAGE AT THEIR BROTHERS AND SISTERS TRULY IS!
YOU KNEW...KNEW THIS WAS COMING...
IF THE PEOPLE OF EARTH DIDN'T UNITE.
I HAD GREAT EXPECTATIONS THEY WOULD.
YET THEY CONTINUED TO WAR OVER THEIR TRIFLING DIFFERENCES.
COMBAT, THEIR ONLY MEANS OF SOLUTION.
TOO SAVAGE TO BE ALLOWED TO JOIN THE COSMIC COMMUNITY...

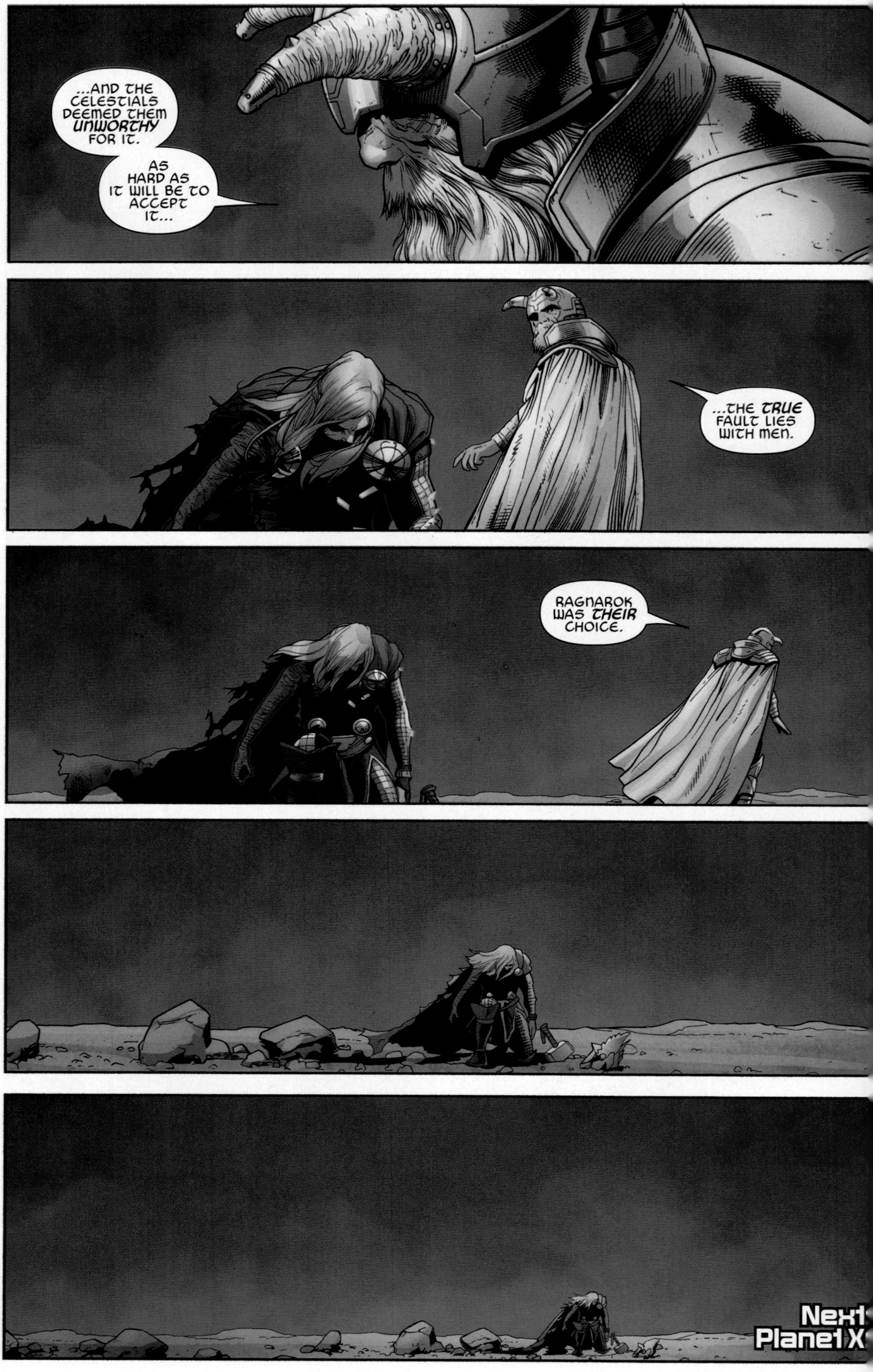
...AND THE CELESTIALS DEEMED THEM UNWORTHY FOR IT.
AS HARD AS IT WILL BE TO ACCEPT IT...
...THE TRUE FAULT LIES WITH MEN.
RAGNAROK WAS THEIR CHOICE.
Next
Planet X

"I'm hooked and I want more *Uncanny Avengers*. Now."
– Doug Zawisza, ComicBookResources.com

"..shocking and ingenious."
– David Pepose, Newsarama.com

"...we're in for something special."
– Ron Richards, iFanboy.com

MARVEL
NOW!

UNCANNY AVENGERS VOL. 1: THE RED SHADOW PREMIERE HC
WRITTEN BY RICK REMENDER • ART BY JOHN CASSADAY
978-0-7851-6844-7 • JAN130755

"*Uncanny Avengers* doesn't waste any time getting to the good stuff."
– Chris Sims, ComicsAlliance.com

MARVEL NOW!

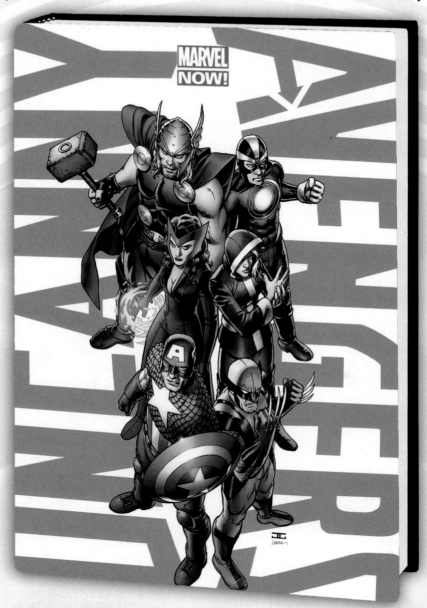

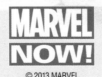

UNCANNY AVENGERS

AR INDEX

TMAUXVKE3A63

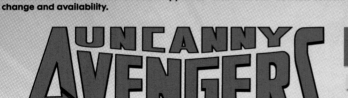

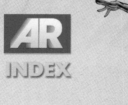

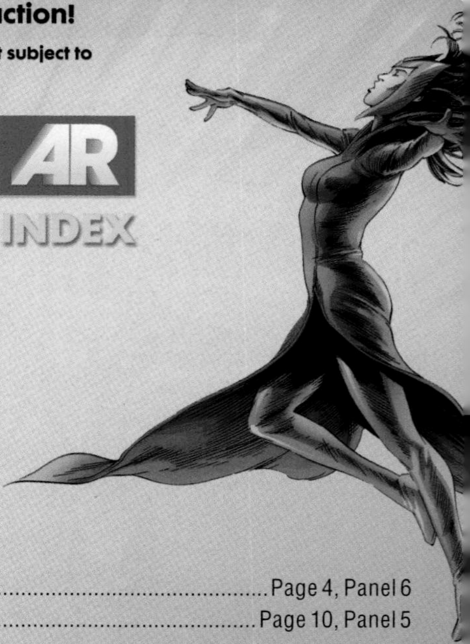